KU-174-265

IMPLEMENTING INNOVATIVE SOCIAL INVESTMENT

Strategic lessons from Europe

Edited by

Susan Baines, Andrea Bassi,
Judit Csoba and Flórián Sipos

First published in Great Britain in 2019 by

Policy Press
University of Bristol
1-9 Old Park Hill
Bristol
BS2 8BB
UK
t: +44 (0)117 954 5940
pp-info@bristol.ac.uk
www.policypress.co.uk

North America office:
Policy Press
c/o The University of Chicago Press
1427 East 60th Street
Chicago, IL 60637, USA
t: +1 773 702 7700
f: +1 773-702-9756
sales@press.uchicago.edu
www.press.uchicago.edu

© Policy Press 2019

The digital PDF version of the Introduction [978-1-4473-5189-4] and Conclusion [978-1-4473-5190-0] are available Open Access and distributed under the terms of the Creative Commons Attribution-NonCommercial 4.0 license (http://creativecommons.org/licenses/by-nc/4.0/) which permits adaptation, alteration, reproduction and distribution for non-commercial use, without further permission provided the original work is attributed. The derivative works do not need to be licensed on the same terms.

British Library Cataloguing in Publication Data
A catalogue record for this book is available from the British Library

Library of Congress Cataloging-in-Publication Data
A catalog record for this book has been requested

978-1-4473-4782-8 hardback
978-1-4473-4784-2 ePdf
978-1-4473-4785-9 ePub
978-1-4473-4786-6 Mobi

The rights of Susan Baines, Andrea Bassi, Judit Csoba and Flórián Sipos to be identified as editors of this work has been asserted by them in accordance with the Copyright, Designs and Patents Act 1988.

All rights reserved: no part of this publication may be reproduced, stored in a retrieval system, or transmitted in any form or by any means, electronic, mechanical, photocopying, recording, or otherwise without the prior permission of Policy Press.

The statements and opinions contained within this publication are solely those of the editor and contributors and not of the University of Bristol or Policy Press. The University of Bristol and Policy Press disclaim responsibility for any injury to persons or property resulting from any material published in this publication.

Policy Press works to counter discrimination on grounds of gender, race, disability, age and sexuality.

Cover design by Andrew Corbett
Front cover image: Shutterstock
Printed and bound in Great Britain by CPI Group (UK) Ltd, Croydon, CR0 4YY
Policy Press uses environmentally responsible print partners

Contents

List of tables, figures, images and boxes

Notes on contributors

Dr Inga Narbutaité Aflaki is a Senior Lecturer in Political Science at Karlstad University, Sweden. The main focus of her research is policy processes and policy change, in particular, on a sub-national level. Recent research includes regional/local innovation support policies that evolve from cooperation between industrial clusters, universities and other regional actors.

Dr George Alexias is a Professor at Panteion University of Social and Political Sciences, Greece, in the Department of Psychology. He teaches Sociology of Health and Illness, Sociology of the Body, and Social Science Research Methods, as well as courses at the Hellenic Open University. His research interests include sociology, sociology of health and illness, sociology of the body, and sociology of genetics, with numerous journal articles, studies and books published. He has participated in many research projects, national and EU-funded, holding both research and team-leading positions.

Dr Gavin Bailey is a Research Associate with the Policy Evaluation & Research Unit at Manchester Metropolitan University, UK. His research has covered a wide range of social problems, including homelessness, youth disengagement, problematic drug use, domestic violence and hate crime.

Susan Baines is Professor of Social Enterprise in the Policy Evaluation & Research Unit at Manchester Metropolitan University, UK. She has published extensively on social enterprise, social innovation and the reform of public services, and has led many research and knowledge-exchange projects on these topics.

Andrea Bassi is Associate Professor of Sociology in the Department of Political and Social Sciences at Bologna University, Italy. His research interests include studies on non-profit organisations in the field of social and health services, systems of measurement of organisational performance, and the social impact of non-profit organisations. He is the author of more than 50 articles on these themes in international and Italian journals, as well as of five books.

Nikola Borosch, MA undertook research for the InnoSI project on labour market integration for migrants and asylum seekers in the city of Münster, Germany. His main research interests lie in the fields of comparative policy analysis and of labour market policy.

Dr Judit Csoba is the Head of the Department of Sociology and Social Policy and Vice Dean for Finance and Grants in the Faculty of Humanities, University of Debrecen, Hungary. Her research fields cover social policy, employment policy, the transformation of welfare systems into workfare ones, the social economy and active labour market programmes.

Alfons Fermin is an independent researcher with expertise in social and urban issues. He works on the nexus between policy, practice and research at the local, national and European levels.

José Pedro García-Sabater is a Full Professor of Operations Management and Industrial Engineering in the Department of Management at the Universitat Politècnica de València, Spain. He is an expert on the mathematical modelling of production, planning and scheduling processes.

Dr Sandra Geelhoed is an Associate Professor at the Research Centre for Social Innovation, University of Applied Sciences Utrecht, the Netherlands. Before that, she worked for more than 20 years on issues dealing with imagined communities and community development as a researcher and teacher at the Ecole des Hautes en Sciences Sociales in Paris.

Danielle Gluns MA is currently researching models of cooperation between local governments and social organisations, under the direction of Professor Dr Annette Zimmer, University of Münster, Germany.

Dr Rob Gründemann has worked since 2007 as a Professor in the Research Centre for Social Innovation, University of Applied Sciences Utrecht, the Netherlands. He has been involved in more than 20 projects at the European level, mainly relating to health in the workplace.

Alexandra Koronaiou is a Professor at Panteion University of Social and Political Sciences, Greece, in the Department of Psychology. She teaches Sociology of Work and Leisure, and Sociology of Media, as well as courses in postgraduate programmes, also at the Hellenic Open University. Her research interests include sociology of work and free time, education, youth and gender issues, political culture and participation, with numerous journal articles, studies and book published. She has long and extensive experience of national and international project management and participation, and she is a member of scientific national and international committees and associations.

José Millet-Roig holds the Chair of Managerial Culture at the Universitat Politècnica de València, Spain. Despite having an academic background and many publications on biomedical signalling, he has developed his career in business development and in creating and enhancing links between local industry and the university. He is editor of *Service Business: An International Journal.*

Dr Dorota Moroń is at the University of Wroclaw, Poland. She researches and publishes on social innovation, non-governmental organisations (NGOs) and the legal basis for NGO activities and their implementation in practice.

Dr Chris O'Leary is a specialist in public policy. He is a senior lecturer in the Policy Evaluation & Research Unit (PERU) at Manchester Metropolitan University, UK, and manages projects that involve multidisciplinary teams and mixed methods. Much of his work before joining PERU was around modelling need and demand in terms of multiple needs, prevention and the integration of services.

Dr Jessica Ozan is a Research Associate with the Policy Evaluation & Research Unit at Manchester Metropolitan University, UK. Her research interests include evaluation methodology, children and youth, and intercultural approaches.

Aida Saez-Mas is an industrial engineer by the Universitat Politècnica de València, Spain. Her postgraduate research interests include the electrical industry in Spain and the effects of energy poverty. Currently she is finishing her PhD thesis related to internal logistics in manufacturing.

Alexandros Sakellariou holds a PhD in Sociology; he is a post-doctoral researcher at Panteion University of Social and Political Sciences and teaches Sociology at the Hellenic Open University. His scientific interests include sociology of religion, politics and religion, youth activism and civic participation, right-wing extremism, radicalisation and qualitative research methods. He has long experience as a researcher in various national and EU-funded research projects and surveys, and he is a contributor co-authoring reports on religious and political issues in Greece.

Flórián Sipos is an Assistant Lecturer at the University of Debrecen, Hungary. He has broad experience in executing and coordinating international research and social development projects. His research activities cover social history, civic engagement and community work.

Dr Kaisa Sorsa is a Principal Lecturer at Turku University of Applied Sciences, Adjunct Professor of Regulatory Studies in the University of Turku and Adjunct Professor of Contract and Marketing Law at the University of Eastern Finland. She has conducted regulatory research in the field of economic changes from both micro- and macro-viewpoints, as well as in the field of regulatory innovations and responsible business.

George Vayias holds a degree in Sociology and he is a doctoral student at Panteion University of Social and Political Sciences, Greece, in the Department of Psychology. He has participated in various research projects, national and EU-funded, holding both research and administrative positions. His research interests mainly include sociology and psychology of youth communities and politics, sociology and psychology of leadership, sociology and psychology of cyberspace, organisational theory, and social media culture.

Aldona Wiktorska-Święcka, Professor of the University of Wroclaw, Poland, PhD, D.S. MBA (Dr habil) is chair of the section of European Integration and Regional Development at the Department of European Studies, Faculty of Social Science, University of Wroclaw, Poland. She has published extensively on urban governance and social innovation. Her research activities cover public governance and public management, political culture, innovations in management and governance.

Dr Michael Willoughby is a member of the Institute for Information and Communication Technologies, Universitat Politècnica de València, Spain. He specialises in topics related to entrepreneurship and new technologies applied to business organisations.

Annette Zimmer is Professor of Social Policy and Comparative Politics at the University of Münster, Germany. She has served on the Board of the German Political Science Association and on the Advisory Board of the German Volunteer Survey. Her research focuses on the topics of social innovation and civil society–government relations. She is the author of many articles and books on these themes.

Acknowledgement

This book is based on research undertaken for 'Innovative Social Investment: Strengthening Communities in Europe' (InnoSI) under the leadership of Professor Chris Fox, Director of the Policy Research & Evaluation Unit, Manchester Metropolitan University. InnoSI received funding from the European Commission Horizon 2020 programme 'Societal Challenges: European Societies after the Crisis', Grant Agreement Number 649189.

ONE

Social Investment in welfare: a sub-national perspective

Susan Baines, Judit Csoba, Flórián Sipos and Andrea Bassi

Introduction

The concept of a Social Investment welfare paradigm has become highly influential in public policy globally (Deeming and Smyth, 2017). At its heart lies the idea that welfare states must invest to strengthen skills and capacities, beginning in early life. 'Social Investment' therefore refers to policies and interventions that aim to build the productive capacities of citizens (Deeming and Smyth, 2015). Typical examples include labour market activation and early years education and care (Hemerijck, 2017). According to the European Commission (2013: 3): '[S]ocial investment policies reinforce social policies that protect and stabilise by addressing some of the causes of disadvantage and giving people tools with which to improve their social situations'. Many countries – including but not limited to members states of the European Union (EU) – have adopted some elements of Social Investment, although uptake is far from uniform (Bouget et al, 2015).

Social Investment calls into question past welfare policy paradigms (Van Kersbergen and Hemerijck, 2012). Indeed, according to its advocates, it amounts to 'a paradigmatic rethink of active welfare states for the 21st century knowledge economy' (Hemerijck, 2017: 66). The scholarly literature on Social Investment focuses heavily on aggregate effects and the macro-comparative analysis of welfare spending (Kuitto, 2016). As a result, debates often remain on an abstract meta-level and make limited reference to local and micro-level implementation and practice. In contrast to most writing on Social Investment, this book brings sub-national contexts to the fore. It does this with original, empirical research evidence about successes, challenges and setbacks from 10 countries.

It is the idea of having a lasting impact that gives Social Investment policies the characteristics of an 'investment' by offering some returns over time. This meaning of the term 'social investment' is somewhat distinct from its more typical usage in the UK and other English-speaking countries to denote financial mechanisms such as Payment by Results (PbR) and Social Impact Bonds (SIBs) for funding social programmes. Financial mechanisms are not the main focus of this book, although we do consider some aspects of financial innovation.

Innovation is an essential element of Social Investment as social policies require constant adaptation to new challenges (Jenson, 2015). Social innovation is concerned with 'the development of what are currently viewed as assets for sustainable development: environmental, human and social capital' (BEPA, 2010). Yet, the emerging scholarly literature on Social Investment has included social innovation to a very limited extent (Ewart and Evers, 2014).

The aim of this book is to advance empirical and conceptual insight into the Social Investment welfare paradigm from a social innovation and a sub-national perspective. Drawing upon multinational research under Horizon 2000 Societal Challenges, chapter authors offer new evidence about the regional and local realities of Social Investment policies and programmes, and original analysis informed by engagement with the service users and local communities affected.

Social Investment

The idea of 'Social Investment' implies that spending on welfare is a long-term investment to improve prospects for economic and social participation (Hemerick, 2013, 2015; Leoni, 2015). Its early origins have been traced to the founding of the Swedish welfare state in the 1930s, and the arguments of social democrats in that country, who viewed social policy as an investment rather than a cost (Deeming and Smyth, 2015). It can also be linked to earlier and often overlooked 'productivist' traditions in British social policy (Smyth and Deeming, 2016). A 'socially investive state' was proposed by Giddens, who argued for 'investment in human capital wherever possible, rather than the direct provision of economic maintenance' (Giddens, 1998: 117). Whereas Giddens advocated activation instead of income guarantees, other prominent scholars have insisted that minimising poverty and income insecurity is a precondition for effective Social Investment, not a substitute (Esping-Anderson et al, 2002; Hemerijk, 2017). Social investment in the UK (aligned with the viewpoint of Giddens), as well as in other English-speaking countries such as Australia, has been described as a 'light' version characterised by investment in human capital alongside low social protection (Deeming and Smyth, 2015). Nevertheless, there is evidence of some convergence around key

Social Investment objectives (Jenson, 2009) and the formation of 'a fairly coherent epistemic community' (Hemerijck, 2017: 3). As a way of framing problems and solutions, Social Investment has become widely shared and gained the backing of influential international organisations such as the Organisation for Economic Co-operation and Development (OECD), the United Nations Children's Fund (UNICEF) and the World Bank (Cantillon and Van Lancker, 2013; Deeming and Smyth, 2017).

The EU, under the Dutch presidency in 1997, introduced the phrase 'social policy as a productive factor' to counter the market-liberal stance, then becoming widely accepted, that welfare interventions are at the expense of economic competitiveness. Social Investment was anchored in the Lisbon Agenda, with the objective to modernise the European social model through a synthesis of competitive markets, knowledge-based investment and social cohesion (European Council, 2000; Morel et al, 2012). The Europe 2020 Strategy reinforced the EU's social dimension and transferred the Social Investment objectives of the Lisbon Agenda into the European economic policy agenda, with the overall objective to lift at least 20 million people out of poverty and social exclusion. Investment in human capital, active inclusion strategies and early childhood intervention thereby became priorities of Europe 2020's social agenda (Social Protection Committee, 2011).

The European Commission adopted the expression 'Social Investment' in 2013. In this book, we take as a working definition words that become embedded in the Social Investment Package (SIP) launched in that year:

> The social investment approach stresses the case for considering certain parts of employment and social policies – and possibly other policy areas, such as education – as entailing investments improving prospects for future employment and social participation, together with more social cohesion and stability … thus stressing the life course dimension of social policies and their long-term benefits for society. (European Commission, 2013: 4)

This definition foregrounds human capital and labour market attachment in the 'life course dimension' of social policies. At the same time, it recognises social participation and cohesion. More recent EU policy initiatives have further emphasised fairness and social justice alongside dynamic labour markets and expanding access to paid work (European Commission, 2017).

In contrast to more redistributive forms of welfare, measures and instruments associated with Social Investment are intended to strengthen people's skills and capacities over the course of their lives. In other words, welfare should '"prepare" individuals, families and societies to respond to the new risks of a competitive knowledge economy … [rather than] "repair" damages after moments of economic or personal crisis' (Hemerijck, 2015: 242). The new risks that people face because of the challenges of post-industrial societies are associated with precarious employment, income volatility, skills that become quickly outdated and changing household structures. All this implies the need for 'capacitating social services' aimed at equipping individuals and families to mitigate increasingly unforeseeable, erratic and heterogeneous hazards (Sabel, 2012; Hemerijck, 2017). Social Investment has three central interdependent functions, known as stocks, flows and buffers, which can promote the fulfilment of the productive function of social policy (Hemerijck, 2017). In more detail, these consist of:

- raising the quality of the 'stock' of human capital and capabilities over the life course;
- easing the 'flow' of contemporary labour market and life-course transitions;
- maintaining 'buffers', mainly in the form of safety nets for income protection and economic stabilisation. People are also 'buffered' through support services that alleviate shocks and stresses (Sabel et al, 2017).

Through stocks, flows and buffers, Social Investment, according to its proponents, stops disadvantage from compounding in the lives of individuals and across generations (Esping-Anderson et al, 2002; Hemerijck, 2017). Critics counter that Social Investment policies may not impact positively on inequalities (Kazepov and Ranci, 2017) and may have flaws when it comes to the protection of vulnerable groups (Cantillon and Van Lancker, 2013). A separate but related strand of criticism concerns making social policy 'the "handmaiden" of economic policy' (Dobrowolsky and Lister, 2008: 132). Morel and Palme (2017) and Bonvin and Laruffa (2017) propose squaring this circle by thinking of human capital not only for economic returns, but also more holistically in terms of capabilities (Sen, 2001), thus opening a way to refocus Social Investment debates around human freedom, democracy and citizenship.

The break from the consensus of the post–Second World War welfare model is highlighted in the words of Palier (2008, translated by Jenson, 2009: 447): that Social Investment means 'going from a welfare state that is a "nurse" to one that is an "investor"'. The Keynesian emphasis on the management of effective demand under the post–Second World War consensus gives way to an emphasis on effective supply, removing barriers to entry into the labour market, discouraging early exit, making transitions less precarious and providing gender equality throughout the life cycle. Social Investment advocates also reject and seek to replace neoliberal principles of welfare retrenchment (Hemerijck, 2017). Three welfare paradigms are set out in Table 1.1.

The extent to which Social Investment represents a fully fledged paradigm is contested. Nolan (2013) emphasises the conceptual and empirical challenges of ascertaining what Social Investment is and what it is not since many policies and instruments have characteristics that are both investive and compensatory. Daly (2012) sees Social Investment as a compromise position that departs from neoliberalism by accepting the reform capacity of the (welfare) state while sharing neoliberalism's enthusiasm for markets, including their use in welfare provision. Echoing Deeming and Smyth's (2015) analysis of light and strong versions of Social Investment, Barbier (2017) discerns two ways of envisioning Social Investment. One way is as an innovative reform strategy that accompanies national systems of social protection. The other way departs from social protection by advocating conditional, targeted, time-limited programmes, sometimes resourced through private finance. This is close to the usage in the UK of the term 'social

Table 1.1: Three welfare paradigms

	Welfare state consensus (post–Second World War)	Neoliberal	Social Investment state
Goals	Full (male) employment and welfare rights	Market efficiencies and flexible labour markets	Growth and competitiveness through improved human capital
Enemies	Giant evils (idleness, want, ignorance, disease, squalor)	High public spending (which 'crowds out' private initiative)	Intergenerational disadvantages; gender inequality
Timescale	Here and now	Ahistoric	Future-oriented
Policy instruments	Benefits to replace income; universal services	Benefit curtailment and service privatisation	Capacitating services with investment in children and active labour programmes

Source: Adapted from Hemerijck (2017)

investment' to refer to Social Impact Investing, meaning the use of repayable finance to achieve a social as well as a financial return. The Cabinet Office (2013), for example, declared that 'social investment refers to capital which enables social organisations to deliver both social and financial returns'. Nichols and Teasdale (2017) position 'social investment' in this sense as a 'micro-paradigm' nested within the overarching frame of neoliberalism. In Barbier's analysis, it is a way of viewing Social Investment that should be strenuously resisted by Social Investment partisans. New commissioning mechanisms such as SIBs, Barbier notes, are mentioned positively in the European Commission (2013) communication on the SIP. SIBs make funding for services conditional on achieving results. The case for them is that they are a way of bringing rigour to interventions and providing the financial and political capital for innovation (Warner, 2013).

Social innovation

European welfare states were designed to offer support against 20th-century social risks. The idea of new risks that do not respond to established, tried-and-tested welfare remedies is the lynchpin of Social Investment. Social innovation is an evocative but somewhat elusive concept that has become influential in scholarship and in policymaking (Grimm et al, 2013; Evers and Brandsen, 2016). In contrast to technological and industrial innovation, social innovation is explicitly about addressing human needs (Marques et al, 2017). Nevertheless, as Jenson (2015) notes, thinking on social innovation has been heavily imbued with the writing of the economist Schumpeter (1983 [1934]), in particular, his influential categorisation on the main types of entrepreneurial behaviour that produce innovations in industry. These are: introducing a new good; introducing a new method of production; opening up a new market; exploiting a new source of raw materials; and organising whole industries in new ways (Schumpeter, 1983 [1934]). Social innovation can be found in four schools of thought from different national and linguistic traditions:

- Centre de recherche sur les innovations sociales (CRISES) in French-speaking Canada, founded by the sociologist Benoît Lévesque in the late 1980s, with an emphasis on the well-being of individuals and communities (Lévesque, 2006);
- studies of urban renewal and development primarily under the direction of the French-speaking Belgian scholar Frank Moulaert,

represented by a series of research projects funded by the European Commission during the 1990s (Moulaert, 2013);

• German and Austrian researchers particularly keen to link the debate on social innovation closely to the legacy of Schumpeter and discourse on innovation in general (Franz et al, 2012); and

• English-speaking business schools and think tanks, for example, the Young Foundation and NESTA (National Endowment for Science, Technology and the Arts) in the UK, and the Stanford Social Innovation Review (SSIR) of the Center on Philanthropy and Civil Society (PACS) at Stanford University, California, in the US.

At its simplest, social innovation refers to 'ideas translated into practical approaches; new in the context where they appear' (Brandsen et al, 2016: 5). The intentionality of social innovation distinguishes it from mere social change (Franz et al, 2012; Grimm et al, 2013). A widely cited definition is:

> The generation and implementation of new ideas about how people should organize interpersonal activities or social interactions to meet one or more common goals. As with other forms of innovation, the production resulting from social innovation may vary with regard to their breadth and impact. (Mumford, 2002: 253)

This definition encompasses activities that seek to improve the production and delivery of specific services, as well as more radical versions where the emphasis is on wide-ranging social transformation (Marques et al, 2017). The latter is the essence of social innovation for Westley and Antadze (2010), who see it as challenging institutions and affecting the distribution of power to make a difference to seemingly intractable social problems.

Within Europe 2020, social innovation features almost as prominently as technological innovation (Sabato et al, 2017). The European Commission has prioritised social innovation to address policy problems because it implies non-standard answers to non-standard risks, as well as notions of co-production based on strengths and assets (BEPA, 2010). Individual social innovations may or may not be successful and their expected benefits may be contested, but they 'raise the hope and expectations of progress towards something better (a more socially sustainable/democratic/effective society)' (Brandsen et al, 2016: 6–7). This notion of social innovation is well aligned with the future-oriented paradigm of the Social Investment state.

The social economy

The SIP insists that resources for social policies are not limited to those from the public sector (European Commission, 2013). The SIP mentions the roles of various non-government entities: non-profit organisations, the for-profit private sector and families. It also comments on the need for more effective support for the social economy and innovation (European Commission, 2013). Recent scholarly writing on Social Investment has put new emphasis on non-government actors, especially the social economy. Ferrara (2017) considers that there is a 'precious asset' to the Social Investment agenda at the grass-roots level, where experiments outside the public sphere are becoming key arenas for solutions to social challenges with links to social innovation. Sabel et al (2017) similarly celebrate piecemeal, decentralised efforts to move in the direction of Social Investment.

The social economy engages with the market but economic activity is not the ultimate goal and social objectives override the drive to generate economic returns. Organisations in the social economy perform many roles in welfare and community functions. They often cooperate with agencies in the public sphere and may help to deliver state priorities (Evers and Laville, 2004), although for some, becoming close to the state implies losing distinctiveness (Billis, 2010). The social economy is defined by the International Centre of Research and Information on the Public, Social and Cooperative Economy (CIRIEC, 2012: 23) as 'organisations of people who conduct an activity with the main purpose of meeting the needs of people rather than remunerating capitalist investors'. Within the CIRIEC definition are two subsectors: (1) the market or business subsector; and (2) the non-market producer subsector. The first subsector includes cooperatives, mutual societies and social enterprises, and the second subsector includes foundations, associations, community organisations and voluntary organisations. By this definition, groups in the social economy are formally organised and usually have a legal identity. In some countries, terms such as 'civil society', 'third sector' and 'community and voluntary sector' are more commonly used, often interchangeably with social economy, although there are some differences. For example, in Italy, the main difference between the concept of social economy and the concept of the third sector is based on the fact that the former includes cooperatives while the latter does not (Bassi et al, 2016).

'Civil society' is a broader term that includes religious bodies, trade and professional bodies, and sports clubs. Informal groups of friends and neighbours are not part of the social economy according to the CIRIEC definition (although informal groups coming together for a common purpose may formalise). Informal groups may be considered part of civil society. Evers and Laville (2004) conceptualise the social economy as occupying a tension field influenced by state policies and legislation, business practices, and the needs and contributions of families. The CIRIEC definition concentrates on the intersection with the state and the market. The other part of this tension field comprises communities and families. All this is encompassed in the idea of 'substantive' economic formations, which are meant to satisfy various needs (Polányi, 1976). The substantive, or *embedded*, economy represents the opposite pole to the formal, market economy. Its characteristics are highlighted in Table 1.2.

Social innovation is often equated with social entrepreneurs, voluntary organisations and community activists taking a special role as pioneers of new ideas (Evers and Laville, 2004). It is also possible for commercial organisations to implement social innovations but it is unlikely that profit will be their primary goal (Marques et al, 2017). In the book, we follow Brandsen et al (2016) in viewing the link between social innovations and organisational forms as an empirical question, not a presupposition.

Table 1.2: Comparison of the distinctive features of the substantive and the formal economy

	Substantive economy	Formal economy
Goal of the economy	Satisfaction of needs	Growth as an end in itself
Motivation of work	Many-faceted motives, incentives and objectives	Financial incentives
Function of work	Work is a natural form of existence	Work is an instrument and/or goal
Independence of the economy	Economic activity interwoven with social relationships	Economic activity as an independent subsystem
Producer/consumer roles	The producer is also a consumer	The producer and the consumer are separate
Degree of solidarity	High collectivity	High individualism and competition

The Innovative Social Investment Strengthening Communities in Europe project

The Innovative Social Investment: Strengthening Communities in Europe (InnoSI) project examined innovative implementation of Social Investment at national and sub-national levels across the EU. The InnoSI consortium consisted of academic research teams and 'impact' partners (mainly non-governmental organisations [NGOs]) in 10 countries: Finland, Sweden, the UK, the Netherlands, Germany, Poland, Hungary, Spain, Italy and Greece. Research included econometric modelling to quantify the economic processes and outputs through which social innovation acts, and assessment of the main policymaking trends using documents and interviews with key national experts. This book is concerned with the most substantial original empirical research from the project, which consists of in-depth, multi-method case studies in 10 EU countries of innovative, strategic approaches to delivering Social Investment policy at a sub-national level. Brief reference is made in Chapter Twelve to policy analysis and national expert interviews.

Case studies have become widely used in social research in order to investigate complex contemporary issues and changes in policies or practices (Byrne, 2009). A case study is an approach to what is studied rather than a research method, and can deploy multiple, complementary forms of data collection (Stake, 2008). Case studies investigate issues or events within their real-life setting and can function as a kind of natural experiment (Yin, 2003; Wolff Kristina, 2007). They aim to develop understanding of causation beyond the idiosyncratic while rejecting any quest for universal laws (Flyvbjerg, 2006; Byrne, 2009). A core characteristic of case studies is the generation of 'rich dialogue between ideas and evidence' (Ragin, 1989: 52).

InnoSI case studies

The national InnoSI teams selected two case studies per country and these were agreed in consultation with the coordinating partner at Manchester Metropolitan University. All cases were innovations in services relating to welfare. All had been implemented, although some were fully completed and others were still in progress. Cases in the planning or inception stage were not included. Typical or average cases are not necessarily the best to advance learning (Flyvbjerg, 2006). The InnoSI case studies were not intended to be 'typical' examples of Social Investment. Rather, they were purposively selected using the local knowledge of academic and non-academic partners. Criteria for selection were meeting characteristics of Social Investment according to the literature, and demonstrating some level of innovation (either absolutely or in context). In other words, they should be both investive and innovative. For example, although education has been called the vanguard of Social Investment (Deeming and Smyth, 2015), education programmes were not part of InnoSI. The case studies, however, included innovative interventions aiming to ensure that education reaches those who use it least. Ten out of the 20 case studies form the basis of the chapters in this book, one for each participating country.

This book is structured in three parts representing the Social Investment themes of: early interventions in the life course; active labour market strategies; and promoting social cohesion and solidarity. Table 1.3 highlights the investive and innovative characteristics of each case.

Research for the case studies involved the evaluation of programme implementation and impact, and, where possible, economic evaluation (Fox et al, 2016). It considered what the Social Investment initiatives set out to achieve and how, using the concept of Theory of Change (ToC), and examined the ways in which these achievements were evidenced. A ToC refers to the 'underlying theory of [the] program' or 'set of assumptions about how and why program activities and resources will bring about changes for the better' (Leeuw and Vaessen, 2009: 15). It allows the understanding of not only whether activities worked, but also how and why, and which aspects of the intervention worked or not, and for whom (Mackenzie and Blamey, 2005). There is a difference between a programme theory developed through a ToC approach and a logic model, although the two are sometimes elided. Logic models examine the relationship between the programme elements (input, processes, outputs and outcomes) on a technical, descriptive level. A programme theory, in contrast, emphasises context and explanation. It examines causal processes through articulating how a programme works, for whom and under which circumstances (Astbury and Leeuw, 2010). The ToC approach can be adapted to suit the evaluation context (Dyson and Todd, 2010).

All the case studies in this book include the perspectives of beneficiaries, collected through interviews, site visits and observation. All the research teams undertook interviews with programme personnel who were decision-makers, service managers and front-line workers. Other stakeholders were also interviewed, as relevant in each case, including leaders of social economy organisations and businesses, educators, local politicians, and volunteers. The national

Table 1.3: Innovative and investment characteristics of case studies

Case study	Social Investment	Social innovation
Part A: Children and families: early interventions in people's life courses		
Early Childhood Education and Care in Emilia-Romagna Italy	Education and early childhood care; support parents' labour market participation	Best practice for the relationship between public, private and social economy actors
Troubled Families in Greater Manchester UK	Improve school attendance; support for parenting; address parental worklessness	Challenging the way services have worked in silos; Payment by Results (PbR) to local authorities
Partnerships between idea-based and public organisations Sweden	Integration of unaccompanied young migrants into Swedish society	More equal long-term collaboration between sectors on new societal challenges
Part B: Labour market activation		
Youth Guarantee Finland	Improve access to education and jobs for young adults	Public–private–people partnership with young people actively shaping their own future
Connecting vocational school graduates with the labour market Greece	Addresses youth unemployment through competencies for the labour market	Forge new links between businesses and vocational education
MAMBA (Action programme for the labour market integration of migrants) Germany	Support migrants to contribute to local labour markets	Inter-sectoral collaboration and networks between originally distinct systems
Assistance from A to Z ('Accompaniment') Poland	Address social and labour market exclusion	Solutions that already existed delivered in new ways; involves representatives of all sectors
Part C: Social solidarity		
'Green Sticht' (diverse neighbourhood) Netherlands	Move vulnerable people from dependency	Integration of self-reliant residents with socially vulnerable ones with regard to housing, work and living
Social Economic Land Programme Hungary	Increase rural livelihood opportunities	Combine environmental and labour market goals
Energy cooperatives Spain	Combat fuel poverty; strengthen community	Foster new kinds of sustainable behaviours

teams all undertook documentary analysis of existing evaluations, management materials, media coverage and other public domain sources (eg websites, reports).

In the InnoSI project, research findings were supplemented with the voices of 'community reporters'. Community reporting is a storytelling movement that uses digital tools such as portable and pocket technologies to help people to tell their own stories in their own ways. Central to community reporting is the belief that people telling authentic stories about their own lived experience offers a valuable understanding of their lives. Community reporters in the InnoSI project were programme beneficiaries, front-line workers, local organisation members and students trained and supported to tell their own stories and gather the stories of others. 'User voice' stories are included in several of the chapters.

Book structure

The Social Investment paradigm puts particular emphasis on early education and the activation and inclusion of children. Part A comprises three chapters about early interventions involving children, families and young people (Chapters Two, Three and Four). In Chapter Two, Andrea Bassi explains the integrated system of early childhood education and care (ECEC) in Emilia-Romagna, Italy. Taking evidence from three contrasting locations in the region, he demonstrates how high-quality ECEC provision is achieved through the co-creation and sharing of knowledge, expertise and experiences that are generated by innovative forms of public governance. A key success factor was a strong focus on continuing professional development activities organised in the form of 'laboratories for social change' – empowering ECEC professionals – rather than as top-down training. With regard to the financing of Social Investment, a significant lesson is the success of flexible combinations of different funding sources (public, philanthropic and private enterprise). This case study provides exemplary evidence of diversified ECEC provision, serving the needs of children and families within local communities and realised with a special focus on accessibility and economic sustainability.

In Chapter Three, Jessica Ozan, Chris O'Leary, Susan Baines and Gavin Bailey report on Troubled Families in Greater Manchester, UK. This is a sub-regional implementation of a controversial national programme in England intended to offer joined-up services targeted at families representing the highest costs to the public purse. Its underpinning principles include early intervention with children and sustained employment for parents. Troubled Families is innovative in using the funding mechanism of PbR, under which local authorities are paid partly through submitting data to demonstrate that they have met outcomes. The evidence shows that, to some extent, the programme supported a shift towards service integration in Greater Manchester as intended. A particular success factor was co-produced family plans, taking the families' perspectives into account. PbR was welcomed by some senior managers but did not prove very supportive of the desired new and positive relationship between public services, communities, individuals and enterprises.

In Chapter Four, Inga Narbutaité Aflaki describes and analyses an innovative form of partnership for the reception and integration of unaccompanied asylum-seeking children in Gothenburg, Sweden. The municipality of Gothenburg works with children who arrive in Sweden without adults. It does this through a form of collaborative partnership (idéburna offentliga partnerskap [IOP]) with nine civil society organisations. Often, housing and care are the only services that asylum-seeking children receive through municipal or contracted service providers. The Gothenburg IOP provides children with a wide variety of complementary services, including psychosocial counselling, access to Swedish social networks through volunteer 'friend' families, tailored leisure time activities and summer work practice opportunities. This IOP partnership is experimental in Swedish local public policy. It has been successful in increasing municipal capacities through new patterns of more equal and long-term relations with civil society.

Labour market activation is at the heart of Social Investment, and this is the theme of Part B (Chapters Five, Six, Seven and Eight). Their emphasis is on social innovation to upgrade human capital and increase access to paid work. In Chapter Five, Kaisa Sorsa introduces the Youth Guarantee and One-Stop Guidance Centres (OSGCs) in Finland. The Youth Guarantee supports young people to gain a place in education and employment to prevent prolonged youth unemployment. The OSGCs are a mechanism for Youth Guarantee implementation, giving young adults tools with which to improve their social situation, for example, enhancing access to education and jobs. This is a social innovation that creates a new form of public–private–people partnership, with young people actively shaping their own future. OSGCs invest in young people's social capital. The Turku OSG, the focus of the case study, achieved its goal of empowering young people by involving them from the very beginning and throughout implementation.

In Chapter Six, Alexandra Koronaiou, George Alexias, Alexandros Sakellariou and George Vayias consider a programme providing work experience for technical education graduates in Greece. This programme was launched to provide education, vocational counselling and work experience to people aged up to 29 years who resided in regions of the highest youth unemployment. It was organised and managed by a consortium of social partners established for the purpose. Enterprises were given the opportunity to employ graduates as interns to extend their workforce and to benefit from fresh ideas. The programme was quite a complex one with very limited time available (just under one year). Nevertheless, there is some evidence of positive effects on various levels, although it is too early to assess the numbers and sustainability of the new jobs created.

The subject of Chapter Seven by Nikola Borosch, Danielle Gluns and Annette Zimmer is the network for the regional labour market integration of asylum seekers and refugees in Münster (MAMBA), Germany. MAMBA was designed by a refugee aid association which coordinates it in partnership with four other local organisations, each partner providing individual support to participants in its particular field of expertise. In addition to working intensively with individuals to improve their job prospects, the MAMBA partners attempt to address structural barriers to labour market integration by raising awareness with employers and providing training for job centre staff. MAMBA is a success story mainly as a result of intensive, time-consuming personal assistance achieved through the fruitful cooperation of very different organisations.

This section concludes with Chapter Eight by Aldona Wiktorska-Święcka and Dorota Moroń, which is about activation and empowerment of the homeless in Wroclaw, Poland. Known as 'Assistance from A to Z', this programme equips homeless individuals with competencies and skills to improve self-sufficiency and access the labour market. It is a local project but related to national and EU active inclusion policy and funded through the European Social Fund. An important innovative element was the use of 'accompaniment', an idea for intensive individual support that comes from France. In the Polish context, the combined use of a wide range of social and professional support was also innovative. The activation and empowerment of a group of such extremely excluded people as the homeless is demanding and requires intensive, individualised interventions adapted to the needs and capabilities of the beneficiaries. Economic evaluation of this case suggests that it was successful in bringing positive results and was a productive expenditure.

Part C is about Social Investment and social solidarity (Chapters Nine, Ten and Eleven). The main focus is on inclusion in social and community life. In Chapter Nine, Alfons Fermin, Sandra Geelhoed and Rob Gründemann explain the innovative creation of a socially diverse neighbourhood called the 'Green Sticht' in Utrecht, the Netherlands. Inspired by the ideas of a charismatic activist preacher, the Green Sticht created an entirely new neighbourhood with an informal support system for socially vulnerable people, and thus circumvented the 'not in my backyard' sentiment present in the city. Residents who choose to move there out of idealism live alongside citizens who are formerly homeless, often with psychological and psychiatric problems. The Green Sticht has become financially self-reliant. It has never been fully replicated, but it has recently inspired two new projects, showing that it is possible to adapt combinations of the main elements and mechanisms that have made it successful and sustainable.

In Chapter Ten, Judit Csoba and Flórián Sipos introduce the Social Land Programmes in Hungary. Social Land Programmes aim to strengthen self-sufficiency and reduce reliance on social aid by helping people with no financial means to engage with small-scale agriculture. The case study investigated eight rural communities participating in a Social Land Programme. Innovative features include bottom-up organisation designed and carried out locally (in contrast to the top-down public employment programmes in Hungary). For local leaders, producing food and improving living standards are its main points. They also see various other benefits that include improving the social and physical environment and passing on positive role models within the family. However, they consider national goals of increased employment and self-sustainability to be over-optimistic.

Chapter Eleven by Michael Willoughby, Jose Millet-Roig, Jose Pedro García-Sabater and Aida Saez-Mas is about a successful energy cooperative in Spain. With rising poverty and energy prices among the most expensive in Europe, the cooperative not only provides a reliable source of clean energy to consumers, but also forms a central part of the community in which it is situated. The case study points to a need for private enterprises to collaborate with local authorities and social services to provide solutions to the drastic situations of poverty that are still prevalent, particularly in areas of Southern and Eastern Europe. The Spanish energy cooperative demonstrates one way in which the social economy can help to shape the future of the welfare state in the absence of state funding and in the face of national policies that are not well aligned.

In Chapter Twelve, Andrea Bassi, Susan Baines, Judit Csoba and Flórián Sipos review Social Investment in theory and praxis, asking whether it is a 'quiet revolution' in innovative local services. This final chapter synthesises the findings, drawing together lessons from the thematic sections. The authors consider the changing roles and responsibilities of different actors, the centrality of the substantive economy, and activation, personalisation and co-creation. They conclude with reflections on the intersection of Social Investment with social innovation, and some implications for decision-makers and for front-line practitioners tasked with implementation.

References

Astbury, B. and Leeuw, F.L. (2010) 'Unpacking black boxes: mechanisms and theory building in evaluation', *American Journal of Evaluation*, 31(3): 363–81.

Barbier, J. (2017) '"Social investment": with or against social protection', in A. Hemerijck (ed) *The uses of social investment*, Oxford: Oxford University Press.

Bassi, A., Ecchia, G. and Guerra, A. (2016) 'Overview report on the role of the social economy in delivering social investment related to social innovation'. Available at: https://ec.europa.eu/research/participants/documents/downloadPublic?documentIds=080166e5a613a6d0&appId=PPGMS

BEPA (Bureau of European Policy Advisers) (2010) *Empowering people, driving change: Social innovation in the European Union*, Luxembourg: Publications Office of the European Union.

Billis, D. (2010) 'From welfare bureaucracies to welfare hybrids', in D. Billis (ed) *Hybrid organizations and the third sector: Challenges for practice, theory and practice*, New York: Palgrave Macmillan.

Bonvin, J.-M. and Laruffa, F. (2017) 'Towards a normative framework for welfare reform based on the capability and human rights approaches', Re-InVEST Working Paper Series D4.1, Leuven: RE-InVEST.

Bouget, D., Frazer, H., Marlier, E., Sabato, S. and Vanhercke, B. (2015) *Social investment in Europe: A study of national policies*, Brussels: European Commission.

Brandsen, T., Evers, A., Cattacin, S. and Zimmer, A. (2016) 'Social innovation: a sympathetic and critical interpretation', in T. Brandsen, A. Cattacin, S. Evers and A. Zimmer (eds) *Social innovations in the urban context*, Berlin: Springer International Publishing, pp 3–20.

Byrne, D. (2009) 'Case based methods: why we need them; what they are; how to do them', in D.S. Byrne and C.C. Ragin (eds) *The SAGE handbook of case-based methods*, Los Angeles, CA, and London: SAGE.

Cabinet Office (2013) 'Social investment: an introduction to the government's approach'. Available at: https://www.gov.uk/government/publications/social-investment-an-introduction-to-the-governments-approach

Cantillon, B. and Van Lancker, W. (2013) 'Three shortcomings of the social investment perspective', *Social Policy and Society*, 12(4): 553–64.

CIRIEC (International Centre of Research and Information on the Public, Social and Cooperative Economy) (2012) 'The social economy in the European Union', European Economic and Social Committee, Brussels.

Daly, M. (2012) 'Paradigms in EU social policy: a critical account of Europe 2020', *Transfer: European Review of Labour and Research*, 18(3): 273–84.

Deeming, C. and Smyth, P. (2015) 'Social investment after neoliberalism: policy paradigms and political platforms', *Journal of Social Policy*, 44(2): 297–318.

Deeming, C. and Smyth, P. (eds) (2017) *Reframing global social policy: Social investment for sustainable and inclusive growth*, Bristol: The Policy Press.

Dobrowolsky, A. and Lister, R. (2008) 'Social investment: the discourse and the dimensions of change', in M. Powell (ed) *Modernizing the welfare state: The Blair legacy*, Bristol: The Policy Press, pp 125–42.

Dyson, A. and Todd, L. (2010) 'Dealing with complexity: theory of change evaluation and the full service extended schools initiative', *International Journal of Research & Method in Education*, 33(2): 119–34.

Esping-Andersen, G., Gallie, D., Hemerijck, A. and Myles, J. (eds) (2002) *Why we need a new welfare state*, Oxford: Oxford University Press.

European Commission (2013) 'Towards social investment for growth and cohesion – including implementing the European Social Fund 2014–2020', COM (2013) 83 final: Brussels.

European Commission (2017) 'Commission communication on the European pillar of social rights', COM/2017/0250 final: Brussels. Available at: http://eur-lex.europa.eu/legal-content/EN/TXT/PDF/?uri=CELEX:52017DC0250&from=EN

European Council (2000) 'Lisbon European Council. Presidency conclusions', 23–24 March.

Evers, A. and Brandsen, T. (2016) 'Social innovations as messages: democratic experimentation in local welfare systems', in T. Brandsen, A. Cattacin, S. Evers and A. Zimmer (eds) *Social innovations in the urban context*, Berlin: Springer International Publishing, pp 161–80.

Evers, A. and Laville, J.L. (eds) (2004) *The third sector in Europe*, Aldershot: Edward Elgar Publishing.

Ewert, B. and Evers, A. (2014) 'Blueprints for the future of welfare provision? Shared features of service innovations across Europe', *Social Policy & Society*, 13(3): 423–32.

Ferrara, M. (2017) 'Accelerator or brake? The EU and the difficult politics of social investment', in A. Hemerijck (ed) *The uses of social investment*, Oxford: Oxford University Press, pp 328–38.

Flyvbjerg, B. (2006) 'Five misunderstandings about case-study research', *Qualitative Inquiry*, 12(2): 219–45.

Fox, C., Caldeira, R. and Grimm, R. (2016) *An introduction to evaluation*, London: Sage.

Franz, H.W., Hochgerner, J. and Howaldt, J. (2012) 'Challenge social innovation: an introduction', in H.W. Franz, J. Hochgerner and J Howaldt (eds) *Challenge social innovation*, Berlin and Heidelberg: Springer, pp 1–16.

Giddens, A. (1998) *The Third Way: The renewal of local democracy*, Cambridge: Polity Press.

Grimm, R., Fox, C., Baines, S. and Albertson, K. (2013) 'Social innovation, an answer to contemporary societal challenges? Locating the concept in theory and practice', *Innovation: The European Journal of Social Science Research*, 26(4): 436–55.

Hemerijck, A. (2013) *Changing welfare states*, Oxford: Oxford University Press.

Hemerijck, A. (2015) 'The quiet paradigm revolution of social investment', *Social Politics*, 22(2): 242–56.

Hemerijck, A. (2017) 'Social investment and its critics', in A. Hemerijck (ed) *The uses of social investment*, Oxford: Oxford University Press.

Jenson, J. (2009) 'Lost in translation: the social investment perspective and gender equality', *Social Politics*, 16(4): 446–83.

Jenson, J. (2015) 'Social innovation: redesigning the welfare diamond', in A. Nicholls, J. Simon, M. Gabriel and C. Whelan (eds) *New frontiers in social innovation research*, London: Palgrave Macmillan, pp 89–106.

Kazepov, Y. and Ranci, C. (2017) 'Is every country fit for social investment? Italy as an adverse case', *Journal of European Social Policy*, 27(1): 90–104.

Kuitto, K. (2016) 'From social security to social investment? Compensating and social investment welfare policies in a life-course perspective', *Journal of European Social Policy*, 26(5): 442–59.

Leeuw, F. and Vaessen, J. (2009) *Impact and development: Nonie guidance on impact evaluation*, Washington, DC: World Bank.

Leoni, T. (2015) 'The social investment perspective as guiding principle for welfare state adjustment', WWWforEurope.

Lévesque, B. (2006) 'L'innovation dans le développement économique et dans le développement social', in J.-L. Klein and D. Harrisson (eds) *L'innovation sociale. Émergence et effet sur la transformation sociale*, Québec: Presses de l'Université du Québec, pp 43–70.

Mackenzie, M. and Blamey, A. (2005) 'The practice and the theory: lessons from the application of a theories of change approach', *Evaluation*, 11(2): 151–68.

Marques, P., Morgan, K. and Richardson, R. (2017) 'Social innovation in question: the theoretical and practical implications of a contested concept', *Environment and Planning C*, 36(3): 496–512.

Morel, N. and Palme, J. (2017) 'A normative foundation for the social investment approach?', in A. Hemerijck (ed) *The uses of social investment*, Oxford: Oxford University Press.

Morel, N., Palier, B. and Palme, J. (eds) (2012) *Towards a social investment welfare state? Ideas, policies and challenges*, Bristol: The Policy Press.

Moulaert, F. (ed) (2013) *The international handbook on social innovation: Collective action, social learning and transdisciplinary research*, Aldershot: Edward Elgar.

Mumford, M.D. (2002) 'Social innovation: ten cases from Benjamin Franklin', *Creativity Research Journal*, 14(2): 253–66.

Nicholls, A. and Teasdale, S. (2017) 'Neoliberalism by stealth? Exploring continuity and change within the UK social enterprise policy paradigm', *Policy & Politics*, 45(3): 323–41.

Nolan, B. (2013) 'What use is "social investment"?', *Journal of European Social Policy*, 23(5): 459–68.

Palier, B. (2008) 'Presentation', in G. Esping-Andersen and B. Palier (eds) *Trois Leçons sur l'Etat-providence*, Paris: Seuil, pp 5–17.

Polányi, K. (1976) *Az archaikus társadalom és a gazdasági szemlélet [Archaic society and the economic approach]*, Budapest: Gondolat Kiadó.

Ragin, C. (1989) *The comparative method: Moving beyond qualitative and quantitative strategies*, Oakland, CA: University of California Press.

Sabato, S., Vanhercke, V. and Verschraegen, G. (2017) 'Connecting entrepreneurship with policy experimentation? The EU framework for social innovation', *Innovation: The European Journal of Social Science Research*, 30(2): 147–67.

Sabel, C. (2012) 'Individualized service provision and the new welfare state: are there lessons from Northern Europe for developing countries?', in C. Luiz de Mello and M.A. Dutz (eds) *Promoting inclusive growth, challenges and policies*, Paris: OECD, pp 75–111.

Sabel, C., Zeitlin, J. and Quack, S. (2017) 'Capacitating services and the bottom-up approach to social investment', in A. Hemerijck (ed) *The uses of social investment*, Oxford: Oxford University Press.

Schumpeter, J. (1983 [1934]) *The theory of economic development. An inquiry into profits, capital, credit, interest and the business cycle*, New Brunswick, NJ: Transaction Publishing.

Sen, A. (2001) *Development as freedom*, Oxford: Oxford Paperbacks.

Smyth, P. and Deeming, C. (2016) 'The "social investment perspective" in social policy: a longue durée perspective', *Social Policy & Administration*, 50(6): 673–90.

Social Protection Committee (2011) *The social dimension of the Europe 2020 Strategy*, Luxembourg: Publications Office of the European Union.

Stake, R.E. (2008) 'Qualitative case studies', in N. Denzin and Y. Lincoln (eds) *Strategies of qualitative inquiry*, Thousand Oaks, CA: Sage, pp 119–49.

Van Kersbergen, K. and Hemerijck, A. (2012) 'Two decades of change in Europe: the emergence of the social investment state', *Journal of Social Policy*, 41(3): 475–92.

Warner, M. (2013) 'Private finance for public goods: social impact bonds', *Journal of Economic Policy Reform*, 16(4): 303–19.

Westley, F. and Antadze, N. (2010) 'Making a difference: strategies for scaling social innovation for greater impact', *The Innovation Journal: The Public Sector Innovation Journal*, 15(2): article 2. Available at: www.innovation.cc/scholarly-style/westley2antadze2make_difference_final.pdf

Wolff, K. (2007) 'Methods, case study', in G. Ritzer (ed) *Blackwell encyclopedia of sociology*, Oxford: Blackwell Publishing, Blackwell Reference Online.

Yin, R. (2003) *Case study research: Design and methods*, London: Sage Publications.

Part A: Children and families: early intervention in people's life courses

Andrea Bassi and Susan Baines

The three case studies included in this section illustrate examples of a core area of the Social Investment paradigm: early interventions in people's life courses and especially investing in children. A core idea of the Social Investment perspective is that the future must be assured by investing in children in order to end the intergenerational transmission of disadvantage (Jenson, 2009). Education has been called the vanguard of Social Investment (Deeming and Smyth, 2015). Hemerijck (2002) proposes a 'developmental' welfare agenda for 21st-century Europe. The concept of developmental welfare provides a common language for giving priority to guaranteeing high levels of employment for both men and women as a fundamental political objective, combining elements of flexibility and security, aimed at facilitating men and especially women in reconciling work and family life. The agenda implies the early identification of problems through investment in early childhood services, as well as family and child-centred interventions.

Jane Jenson (2015: 98), in a rare attempt to link Social Investment and social innovation, comments that 'the emerging knowledge based economy requires significant investment in human capital [that] must begin with the youngest children and early childhood education'. However, there are criticisms of this as an overly instrumental conceptualisation of children that displaces both their right to a childhood and interest in their present welfare. Ruth Lister (2003) deplored the 'emergent social investment state' in the UK under New Labour in the early 2000s. She opposed, in particular, the implication that children should be seen as 'citizen-workers of the future' rather than the 'citizen-child of the present'.

The three case studies in this book are concerned with children and families, but in very different ways. Chapter Two analyses early childhood education and care (ECEC) services, which are not only a principal policy area of the Social Investment package (European Commission, 2013), but also, according to the Europe 2020 Strategy, an essential requirement to achieve smart, sustainable and inclusive growth. ECEC services in the Emilia-Romagna region of Italy include new types of services to meet the changing needs of families. These

ECEC services aim to be universal while responding to local needs. The education and care services support mothers to combine family life and employment but the overall emphasis of most participants is one of child development. The three different services included in the Italian case study have in common a strong commitment towards working with families in a participatory and inclusive way that values the contribution that each parent can bring. The professionals advocate dialogue with the parents and families of the children in order to learn from their experiential understandings. The adoption of a 'welcoming approach' towards parents, sustaining their informal involvement in the everyday life of childcare and education provision, seems to be a key success factor for developing mutual relationships of trust between educators and families, especially in contexts where childcare outside the family is not always seen positively. Children, including very young children, are viewed as citizens and bearers of rights rather than future productive workers.

Troubled Families is a targeted national programme in England intended to 'turn around' families with multiple problems. The national programme emphasises that the cost of these families to the public purse is out of proportion to their numbers. In this sense, it fits the model of conditional, targeted, time-limited programmes that Barbier (2017) sees as counter to the strong Social Investment paradigm. Nevertheless, the underpinning principles of the programme align with the paradigm through its emphasis on early intervention with children, and sustained parental employment. Troubled Families has been highly controversial, with critics deploring an element of stigmatisation in which families are presented as causing trouble ('neighbours from hell') rather than beset by troubles such as poverty and poor health. The case study in Chapter Three focuses not on the national programme, but on its implementation in the conurbation of Greater Manchester, where it forms part of the recent devolution agreement with central government. It therefore has in common with ECEC a strong emphasis on local solutions. As in Emilia-Romagna, new collaborations and partnerships have been put in place with some success, although the aim of integrating services within a subregion is rather different.

Social Investment also implies responding to increasingly diverse populations. Early intervention in life-course models does not at first sight seem to fit very well with responding to immigration when beneficiaries have not been born in the country that hosts them and may have family ties and emotional links overseas. Chapter Four is about a creative local response in Sweden to the recent influx of children who arrive in the country without parents or other responsible adults. The family-centred approaches of Chapters Two and Three are therefore not possible. Many of the children have complex needs as a result of traumatic experiences of war and flight. Instead of working with the children's own families, the programme partners help to form substitute 'friend families' with local volunteers. The first priorities are securing shelter and improving psychological well-being but there is also education for future life in Sweden and an element of workforce preparation through practical work experience. The long-term goals for working with a group of highly disadvantaged young people in this Swedish case fit the Social Investment paradigm, although increasing future human capital does not appear to be a strong driver for the partners, who are more interested in humanitarian issues.

References

Barbier, J. (2017) '"Social investment": with or against social protection', in A. Hemerijck (ed) *The uses of social investment*, Oxford: Oxford University Press.

Deeming, C. and Smyth, P. (2015) 'Social investment after neoliberalism: policy paradigms and political platforms', *Journal of Social Policy*, 44(2): 297–318.

European Commission (2013) 'Towards social investment for growth and cohesion – including implementing the European Social Fund 2014–2020', COM (2013) 83 final: Brussels.

Hemerijck, A. (2002) 'The self-transformation of the European social model(s)', in G. Esping-Andersen, with D. Gallie, A. Hemerijck and J. Myles (2002) *Why we need a new welfare state*, Oxford: Oxford University Press.

Jenson, J. (2009) 'Lost in translation: the social investment perspective and gender equality', *Social Politics*, 16(4): 446–83.

Jenson, J. (2015) 'Social innovation: redesigning the welfare diamond', in A. Nicholls, J. Simon, M. Gabriel and C. Whelan (eds) *New frontiers in social innovation research*, London: Palgrave Macmillan, pp 89–106.

Lister, R. (2003) 'Investing in the citizen-workers of the future: transformations in citizenship and the state under New Labour', *Social Policy & Administration*, 37(5): 427–43.

TWO

Investing in the future!
Three case studies of social innovation in the Emilia-Romagna Early Childhood Education and Care services system

Andrea Bassi

Introduction

This chapter is about the Early Childhood Education and Care (ECEC) services in Emilia-Romagna, Italy. It considers the extent to which these integrated ECEC services are beneficial to children, families and society at large, and assesses them as possible best practice with regard to the partnership between public, private for-profit and non-profit actors. The rationale for the selection of these services (focusing specifically on children aged three and under and their families) is the relevance of the policy area for the theme of Social Investment. The chapter adopts the theoretical framework of social innovation from Westley and Antadze (2010) and applies Hochgerner's (2011) four-dimensional scheme of social innovation – resources, authority flows, routines and beliefs – as elaborated by Bassi (2011).

Analysis of the data collected shows that no one model fits all. Rather, the key success factors for increasing the availability and the affordability of ECEC provision seem to reside in the flexible combination of different funding sources coming from the public sector as well as from the not-for-profit sector and private enterprises. This happens within a comprehensive framework of public policies that responsively addresses the needs identified within each community while striving for universalism. In this sense, the case studies provide exemplary instances of how diversified ECEC provision serving the varied needs of children and families within local communities could be realised, with a special focus on accessibility and economic sustainability. Besides addressing the issues of sustainability and accessibility, the case studies shed light on how the pedagogical quality of ECEC provision and its ongoing improvement could be nurtured through the co-creation and sharing of knowledge, expertise and experiences generated by innovative forms of public governance (local and regional networks, partnerships with parents, coalitions for policy advocacy, inter-agency collaboration).

Social innovation in ECEC services in Emilia-Romagna

This research studied ECEC services in the region of Emilia-Romagna, adopting a realist evaluation approach. In order to verify the potentialities of these services in terms of social innovation – within a Social Investment policy framework – a multiple case-study research approach was adopted. This chapter is therefore based on a case-study design involving in-depth research with three out of the 1,206 services active in the region. The process by which the three cases were selected is set out in the following before going on to discuss their characteristics.

The most difficult task in a research programme based on a case-study approach concerns the selection of the unit of analysis. In order to identify the case-study services, the research team proceeded as follows. First of all, they contacted the head of the ECEC services system in the Emilia-Romagna region, explained the research design and asked them to offer the support of the ECEC services offices. After discussion with the public official working in the ECEC services office at the regional level, selection criteria were agreed upon and 12 services were identified, from which the research team chose six. The cases to be included in the research were selected following four main criteria:

1. Geographic distribution: western, central and eastern areas of the Emilia-Romagna region (mountain/hills; plain; seaside);
2. Municipality dimension: small (up to 15,000 inhabitants); medium (up to 100,000 inhabitants); and metropolitan areas (250,000 to 500,000 inhabitants);
3. Ownership structure, with the principal delivering organisation being public, private for-profit or private non-profit; and
4. Services typology, following the classification defined by the Emilia-Romagna regional government ([a] Nurseries/kindergartens; [b] Integrative/complementary services; [c] Home services; and [d] Experimental services).

After the first two site visits, the team realised that it would not be possible to conduct all six case studies in sufficient depth given the duration of the Innovative Social Investment: Strengthening Communities in Europe (InnoSI) study. In agreement with the public official responsible for ECEC services, the number of case studies was therefore reduced to three, selected according to the ECEC services typology. They were: the *Filonido* nursery in the city of Bologna for type a; *La Gabbianella* and *L'Albero delle Meraviglie* in the town of Comacchio for type b; and *Il girotondo Intorno al Bosco* in the village of Serramazzoni for type c. The team also tried to take into consideration the other characteristics. In terms of geographic distribution, Bologna is on the plain (centre), Comacchio at the seaside (east) and Serramazzoni in the mountains/hills to the west. With regard to the municipality dimension, Bologna is a city (387,500 inhabitants), Comacchio is a medium-sized town (22,600 inhabitants) and Serramazzoni has only 8,200 inhabitants. The Bologna nursery is owned by a big social enterprise consortium, while in Comacchio, the owner is a medium non-profit organisation, and in Serramazzoni, the owner is a small for-profit business. It was not possible to include in the sample a public ECEC service centre.

In common with all InnoSI case studies, the research in Emilia-Romagna utilised a variety of sources of data, as indicated in Chapter One. It included: official documents (eg laws enacted by the regional government and regulations enacted by municipalities); unofficial documents (such as meeting minutes); grey material (research reports and evaluation reports by public bodies and research institutions); face-to-face interviews with representatives from the public administration, non-profit organisations, private corporations and parents' associations; focus groups with representatives of the aforementioned organisations; and on-site observation of ECEC service centres. The following subsections draw upon these data to elaborate on each of the three services in turn.

The home-care ECEC service in Serramazzoni

Serramazzoni is situated in the first buttress between the plains and the mountains of the Modena province. The educational service called 'The wandering around the woods' was founded in 2005 thanks to an agreement between the municipality of Serramazzoni and a private entity, meeting the requirements of Regional Law n. 1/2000. The obligations identified for the manager are as follows: organising and providing the necessary means for the execution of the service; providing educational staff and personnel for general services in the numbers needed to meet the requirements of the legislation; providing the necessary tools for the service; and providing the purchase of equipment and furniture, and the ordinary and extraordinary maintenance of the location. The municipality has the responsibility for organisational and administrative support services, including service user information and receipt of applications for admission, as well as the determination of the monthly rates charged to families.

The educational service 'The wandering around the woods' takes children from nine months to three years, providing services to nourish their growth and to complement and support the role of parents. It is located inside a historic building (of the 17th century) with characteristics typical of mountain areas. It consists of two services: (1) a 'Small Educational Group' in an apartment on the ground floor; and (2) 'Educator Homecare' placed in the home next door. The service operates five days a week, from Monday to Friday, with full-time operation from 08:00 to 16:00. The 'Small Educational Group' offers sessions for seven children from the age of nine months up to 36 months, led by two educators. The 'Educator Homecare' service offers sessions for five children from the age of 12 months up to 36 months, led by two educators.

The 'complementary ECEC service' in Comacchio

In terms of scenic and historical aspects, the town of Comacchio is one of the major centres across the Po River. Comacchio was born from the union of 13 small islands formed by the intersection of the Po estuary with the sea. For this reason, it has had to base its urban and economic development on the element of water. The municipal childhood centre called *L'Albero delle Meraviglie* (The Centre of 'Wonder Tree') was founded in 1988 as a pilot. It was the first time that the city of Comacchio assumed direct responsibility for early childhood education. The problems it faced were related to the development of boys and girls in the early years, the support of parents' roles and the facilitation of parent–child relationships (Andreoli and Cambi, 2001).

The young mothers who had worked to encourage the initiative, some of them in possession of only basic training in education, lent their work on a voluntary basis. The service is situated in the building of an elementary school, but the school director withdrew the collaboration two years later and the initiative was interrupted for more than a year. In 1992, voluntary mothers founded 'Libellula', an association of volunteers (charity) registered in the regional register, to which the municipality school and education office entrusted the management of the *L'Albero delle Meraviglie* for the next four years. In 1997, the association had to give up the management of the service but it continued its educational and outreach activities, providing the parents with training sessions and courses pre-birth. Following changes in its institutional and statutory structure, it transformed itself into a cooperative called 'Girogirotondo'. From the school year 1998/99, the cooperative took over the management of *L'Albero delle Meraviglie*, progressively expanding the range of offers and extending their activities into the neighbouring territories with various initiatives aimed at different types of users (Andreoli and Cambi, 2001). This service can be credited with two significant achievements. It provided an opportunity for the youngest, which was totally lacking in the territory, and it created an opportunity for professional training and job placement for young women.

The children's day-care service, *La Gabbianella* (The little seagull), is an educational service run by the Girogirotondo cooperative. It was founded in 1999 in response to the needs of the families for a day-care service for young children. The service hosts up to 24 children aged from 12 to 36 months, entrusted to educators for up to five hours daily. During the year, it follows the calendar of the public school holidays. However, it is open the entire year (from September until the end of August) in order to keep continuity of the service in place and to meet the demands that come from a tourism-oriented area. This yearly opening period is a major improvement, aimed at strengthening the 'educational offer' of the territory and helping parents working in tourist accommodation services (beaches and restaurants) during the summer. Today, it is an alternative/integrative service for those families who do not choose a full-time ECEC service, but who still want part-time day care in which their children can enjoy significant experiences of socialisation, playing, exploration and first separation from the family environment and parents.

The Children and Parents Centre of *L'Albero delle Meraviglie* is open every afternoon from Monday to Saturday from 16:30 to 19:30 (each afternoon being reserved for a different age group), and on Saturday, from 9:30 to 12:30. It is a type of service characterised by the presence of children and parents (or other adult family members) who interact together. The centre must therefore be understood as a 'co-educational' site, a system in which each part (space, time, the role of adults, relationships) evolves and changes in relation to others in a reciprocal relationship. The centre promotes opportunities for socialising and playing in a meeting space designed to encourage the processes of growth and development of skills by creating an atmosphere of sociability and trust, both through experience in the peer group and in the relationship with adults (Musatti, 2004). Image 2.1 shows how front-line workers visualise it as a space where children and parents can play together, and be engaged in a multiplicity of activities with the help of professional educators.

Image 2.1: Illustration of the 'Children and Parents Centre' from the point of view of a front line-worker

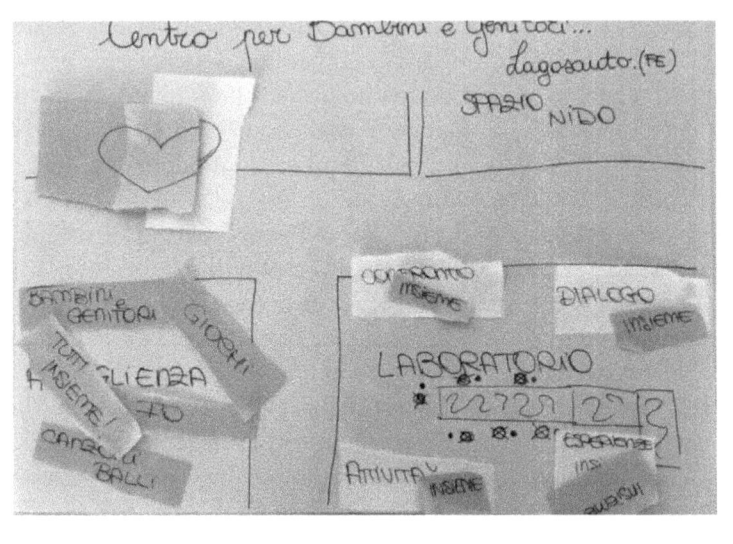

The 'Filonido' nursery in Bologna

Filonido is a 'corporate welfare' nursery centre that was inaugurated in September 2011 as a 10th structure designed, built and managed in the province of Bologna by a cooperative consortium called 'Karabak'. The challenge started from analysis of customers' requests by the municipality of Bologna, together with the Emilia-Romagna region and the companies of the trade fair, and from a local context study about needs, desires and medium- to long-term perspectives. Thus, the Filonido project was preceded by an analysis aimed at describing the specific characteristics in terms of city planning and socio-economic background of Bologna's San Donato district, as well as identifying the demand for educational services for early childhood.

In 2009, the Emilia-Romagna region and the municipality of Bologna signed an agreement for the construction of a public and 'corporate welfare' crèche, located in the district of San Donato in Bologna, open to the community. For the construction of the crèche, the region invested €2 million and the municipality of Bologna made available the land where it is built. Moreover, it identified the Karabak consortium as the project manager and supervisor for a period of 30 years by using a public tendering procedure. The Karabak consortium is made up of five cooperatives: two 'social cooperatives' (Dolce and Cadiai); one catering (food service) cooperative (Camst); one construction cooperative (Manutencoop); and a maintenance cooperative (CIPEA). The agreement includes three companies: Unipol Finance Group, Legacoop and Hera Group. Based on that, the Filonido nursery hosts a certain number of children of the workers (mainly mothers) of these companies/organisations.

The agreement, approved by the Emilia-Romagna region, the municipality of Bologna and three participating services companies, lays down the commitment of the partners. The average cost of a child place is around €800 a month. The fee paid by the families depends on income and the remaining amount of the full cost of the service is paid by the municipality. The differences in cost related to the places reserved to the employees of the corporations are paid by the corporations. At the end of the concession, the building will be owned by the city of Bologna.

The Filonido project was possible thanks to a partnership between public and private institutions, based on sharing a common goal: giving families some concrete answers to their work–life balance needs. Filonido represents an exemplary implementation of *community welfare* based on providing services through a net of different organisations. The nursery is an educational social service of public interest that works with families and it is aimed at educating the children according to municipal educational guidelines. Filonido accommodates 81 children aged three months to 36 months, including 20 places agreed upon with the municipality of Bologna, 12 with private or voucher, and 49 with the Emilia-Romagna region and some companies belonging to the Bologna Exhibition Centre (Unipol Finance Group, Legacoop Bologna and Hera Group).

Key findings: implementation and impact

This section summarises the main findings emerging from the three in-depth case studies described earlier. To do this, it utilises the rhetorical format of questions and answers.

First question: are the three case studies analysed examples of Social Investment?

The answer is 'yes' but in peculiar different ways. The Bologna ECEC service centre is a clear example of Social Investment given the fact that it offers a very high-quality nursery service, at the price established by the local authority, to a very broad range of employed women (the centre has the capacity to host up to 81 children aged 0–3 years old), in the proximity of their workplace. The centre, indeed, is located in a very high-density office district (the so-called 'Fiera district') that is characterised by the concentration of many private enterprises (consultancy, financial and commercial intermediaries), cooperative enterprises (insurance, bank services, umbrella organisations giving services to their membership) and public agencies (the regional government), with a high level of women in the workforce. The possibility to entrust their children to a very modern and functional nursery service – with a flexible time schedule – near their work allows them to conciliate their working life with their family life, and to ameliorate their life–work balance. It is about very high-skilled, well-educated, middle-class women who occupy middle- to high-level job positions in the tertiary sector of the economy.

The two Comacchio ECEC service centres, on the other hand, are an example of Social Investment in the sense that they offer a 'space', a place where people of different generations, ethnicity, religions and cultures can meet in a safe and controlled environment in order to pursue the education of their children. It is a particularly important facility, especially in a traditionally deprived and isolated geographical area, and a key actor of the community in the effort to build an inclusive and cohesive society.

The Serramazzoni ECEC service centre is an example of Social Investment given the fact that it offers a nursery service – in a small, informal, friendly and familiar setting – to families that would otherwise not have the possibility to obtain highly qualified care for their children. Taking into consideration that the municipality of Serramazzoni is a small village on the hills outside the big city of Modena, in a very industrialised area with many young families without relatives in the neighbourhood, the Home Centre represents the only possibility for the parents to conciliate their job careers (especially for women/mothers) with the desire to have children. This is clear from many interviews. For example, a mother with three children of different ages, and all of them enrolled in the Home Centre, said: "if the Home Centre was not there, I would not have been able to work – I should have been forced to stay at home, caring for my children".

Second question: are the three case studies analysed examples of 'social innovation'?

This question can be answered positively but in relation to specific dimensions for each case. The theoretical framework is that social innovation happens when it is activated by some actor (individual or collective) in a system of interaction (relational network). Four main dimension of social action – resources, authority flows, routines and beliefs – are illustrated in Figure 2.1. A change in one of the four dimensions of the relational field of action is able to 'activate' additional changes in the other three dimensions (positive feedback). Only when and if the changes interact with each other, reaching a certain level of intensity (scale), does the entire system of interaction change (saturation effect) in a substantial, stable and somehow permanent way. So, in order to start a social innovation process, a socially innovative entrepreneur (who may be an individual or a group) is needed. In order to allow the social innovation to diffuse and reach a scale of sufficient (critical) mass to become adopted by the majority of the actors in the system of interaction, it is necessary that a certain number of preconditions should be complied with. It is a long-standing process with several forward and backward steps, and the final success of a social innovation process is related to the level of 'path dependency' or 'path-breaking' present in the system of interaction.

The Bologna ECEC service centre can be understood as an outstanding example of social innovation from the point of view of an original and unusual combination of economic and financial

Figure 2.1: Social Innovation Compass, representing the complex process of social innovation and its broad impact in the social system

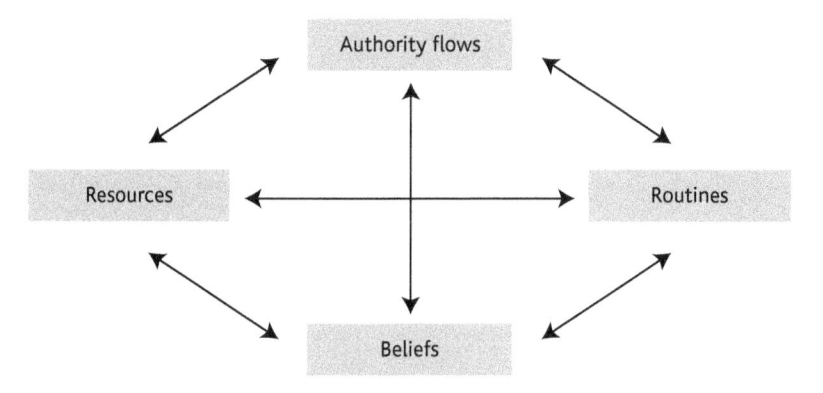

Source: Elaboration of Andrea Bassi from Westley and Antadze (2010)

resources (see the 'left quadrant' in the Social Innovation Compass in Figure 2.1). Figure 2.1 represents the social innovation process as an 'emerging phenomenon' that arises from the interaction (virtuous circles) of the four main dimensions of social action.

As has been described earlier, the peculiarity of the Filonido nursery is the very innovative arrangement of public, private for-profit and private non-profit actors that made it possible to (literally) build a new nursery centre in the Fiera district in the city of Bologna. The network of actors is illustrated in Figure 2.2. It was enabled, in particular, by the following combination of actors and actions:

- the municipality of Bologna gave the land (for a 30-year period);
- the Emilia-Romagna regional government provided a loan of €2 million;
- the cooperative movement set up a consortium (of five members);
- the Karabak consortium built the new centre;
- the Dolce cooperative runs the centre;
- the Camst cooperative supplies the food service; and
- the Emilia-Romagna region, the Hera Corporation, the Unipol Corporation and the Legacoop umbrella association pay for a certain number of places in the nursery for the children of their employees.

The social innovation element of the Comacchio case study consists of an attempt to modify the 'cultural orientations' and the 'beliefs and

Figure 2.2: Networks of actors involved in the Filonido nursery centre

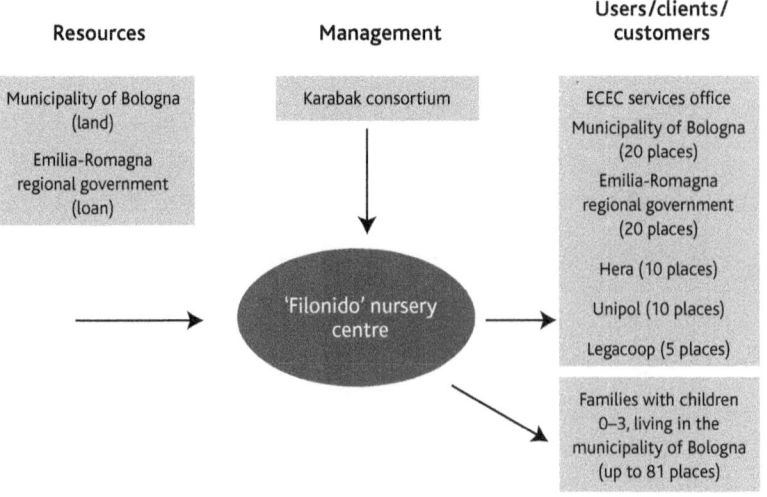

values' of the local community towards childhood and adolescence (see the 'bottom quadrant' of the Social Innovation Compass in Figure 2.1) in an isolated, deprived area of the country. Until the end of the 1980s, the territory suffered from a lack of attention to early childhood education. There were no services for early years child development, support for parents or facilitation of parent–child relationships. Only the successful interaction of international, national, regional and local actors could create the fertile environment for the development and growth of a germ of experimentation around which a bunch of activities and projects took root that are still going on and were able to multiply themselves in a plurality of services and facilities.

The social innovation element of the Serramazzoni case study consists of an attempt to modify the authority flows of the local community in regards to the system of services towards childhood in a dynamic and lively small community situated in one of the most developed economic and productive territories of the region (see the upper quadrant of the Social Innovation Compass in Figure 2.1). The growing demographic trends of the beginning of the 2000s, with the increasing number of young families with infant children, both parents working outside the home and without relatives living nearby, brought pressure on the local administration to implement ECEC services. The impossibility of building a nursery centre – due to the high investment cost – pushed the municipality to promote research for a new settlement and innovative solutions, a possibility that was allowed by the new regulation framework enacted by the regional government in 2000. Article 3 of the new law (n.1 of January 2000) differentiates the plurality of ECEC services available and introduces the typology of 'Home Educator Service'. So, the Serramazzoni case study constitutes a clear example of the combination of different elements that changed the flow of authority in the local community, giving voice to the requests of families with infant children, and creating a 'new market' for ECEC services in which new private providers could find an opportunity to develop their businesses.

Third question: what are the main commonalities that the three case studies share?

Despite many contextual variations, the process of activation of an innovative ECEC service follows a common pathway. This can be summarised in the following six phases:

- Phase 1: An activist or a civil society association (women, parents, workers' union, neighbourhood committees, social movement, etc) (Forno and Graziano, 2014) puts in place an advocacy campaign, pushing the local administration (municipality) towards the adoption of deliberation in order to activate an ECEC service.
- Phase 2: After a long period of negotiation (bargaining), the public administration enacts a resolution that establishes the institution of the ECEC service, sometimes as a pilot or experiment for a limited period of time, usually from one up to three years.
- Phase 3 consists of resistance and opposition. Usually, the institutional regulation framework is not very open to experimentation, pilot projects and innovative services. Inside public administration bodies (at the different government levels: regional, provincial and municipality) employees try to impede any kind of deviation from the routine, 'business as usual' way of working.
- Phase 4: After a certain period of activity, the ECEC service results as a very successful policy and coalitions of supporters are formed in order to sustain the initiative. The municipality is pushed to extend the period of experimentation or, often, to adopt the initiative as a permanent policy.
- Phase 5: At this point, workers who opposed the establishment of the service in the first phase recognise the success of the idea and, unable to obstruct it, start a strategy of acceptance, at first passively and then more and more actively.
- Phase 6: Once the ECEC service becomes a permanent activity, the citizens as customers and the workers as care deliverers, individually or in association (Guidi and Andretta, 2015), are usually able to obtain an extension of both the period and the times of opening, or the activation of additional complementary services.

This very long, time-consuming process shows several features that can be summarised as follows:

- it is clearly a bottom-up process (starting in civil society and moving towards the public administration);
- it requires the presence of a 'social' entrepreneur (usually a woman or a group of women);
- it puts in place a multi-level interaction system with a plurality of actors (global, national, regional and local);
- it activates a complex network of networks (economic, political, social and cultural);

- it consists of emerging phenomena, springing off from the system of interaction in an unintended and unexpected way;
- it requires the combination of several preconditions, among which a very key role is played by the bundle of resources present in the territory; and
- it represents an institutionalisation process through which new practices and ways of thinking enter into mainstream policy.

Learning points and policy implications

It is possible to identify the following lessons to be learned that emerged from the three case studies. *Social innovation initiatives are highly context dependent*, not only in the sense that what can be understood as an 'innovation' in one territory is not in another one, but because social innovations are strictly interwoven and interlocked with a network of actors (defined by the relational system of interaction) that are embedded in a specific economic–political–social–cultural environment. At the beginning of a social innovation process, there is usually the action of a person or of a group of people that play the role of 'entrepreneur', not only, nor primarily, in an economic sense of the term, but more widely from a social, political and cultural perspective. *The public sector is not always an obstacle* to the development and the diffusion of social innovations. On the contrary, in order to be effective, stable (scaling up), durable and sustainable social innovations require a crucial role to be played by the different agencies of the public administration. *The private for-profit sector* can play an important role in social innovation initiatives, but usually – in the field of social, health and education services – is not the actor who starts the experimentation process that results in the social innovation initiative. *Civil society organisations* at different levels of social action– micro, meso and macro – play a crucial and central role in the creation of the small, locally based, experimental, pilot activities, projects and actions that constitute the favourable environment in which social innovations can start, grow and develop.

Social innovations are more effective (and sustainable) when they are able to *trigger a virtuous circle that activates processes of change* in all four dimensions of the 'social innovation diamond' (or compass): (1) resources distribution; (2) authority flows, regulation and actors' roles; (3) routines, social norms and relationships; and (4) values and beliefs. Social innovations often emerge *as unintended consequences* of social action put in place by social actors who want to solve an immediate, concrete and urgent need of their individual members (or families).

From the case studies analysed, it clearly emerges that the rationale driving the Emilia-Romagna region's public investment in ECEC services since the 1970s – as well as their ongoing quality improvement – was a *rights-based rationale* combined with a *social justice rationale*. Children, including young children, were viewed since the very beginning of ECEC in Emilia-Romagna as competent human beings and citizens, and as bearers of rights. Therefore, the ongoing improvement of early education and care services was driven by the commitment of ECEC professionals (educators and pedagogical coordinators) to observe children and to constantly revise their practices by reflecting on children's experiences and progress, as well as for promoting the *participation* of families and local community members in the life of the services (in Box 2.1, two fathers share their experiences of participation). At the same time, this commitment was accompanied by an awareness that pedagogy, civic engagement and political engagement are strictly linked; this awareness, in turn, had profound implications for the way in which ECEC policy-making processes were shaped at the local and regional levels.

Box 2.1: Parents get engaged with the day-to-day work of ECEC centres

The ECEC case studies all share a strong commitment towards working with families in a participatory and inclusive way. Parents expressed much appreciation of opportunities to get engaged in the life of the ECEC centres. 'Educator for a day' is implemented – in slightly different ways – across all the services included in the case study. Within 'educator for a day', each parent who wishes to spend a day in the ECEC centre is given the opportunity. In some cases, they are also invited to run a small activity with children based on their expertise; in others, they are invited to the centre during particular occasions to spend time with their children (eg lunch, tea breaks, festivals or field trips). The following two extracts are from fathers talking about 'Educator for a day':

"Before my first child started to attend the small educational group, my wife and I were strongly against childcare but we were both working parents and we had no choice really ... [but] thinking back, I am now convinced that it was the most important experience my child could have ever have had from an educational point of view! And I realised that as a parent while being there with my child. When I accompanied him in the morning, I used to spend even half an hour on the armchair in the playroom. I played not only with my child, but also with the other children, while the educators were offering me a coffee.... Then I became the first father to be involved in the project 'educator for a day'." (Italian father)

"When I entered the service as 'educator for a day', I saw with my eyes the things that children are able to do when they are together, older and younger ... they help each other and they learn to care for each other!" (Peruvian father)

References

Andreoli, S. and Cambi, I. (2001) 'Un viaggio attraverso i centri per bambini e famiglie dell'Emilia-Romagna: l'Albero delle Meraviglie', *Quaderno GIFT (Genitorialità e Infanzia tra Famiglie e Territorio)*, no 9, pp 28–46.

Bassi, A. (2011) 'Social innovation: some definitions', in Centro de Investigacion de economia y sociedad, *Boletin CIES*, no. 88, Barcelona.

Forno, F. and Graziano, P.R. (2014) 'Sustainable community movement organisations', *Journal of Consumer Culture*, 14(2): 1–19. Available at: http://joc.sagepub.com/content/early/2014/03/19/1469540514526225

Guidi, R. and Andretta, M. (2015) 'Between resistance and resilience: how do Italian solidarity purchase groups change in times of crisis and austerity?', *Partecipazione e conflitto*, 8(2): 443–77. Available at: http://siba-ese.unisalento.it/index.php/paco/issue/view/1322

Hochgerner, J. (2011) 'The analysis of social innovations as social practice'. Available at: https://www.zsi.at/object/publication/1566/attach/The%20Analysis%20of%20Social%20Innovations%20as%20Social%20Practice.pdf

Musatti, T. (2004) 'Early educational settings in Italy: the social context and educational prospects', *Prospects*, 34(4): 447–56.

Westley, F. and Antadze, N. (2010) 'Making a difference: strategies for scaling social innovation for greater impact', *The Innovation Journal: The Public Sector Innovation Journal*, 15(2): article 2. Available at: www.innovation.cc/scholarly-style/westley2antadze2make_difference_final.pdf

THREE

Troubled Families in Greater Manchester

Jessica Ozan, Chris O'Leary,
Susan Baines and Gavin Bailey

Introduction

Troubled Families in Greater Manchester (GM) is a sub-national implementation of an England-wide programme intended to offer joined-up services targeted at families with multiple needs (eg crime, antisocial behaviour, truancy, unemployment, mental health problems and domestic abuse). The underpinning principles of the programme align with the European Social Investment paradigm through its emphasis on early intervention with children, behaviour change and sustained employment. The funding mechanism is a version of Payment by Results (PbR), a form of outcome-based commissioning (Fox et al, 2018), under which local authorities are paid partly through submitting data to demonstrate that they have met outcomes. Troubled Families has been controversial. The government and some popular media declared it an overwhelming success in 'turning around' families (DCLG, 2015) but the national evaluation reported no significant impact. It has been criticised as a policy that individualises societal problems, penalises the socially excluded and justifies cuts in public spending (Levitas, 2012, 2014; Jensen, 2013; Hayden and Jenkins, 2014; Arthur, 2015; Crossley, 2015).

GM is a subregion in the north-west of England, which includes the cities of Manchester and Salford and surrounding towns and villages. There are 10 local authorities in GM, which administer education and social services, housing, roads, and public spaces. In 2012, a number of central government functions were devolved to the Greater Manchester Combined Authority, and a directly elected mayor for GM was first elected in May 2017. The Troubled Families programme in GM was part of the devolution deal (Bate, 2017). There, senior managers see Troubled Families as a catalyst to general public service reform, especially more integrated working across the various services provided directly by the boroughs and contracted to external suppliers, including social economy organisations. The GM approach to reform is underpinned by a set of common objectives:

- A new relationship between public services and citizens, communities and businesses that enables shared decision making, democratic accountability and voice, genuine co-production and joint delivery of services.
- An asset based approach that recognises and builds on the strengths of individuals, families and our communities rather than focusing on the deficits.
- Behaviour change at the community level that builds independence and supports residents to be in control
- A place based approach that redefines services and places individuals, families, communities at the heart
- A stronger prioritisation of well-being, prevention and early intervention
- An evidence led understanding of risk and impact to ensure the right intervention at the right time
- An approach that supports the development of new investment and resourcing models, enabling collaboration with a wide range of organisations. (Greater Manchester Combined Authority, 2016)

The Troubled Families programme is innovative not so much in the interventions on offer, but because of its inter-agency case management, individualised approaches, the co-production of family plans by key workers and family members, and its funding mechanism. All 10 local authorities took part in Troubled Families. The case study focused on two of them in order to offer a meaningful insight into the programme.

Turning around 'troubled families'

The term 'troubled families' emerged in British social policy in 2010, originally in the context of Community Budgets. Community Budgets were intended to develop local solutions to local problems and improve the efficiency of contact between public services and service users (House of Commons Communities Local Government Committee, 2014), enabling local authorities to take a holistic approach to families that experience problems and often cause problems, putting high costs on the public sector (DCLG, 2014: 7). Sixteen local authority areas in England were selected to pilot Community Budgets in October 2010. Following riots in several English cities in the summer of 2011, families that cause problems came to the fore as a policy concern (Jensen, 2013; Arthur, 2015). This was emphasised in the words of then Prime Minister David Cameron:

> Officialdom might call them 'families with multiple disadvantages'. Some in the press might call them 'neighbours from hell'. Whatever you call them, we've known for years that a relatively small number of families are the source of a large proportion of the problems in society. (Cameron, 2011)

In December 2011, Cameron announced new pilots under the name 'Troubled Families'. Their aim was to bring together professionals from diverse services to provide 'a single point of contact for the first time for particular families — working out what the family needs, where the waste is and lining up the right services at the right time' (Cameron, 2011, cited in Bond-Taylor, 2015: 375). GM was one of the original Troubled Families pilot areas. The next year, the Troubled Families programme was rolled out nationally. It is administered by a central government department, the Department for Communities and Local Government (DCLG), and covers England only (Bate, 2017). The aim of the programme was to 'turn around' the lives of these families, meaning that all three of the education and crime/antisocial behaviour outcomes were achieved (ie children having fewer exclusions and unauthorised absences, a reduction in antisocial behaviours across the family, and a reduction in children's offending rates), or that an adult moved off out-of-work benefits into continuous employment (Bate, 2017).

The Troubled Families programme intended to achieve these outcomes through engaging families with a key worker, who offered a personalised approach to the whole family, improved access to local services through an inter-agency approach and built the family's capacity to know where to seek relevant support in the future. To some extent, the activities revolve around changing the outlook, expectations, access and confidence of vulnerable families in order to promote their resilience and independence. The distinctive feature of the programme is that it offers a prompt coordinated response to families' needs. It also generates a plan, based on information received from other agencies, and co-produced by the key worker and the family. Troubled Families is a non-statutory intervention in that families are not compelled to sign up. It can, however, be seen as only semi-voluntary because families may at the same time be facing coercive action such as threats of eviction or prosecution for persistent absence from school (Hayden and Jenkins, 2014). The head of the national programme described Troubled Families as 'distinct from traditional support because it is much more assertive' and it holds out the threat of sanctions (Casey, 2013: 460).

The programme has been said to illustrate a break with the post-war welfare consensus, with a shift towards the 'neoliberal' political project in British social policy (Butler, 2014; Crossley, 2016). One of its most vocal academic opponents, Ruth Levitas, commented that Troubled Families has made a leap from families with troubles (eg poor health and low income) to families that are 'troublesome' and, in this way, has been 'successful in feeding vindictive attitudes to the poor' (Levitas, 2012: 8). Variations on this theme have been taken up by other academics and commentators. Arthur (2015) argues that Troubled Families fails to take account of the multiple disadvantages faced by families struggling with austerity, adversity, truancy and youth antisocial behaviour. Hayden and Jenkins (2014) and Daly and Bray (2015) object to the emphasis on changing behaviour rather than material circumstances. In the analysis of Welshman (2012), 'while the Government talks about "history repeating itself" in families and between generations, the history that has really been repeated here has been that of a flawed discourse'.

However, the small body of primary research evidence from the local implementation of Troubled Families is somewhat more positive than these policy commentaries. Bond-Taylor (2015) reported evidence from families that although empowerment from participation was only partial, they found key workers' advocacy for them empowering. Hayden and Jenkins (2014) conclude that despite the national programme's flawed logic, there is evidence that it has helped local families with multiple problems, and that the programme can be 'usefully subverted' by local authorities for the benefit of vulnerable families (Hayden and Jenkins, 2015).

The programme underwent two phases. Phase 1, which ran from 2012 to 2015, received £448 million and focused on crime, antisocial behaviour, truancy and unemployment (Bate, 2017). It defined troubled families as households meeting three of four criteria: (1) they include individuals involved in crime and antisocial behaviour; (2) they have children not in school; (3) they have an adult on out-of-work benefits; and (4) they cause high costs to the public purse (DCLG, 2014). The government estimated that there were 120,000 families in England who would satisfy the requirement of meeting three of these four criteria.

An expanded version of the programme (Phase 2) was launched in April 2015 for a five-year period and targeted additional problems such as domestic violence, health, drug abuse, mental health and children at risk, with £920 million allocated to help an additional 400,000 families (Bate, 2017). The target population for the expanded Troubled Families programme is families with multiple problems who will benefit from an integrated and whole-family approach (DCLG, 2015). The criteria for inclusion are much broader than for Phase 1. To meet the threshold, families need to satisfy two out of the six following criteria (DCLG, 2015): (1) parents and children involved in crime and or antisocial behaviour; (2) children who have not been attending school regularly; (3) children who need help – children of all ages who need help, are identified as in need or are subject to a Child Protection Plan; (4) adults out of work or at risk of financial exclusion or young people at risk of worklessness; (5) families affected by domestic violence and abuse; and (6) parents and children with a range of health problems.

English local authorities delivering the Troubled Families programme are paid partly through engaging families and partly through demonstrating to central government that they have met programme outcomes. This PbR element is intended to encourage local authorities to focus on outcomes rather than processes. Each local authority receives a set amount of money for each family that it identifies and includes in the programme (up to the number of troubled families estimated by the DCLG). This is referred to as the 'attachment fee', and is £1,000 per family. The DCLG then sets out a number of 'success' criteria for the programme, and for each troubled family attached to the programme that meets these success criteria, a further payment is made. The DCLG states that 'A results based payment of £800 will be offered for each family for whom the local authority claims to have either (a) achieved significant and sustained progress, or (b) moved off out of work benefits and into continuous employment' (DCLG, 2015: 38). It is for the local authority to determine how 'significant and sustained progress' is measured.

The Innovative Social Investment: Strengthening Communities in Europe (InnoSI) case study focused on Phase 2 and its implementation in GM between January and October 2016. The DCLG's estimate for GM was 27,000 troubled families, compared to around 8,000 under Phase 1. GM was the only conurbation-wide early adopter of Troubled Families Phase 2. Combined authorities were established in England under the Local Democracy, Economic Development and Construction Act 2009 with the remit to coordinate strategies, policies and services across local authorities. GM was the first in the country. In 2014, GM's devolution agreement set out new powers and responsibilities for the Combined Authority. This provided opportunities for developing new delivery models in the second phase of Troubled Families, alongside other initiatives across the conurbation, including the expansion of the Working Well programme (Manchester City Council Health and Wellbeing Board, 2015).

The main actors in GM Troubled Families are the Combined Authority and 10 local boroughs, with civil society organisations in some boroughs. The ambitions of the Combined Authority include breaking new ground in combining health and social care budgets, and innovative, 'integrated' solutions to crime, policing, worklessness and related health problems. Senior managers in GM described the programme as a catalyst to more general public service reform, especially better integrated working across the various services provided for families. In GM, there is much stronger emphasis in Phase 2 than in Phase 1 on Troubled Families as a vehicle for the transformation of services through more integration/coordination. Each of the 10 GM districts contributes proportionally towards achieving the goal of significant and sustained progress for families, using a range of evidence-based interventions/service solutions, following a broad set of GM-wide principles and working towards a common Family Outcomes Plan. Using common principles rather than a single standardised approach reflects different local needs.

The Theory of Change articulated in one of the local authorities as part of the case study indicates that mental health, drugs/alcohol and domestic violence crime were identified as the 'toxic trio'. They require a quick response as they represent safeguarding issues. Other anticipated outcomes include health, education and employment. The latter is perceived as the ultimate goal in Phase 2 of the programme. The programme's input includes referrals, co-located services involving multi-agency staff, training to support new ways of working and funding that has a PbR component. Key activities comprise an early help assessment, the triage of cases, allocation meetings, evidence-based interventions and monitoring.

Key findings: implementation and impact

Implementation

The Troubled Families programme implemented in GM is targeted at a wider population than the national programme, even given the use of local discretion. It is now integrated under early help and support. The programme in GM is part-funded through the national programme (aimed at those families that meet the national criteria, and national criteria with local discretion) and through local resources (aimed at families locally defined as troubled families but not eligible for the national programme). It also provides discretion for each of the 10 local authorities in GM in implementing the programme.

Our case study research found that senior managers recognise that Troubled Families is part of something bigger (public service reform and devolution) and each local authority has been able to take different approaches to the design and delivery of the intervention. The local programmes all follow GM-wide principles and work towards a common Family Outcomes Plan, using specific approaches (whole-family, life-course, strengths-based, place-based) in order to achieve better outcomes for complex needs and people at risk. Priorities are determined by the family, who is empowered to access services. The programme is generally perceived as a means to reduce demand on public services.

Nevertheless, the implementation of the programme is largely influenced by the local context, which determines how the programme is delivered, which services are involved and what needs are addressed. For instance, at the time of implementation, some local authorities were working towards their Ofsted[1] improvement plan while others were focusing on integrated health and social care. To some extent, when implemented at a local level, the national agenda loses its importance: "We are all partners – police, fire, voluntary sector.... It doesn't matter what the national agendas are. We have to work within them, but it's what happens on the streets of [Local Authority 1] that is important" (Troubled Families Lead LA1).

The programme is also implemented under different names in different local authorities (eg Supporting Families Pathway, Early Help Hub, Helping Families, Confident Families). To some extent, this reflects its links to different programmes available locally. However, it also reveals wider issues with the terminology employed for the programme. The term 'troubled families' was considered problematic by a majority of interviewees, some of whom indicated that families often reacted negatively to the name as they felt labelled and stigmatised.

There is a common understanding that a better coordination of services can stop the escalation of problems and address families' needs in a seamless way. In GM, the Troubled Families programme has been systemising some elements of service integration (eg single case workers operate across traditional boundaries, and there is a single front door for families with complex needs where a single assessment is undertaken so that families do not repeat their stories again and again). Through the establishment of hubs and the co-location of its teams, the programme has, to some extent, supported an important cultural shift from inter-agency working to service integration. This allows for better communication and information sharing, which supports a holistic view of the family's needs and rapid response. Yet, this does not come without challenges and service integration can raise anxiety among professionals as they worry about losing their job or professional identity: "So, there is mistrust from staff, they are worried about what is going on. They think integration means no more job" (Troubled Families Staff 4).

The PbR element is used in various ways to pay for different elements depending on the borough's local context. Some, but not all, boroughs pass on a proportion of the PbR to commissioned services. Information required to claim for PbR is collected during triage and a Troubled Family case number is generated by the system. Key workers are then responsible for updating the system on a regular basis (every few months) and fill in a snap survey when they close a case. In each borough, an analyst is responsible for "making sure the boxes are ticked, making sure that it is measured" (Troubled Families Staff). It is important to note that the framework is slightly different in each local authority, depending on the type of information that the systems can provide. Analysts meet on a monthly basis to discuss challenges and make sure that data are recorded consistently across GM.

Impact of Troubled Families

Attribution is an issue in a context where several programmes with similar objectives target the same population (eg Whole Place Community Budget and Families in Multiple Need programmes). The claims made through PbR suggest that a high percentage of families (~100%) were 'turned around' by the programme. However, the indicators used to assess those outcomes have been criticised by academics, the media and managers of the programme. In the summer of 2016, several British newspapers reported that the government had failed to publish a highly critical independent evaluation of the Troubled Families programme. When the report was published (Day et al, 2016), it concluded that the programme had no systematic or significant impact on family outcomes in terms of employment and crime reduction. Day et al (2016) recognise that several factors could have contributed towards this finding, including data issues.

The analysis undertaken for this case study identified some successful elements of the programme in GM. For instance, teams communicate well and information is shared in order to offer a personalised approach to families. The majority of families engage with the programme and speak highly of their key workers. There is some evidence that the programme is shifting dynamics through creating better relationships between families and public services (examples of testimony to that effect are shown in Box 3.1). It also empowers families and gives them a sense of agency through co-producing the family plan, using strength-based approaches and providing information about the services available to them. Families reported an increase in confidence and self-esteem.

Box 3.1: Changing dynamics between families and public services

Establishing new dynamics and relationships with public services was one of the mechanisms identified as supporting better outcomes for families involved in the programme. This new type of relationship, which is part of the new public service reform, enables a personalised approach to the family's needs. It is an important trigger to change as some vulnerable families may have experienced unsuccessful/difficult contact with services in the past. A shift in this dynamic would allow them to engage with the services on offer. Community reporters' videos and interviews with families point out a strong history of distrust of social workers and other professionals such as teachers or doctors. There is a clear concern that once social workers get involved, they would stay engaged for long periods of time and might take children away from their parents:

> "They say he has Asperger and ADHD, but I know he is schizophrenic. Otherwise, why would he kick off like that? I am his mother, I know what he is like.... I was depressed, it was much worst the second time, much deeper. All of us was in a bad place. Social services came in and judged me 'You are emotionally neglecting your children!'... All I have ever done was at the best of my ability." (Greater Manchester, Mother 3)

The key worker introduced by the Troubled Families programme appears to have shifted those dynamics through establishing a positive relation with families, one where they feel empowered and respected:

"Every single time she came, she will never say anything negative to me. She would boost me." (Greater Manchester, Mother 5)

"They get to know you as a person, not just as what your problems are. It's almost like a friend." (Greater Manchester, Mother 2)

"She was asking what I wanted to do. Normally, you got told. If someone came in and said 'You need to do this', I'd respond differently, 'cos someone is telling you how to be a parent." (Greater Manchester, Mother 1)

The programme also referred families to evidence-based interventions such as parenting courses. These generic courses are not always suited to individuals. This is illustrated in a story told by a mother of four children aged five to 12 about attending a parenting course. She felt that far from being personalised to her individual needs as a parent, the course was concerned with following guidelines set out in an American book. She found it "quite patronising" and she "didn't really get much from it". She explains how attendees were rewarded with stickers for making contributions in line with the programme's teachings. She felt that she was treated like "a school child" and was "presented with a load of rules". However, she did value the social interactions that going on the course provided between herself, the other attendees and trainers. This story, and others collected with a small group of families from Manchester who have experienced support provision as part of Troubled Families, can be viewed at: https://communityreporter.net/story/my-experiences-parenting-programme

However, some front-line workers noted that, in practice, their work had not significantly changed since the introduction of the Troubled Families programme. They were already focusing on empowering families and using a strength-based approach. There was nevertheless a positive perception of the training received (eg Signs of Safety) and a recognition that, through the programme and recent changes made to the services, the approach was becoming systematised and other staff members had to change their approach.

Some interviewees working on the Troubled Families programme consider that PbR has supported a cultural shift within their organisation, one where front-line workers became more aware of different funding streams and their impact on service delivery. Yet, front-line workers were much less aware of PbR than strategic managers, and those who did typically commented on the requirements for paperwork and monitoring rather than practice. Senior and middle managers demonstrated an understanding of the funding stream and expressed opinions about its benefits and limitations:

> "PbR is a double-edged sword – not always helpful when trying to facilitate conversations with partners. There is a perception that PbR should be distributed [laughter] … but sometimes it can be helpful in a strategic discussion internally … the fact that there is an income stream that is performance related can be helpful." (Troubled Families Lead 3)

Senior and middle managers perceive a stronger focus on evidence and monitoring as an opportunity to help teams keep track of real progress. In the words of one senior manager: "you might think you are doing well, but then you see there is no improvement". Interviewees claim that PbR is central to the way in which they capture their work, but it does not influence their decision-making: "[PbR] is a massive consideration. There is an awareness. It doesn't drive the nature of the work, but it makes sure that you record things" (Troubled Families Lead 8).

Overall, PbR is viewed as a political process, one that pleases the country's ministers (Troubled Families Lead 6). The central benefit of this approach seems to be its potential as a catalyst for change. Some participants perceived it as a means to systematise service integration through incentivising partners. Yet, the processes are time-consuming and the prime benefit appears to be at a strategic level rather than for family outcomes.

The analysis undertaken for the case study also points out that some of the supporting factors are not yet in place for the programme to be effective. The lack of mental health services available to the families creates serious issues for the programme. A great majority of families engaged in the programme present mental health issues and this theme was identified as one of the first outcomes to be improved in order to successfully address other challenges. Consequently, while the programme theory might be plausible, it is unlikely to be successful if services are not available. This is especially the case given the time frame associated with the programme (12 months) and pressure to meet PbR targets at a stage where key services have not yet been accessed by the family.

Learning points and policy implications

Troubled Families was a highly complex intervention at a number of different levels. Troubled Families was targeted at families with multiple needs. These families may include individual members not experiencing problems, and the families often received a number of other interventions (some of which overlapped with Troubled Families services) aimed at addressing different parts of their needs profiles. It is also the case that families receiving the intervention will probably have been the target of previous programmes aimed at addressing their problems. This complexity comes through strongly in the national evaluation of the Troubled Families programme, as well as, to some extent, in the case study work presented here. It has a number of implications. First, in terms of policy design, one of the objectives of Troubled Families was to reduce the number of contacts with public sector agencies experienced by target families, thereby improving the service experience, with the intent of increasing engagement with services and thereby increasing the likelihood of achieving outcomes. However, that policy objective affected the design of Troubled Families at the programme level only, and may not have accounted for the wider service provision and social programmes targeted at these families. This has significant implications for the future design of programmes intended to address multiple, often 'wicked', problems, and relates to the question of how to design such programmes in a way that really does take account of the whole picture of activity experienced by the target population.

The complexity in terms of service user needs also feeds through to the outcomes expected from the programme, and how those outcomes were measured. Multiple, often interrelated, outcomes across a broad range of social policy areas were expected from the programme. One significant issue here is temporality, that is: over what time period could outcomes be expected, and over what period should they be measured? Responding to questions at the House of Commons Public Accounts Committee, the Permanent Secretary of the DCLG suggested that the programme's design focused too much attention on short-term outcomes (House of Commons Public Accounts Committee, 2016). There has also been significant criticism of the programme because it relied on service providers to collect and report data on programme achievements and outcomes (Crossley, 2015). This reliance on provider-generated data might explain the high success rates reported at early stages of the programme's roll-out, and the disconnect between these and the findings of the national evaluation, which did not find any evidence of significant impact (Day et al, 2016). While, in reality, it might be implausible for the commissioner or some third party to be responsible for collecting programme monitoring data, a clear implication from Troubled Families is the need for some independent audit and evaluation of these data and the outcomes claimed.

Over and above the complexity in the programme in terms of its target population and the outcomes expected, the programme also presents a multifaceted and nested form of social innovation. The programme was designed to be both innovative and to generate innovation. It is innovative in terms of its use of PbR, but it is also intended to generate innovation in how services were commissioned and in the local configuration of services. Of course, like policy change more generally (Howlett and Cashore, 2009), there can be a 'dependent variable problem' in terms of determining what constitutes examples of social innovation. The trouble with the Troubled Families programme is that potential examples of social innovation range from micro, service-level changes through to meso, programme-level changes. These range from how service users engage with individual public services through to different ways of organising and integrating services, and even a changed relationship between central and local government in terms of these types of project-based social programmes. Moreover, it is important to stress that although these are potential examples of social innovation, in most cases, these are not entirely new services. Rather, they are often existing services but reconfigured and repackaged to take advantage of new funding streams.

This case study demonstrates the challenges of evaluating such social programmes. These challenges exist not just because of the complexity of the intervention, or the multiple needs experienced by the target population. More significantly, such evaluations increasingly rely on secondary data to measure impact, and these data often come with a number of limitations and imperfections. The national evaluation of the Troubled Families programme sought to deal with these, in part, by using two different approaches to quantitatively measuring impact. In this case, the qualitative research also gave a different picture of the programme to that generated by the impact evaluation. However, a more significant implication is the role of evaluation and other such evidence in relation to policymaking. In this case, policymakers were quick to champion the success of the programme when initial monitoring data suggested high levels of service user access and outputs generated, but were slow to respond to the evaluation, which failed to find any evidence of impact.

Note

[1] Ofsted is the Office for Standards in Education, Children's Services and Skills. They inspect and regulate services that care for children and young people, and services providing education and skills for learners of all ages. Linked to the Department for Education, their report can include an improvement notice. They have the power to dismantle services and change lines of funding.

References

Arthur, R. (2015) 'Troubling times for young people and families with troubles – responding to truancy, rioting and families struggling with adversity', *Social & Legal Studies*, 24(3): 443–64.

Bate, A. (2017) *The Troubled Families programme (England)*, London: House of Commons Library.

Bond-Taylor, S. (2015) 'Dimensions of family empowerment in work with so-called "troubled" families', *Social Policy & Society*, 14(3): 371–84.

Butler, I. (2014) 'New families, new governance and old habits', *Journal of Social Welfare and Family Law*, 36(4): 415–25.

Cameron, D. (2011) 'Full transcript, David Cameron, speech on troubled families, Sandwell Christian Centre, Oldbury, 15 December 2011', *New Statesman*, 15 December. Available at: http://www.newstatesman.com/uk-politics/2011/12/troubled-families-family

Casey, L. (2013) 'Working with troubled families', *Families, Relationships and Societies*, 2(3): 459–61.

Crossley, S. (2015) *The Troubled Families programme: The perfect social policy? Briefing Paper 13*, London: Centre for Crime and Justice Studies.

Crossley, S. (2016) 'Realising the (troubled) family, crafting the neoliberal state', *Families, Relationships and Societies*, 5(2): 263–79.

Daly, M. and Bray, B. (2015) 'Parenting support in England: the bedding down of a new policy', *Social Policy and Society*, 14(4): 633–44.

Day, L., Bryson, C., White, C., Purdon, S., Bewley, H., Kirchner Sala, L. and Portes, J. (2016) *National evaluation of the Troubled Families programme, final synthesis report*, London: DCLG.

DCLG (Department for Communities and Local Government) (2014) *Understanding troubled families*, London: DCLG.

DCLG (2015) *Financial framework for the expanded Troubled Families programme*, London: DCLG.

Fox, C., O'Leary, C., Albertson, K. and Painter, G. (2018) *Payment by Results and Social Impact Bonds: Outcome-based payment systems in the UK and US*, Bristol: The Policy Press.

Greater Manchester Combined Authority (2016) 'Framework for integrated public service reform'. Available at: http://www.greatermanchester-ca.gov.uk/download/meetings/id/860/8_gmca_reform_board

Hayden, C. and Jenkins, C. (2014) '"Troubled Families" programme in England: "wicked problems" and policy-based evidence', *Policy Studies*, 35(6): 631–49.

Hayden, C. and Jenkins, C. (2015) 'Children taken into care and custody and the "troubled families" agenda in England', *Child & Family Social Work*, 20(4): 459–69.

House of Commons Communities Local Government Committee (2014) *Community Budgets 2013*, London: The Stationery Office.

House of Commons Public Accounts Committee (2016) *Troubled Families progress review*, London: The Stationery Office.

Howlett, M. and Cashore, B. (2009) 'The dependent variable problem in the study of policy change: understanding policy change as a methodological problem', *Journal of Comparative Policy Analysis: Research and Practice*, 11(1): 33–46.

Jensen, T. (2013) 'Riots, restraint and the new cultural politics of wanting', *Sociological Research Online*, 18(4): 7.

Levitas, R. (2012) *There may be trouble ahead: Britain's what we know about those 120,000 'troubled' families*, PSE Policy Response Paper # 3, Bristol: Poverty and Social Exclusion in the UK.

Levitas, R. (2014) 'Troubled families in a spin'. Available at: http://193.104.168.102/sites/default/files/attachments/Troubled%20Families%20in%20a%20Spin.pdf

Manchester City Council Health and Wellbeing Board (2015) 'Complex dependency and troubled families: report for resolution item 7, 10th June'. Available at: https://secure.manchester.gov.uk/download/meetings/id/18945/7_complex_dependency_and_troubled_families

Welshman, J. (2012) '"Troubled families": the lessons of history, 1880–2012', *History and Politics*. Available at: http://www.historyandpolicy.org/papers/policy-paper-136.html#S1

Innovative voluntary and public sector partnership for the reception and integration of unaccompanied asylum-seeking children in Gothenburg, Sweden

Inga Narbutaité Aflaki

Introduction

Since 2014, the Swedish welfare state has been facing the major policy challenge of accommodating and integrating asylum-seeking children without parents, so-called unaccompanied minors. This inflow, amounting to 40% of all those registered in the European Union (EU) member states, was the largest in Europe and historically unprecedented. This chapter discusses the potential of a form of partnerships, novel in Sweden, between local government and civil society organisations (CSOs) in Social Investment. The case in focus is a unique partnership between Gothenburg municipality, or, more precisely, its Social Resource Department (SRD), and nine value-based CSOs, aiming to address some of the public policy challenges associated with the reception and integration of unaccompanied children. Its major beneficiaries were a shifting group of about 100–150 unaccompanied minors, aged 18 or younger, who were residing in partnership youth housing units during their asylum-seeking process and initial stay in Sweden. All these minors were allocated to Gothenburg municipality by the County Administrative Board.

Voluntary partnerships between value-driven CSOs and the public sector (voluntary and public sector partnerships; henceforth, IOPs) on varying social and welfare issues of public interest have started spreading since the first Swedish pioneering case in Västerås municipality in 2012. IOPs are envisioned by their major promoters as an innovative form of cross-sector collaboration that is distinct from state and CSO relations in social and welfare services in terms of state grants and market-based contracts. The partnerships aim at respecting and highlighting the uniqueness of CSOs through more transparent and equal collaboration terms guided by principles detailed in the national compacts (Regeringskansliet, 2009, 2010). As this form of governance is just emerging, it faces its own challenges in how to make the most of the CSO potential.

The aim of this chapter is to highlight how IOPs may serve as innovative social investments in local contexts. What follows describes the background to the partnership on integrating unaccompanied minors and the envisioned Theory of Change (ToC). It then explores and exemplifies partnership outputs and their early impact on targeted children, followed by an overview of major implementation challenges and success factors. It concludes with reflections on future policy implications.

Gothenburg partnership: experimental Social Investment through new trust-based relationship

Why was the partnership needed?

Over the past years, the number of unaccompanied asylum-seeking children to Sweden has increased dramatically, from 388 in 2004 to 35,369 in 2015, while the total number of asylum seekers in 2015 was about 160,000,[1] leading the government to call the situation a 'refugee crisis'. The unprecedented influx of asylum-seeking children between 2014 and 2016 is illustrative of how relatively strong state policy capacities may still be strained even in the Nordic welfare model. The immigration wave has escalated local government challenges of finding suitable forms of accommodation and school placements, attending to children's psychosocial and physical health, and providing meaningful activities. In 2014, pressed by increasing immigration, the national government delegated new responsibilities for unaccompanied minors to all the 290 municipalities, disregarding their objections. The municipalities such as Gothenburg, which had voluntarily acted as reception municipalities until 2014, were no longer in control of the volume of minors allocated to them. As this was a breach of the traditionally strong local self-government principles, the local governments were forced to consider new policy solutions.

Until 2015, the local government in Gothenburg had been the sole provider of children's reception services. In the face of the wave of immigration, municipal services proved increasingly inflexible, fragmented and insufficient. Interestingly, the legal pressures and the immigration wave also served as *a window of opportunity* for an experimental reception model in Gothenburg, a municipality with a long tradition of state–third sector collaboration through commissioned services and grants, as well as established trust relationships. Also, national, regional and local compacts on greater CSO involvement in welfare policies prepared the ground for experimental IOP collaborations. Driven policy entrepreneurs from both sides capitalised on the external pressures and a favourable political climate (Narbutaité Aflaki et al, 2017) to initiate a unique partnership in terms of the number of partners and ambitions. It offered the, yet untested in Sweden, Social Investment approach to the reception and integration of unaccompanied minors.

Theory of Change

The partnership's *aim* was to make a contribution to the well-being of unaccompanied children, from their first months in Sweden to their gradual inclusion in society, through an experimental, holistic policy, acknowledging their human value and rights. In the formal partnership agreement, these aims were formulated as 'integrat[ing] housing [of unaccompanied children] with joint, coherent efforts to increase opportunities to meaningful leisure activities and integration into society' (IOP Göteborg, 2016: 2). The implicit partnership logic was that achieving an adequate reception requires a legitimate collaboration model, allowing local government to tap into CSO potential, resources and knowledge, not only by offering public finances, but also by treating CSOs as equal partners. Partnership was seen as a major mechanism for achieving greater service diversity, relevance and integration than each partner (including local government) was capable of on their own. After a series of open dialogues, the formal partnership agreement was signed in April 2015 between seven, and later nine, value-based CSOs and the SRD of Gothenburg municipality for a period of at least five years with an option to renegotiate after three years.

The mix of actors and resources

Gothenburg partnership developed its ToC – the partnership aim, structure and services – by collaborative stakeholder-led processes where local government and CSO influence were balanced against each other in common decision-making structures (Partnership Board, Collaboration Group). This ToC design was unique in that both parties could contribute to defining the norms or rules of engagement beforehand. This design allowed for continuous interplay between parties, even in institutional changes, regarding partnership aims and reasonable ways to fulfil them through individual and jointly coordinated efforts.

Partnership goals were implemented on the basis of two service pillars representing two different types of services and control relationships between the municipality and CSOs: (1) youth housing with basic service and care; and (2) complementary (often volunteer-based) services. In the *housing service* pillar, initially four, but later six, partner organisations (Bräcke Diakoni, Skyddsvärnet, Reningsborg, Göteborgs Räddningsmission, Karriärkraft, Göteborgs Stadsmission) with experience in providing commissioned care services ran several individual residential homes (also referred to as youth housing) under municipal and national supervision. The decision regarding children's placement in a relevant form of housing, including residential homes, rested with 10 municipal district councils, but SRD, as a central supporting unit with its own housing services, had the final responsibility to find the specified housing form. In other words, to exploit the partnership potential and fulfil its aims, the municipal partner had to coordinate its efforts with other municipal units (the districts) in order to place sufficient numbers of children in the residential care homes offered by CSOs.

Interestingly, in this arrangement, the municipal partner still remained a monitoring actor accountable to the National Health and Social Care Inspectorate for service quality, while CSOs, in their role as partners, aspired to some freedom of action in implementing their ideas, organisational values and individual care models in housing services. The ToC in this service pillar thus had to be developed in such a way as to avoid overly detailed steering or the usual principal–agent relations, and rely more on CSOs' competences, specificity and dialogues. Occasionally, the municipal partner was still perceived as the 'big brother' (CSO Housing Director 5) but was, especially in the early phase, prepared to soften its steering mode to become a supportive leader.

In addition to the housing and care services under municipal jurisdiction, CSOs agreed to successively develop and provide several integration services without claiming full public funding, thus securing added partnership value. These services were provided by an organisational mix where traditional advocacy organisations (Swedish Red Cross, Save the Children, Individuell Människohjälp) played a dominant role.

Such a service arrangement was enabled through an innovative co-funding model. The bulk of the financial contribution came from state funding allocated through the National Migration Board to Gothenburg municipality for placing the children in a suitable and legally stipulated form of housing, while partner organisations covered some remaining integration service costs. The state compensated municipalities based on a lump sum per child per day (until July 2017: 1,900 SEK), of which local government allocated a major part (1,750 SEK) to each partner CSO for its housing services. This meant that the municipality kept a fraction of the lump sum (150 SEK) for its administrative costs. While the municipality compensated its partners by a somewhat higher amount (increased by 50 SEK per child per day) for services compared with other directly subcontracted actors, the partners received a lower budget than municipally run housing services and significantly lower than private subcontracted actors. This so-called surplus money was to be used to co-fund the development of complementary services accessible to all children residing in partners' housing.

The initial partnership funding arrangement during 2015 and 2016 may be seen as quite generous as it also compensated housing providers – in line with national regulations (Regeringskansliet, 2016) – for their readiness to receive children, that is, for occasionally vacant places. In this way, partners could develop new services that the Partnership Board deemed of common importance without additional public funding and by contributing their own resources. Partners had to agree on the share of commonly pooled resources for each new service depending on their importance and organisational capacities. Indeed, this arrangement also meant that advocacy organisations not engaged in housing services were allowed their share of the pooled resources, which established trust and solidarity among the CSOs.

In sum, it is possible to distinguish three major *innovative* partnership institutional design and management characteristics: (1) collaborative or dialogue-based decision-making; (2) softer trust-based steering in regulatory housing services without suppressing CSO specificity and advocacy; and (3) a solidary resource pooling and sharing model. The first two aspects, explored later, are seen here as possible new ways for public agencies to interact with CSOs, and thus as relational or *systemic innovation* (Windrum, 2008) or *innovation in governance* (Evers and Brandsen, 2016) in the Swedish context. The latter represents an *innovation in financing mode* (Evers and Brandsen, 2016). Arguably, all these innovations have contributed to increased partnership effectiveness and impact.

Innovative activities and services

Newcomer children residing in partnership housing were offered a variety of services in addition to the care and integration initiatives provided by housing staff. Among these were crisis and trauma counselling, establishing relationships with a Swedish family volunteering to sponsor a child, work experience during summer, and a variety of organised leisure activities with opportunities to establish contacts with CSOs, learning more about Sweden and their city, and practising language and developing new skills through contacts with voluntary organisations. All these services were designed as mutually complementary to avoid overlaps and intended to have a cumulative effect. What is more, several partner organisations offered housing staff training in areas ranging from deepened knowledge of children's countries of origin to suicide prevention in order to assist them in helping staff to deal with this new group with complex needs. Where possible, partners achieved service integration. When successful, housing staff were often envisioned as a connecting node for a variety of partner services. For example, expert referral of children to the crisis counselling coordinated by Skyddsvärnet was not required, as in the municipal counselling services, but the service was provided on request by housing staff based on their assessment of children's needs, thus involving them in a new role. Also, the coordinators of sponsor families ('fadderfamilj') were dependent on staff involvement and ability not only to inform about their services, but also to motivate participation and assist newcomer children in applying for the services. Coordinators also relied on staff judgement as to when the youngsters were deemed ready for receiving a service. The value of service coordination and intermediation lay in directing youngsters to a range of relevant but otherwise non-available services, so bridging some municipal policy gaps. Such a holistic approach, using specific partner resources in service development based on tailoring, personalisation, complementarity, coordination and sustainability, may be seen as a local *policy innovation* (Windrum, 2008), while policy reliance on CSOs per se was less novel.

During 2016, around 270 children received housing and supplementary integration services from the partnership (Bräcke diakoni, 2017). It is noteworthy that some of the services, such as sponsor family support or more specialised staff training, were not offered by the public authorities and clearly represented *service innovations* (Windrum, 2008) in the unaccompanied minors' local reception policy. Some services shared innovative elements in service delivery (Windrum, 2008), such as in trauma or crisis counselling, involving volunteering professional therapists and access for all children at short notice and for as long as the children wanted therapy. This stands in contrast to municipal child psychiatrist services, targeting only children who were approved by their social secretary. Even for the eligible children, the waiting time was long and the therapy provided was more limited. Partnership summertime leisure activities partly overlapped with municipal summer services but were smaller in scope and specifically tailored to the needs of partnership children, expressed through a voluntary reference group. The reference group, initiated by a partnership leisure coordinator, invited youngsters from all 10 partnership housing units to practise democratic representation in planning joint activities. Other services, such as on-the-job training, were rather similar to municipal ones in terms of aims but targeted a broader group of children, also including those without permits and younger than 16. Each individual service, albeit to a varying extent, was found to contribute to the children's well-being and integration (see Box 4.1). All in all, because of their broader access and by complementing already-available services aiming to increase children's well-being and capacities, some partnership services may be classified as *innovations in (minors') rights* (Evers and Brandsen, 2016).

Key findings: partnership service implementation and impact

The partnership evaluation for the Innovative Social Investment: Strengthening Communities in Europe (InnoSI) project has combined an ongoing process analysis with attempts to capture some early visible partnership effects for the targeted children. The assessments build on a thorough document analysis and 40 semi-structured interviews and conversations with the steering group and the collaboration group participants, as well as housing directors, including focus group interviews with staff from five youth housing units and five children. The researcher experienced major difficulties in recruiting partnership children for interviews, which limited the primary data. Additional second-hand data from interviews with five more children in the partnership residential care homes (Schneider, 2016) were included. We also need to keep in mind that services were to be continuously developed and adapted to children's changing needs. In addition, the partnership was gradually forced to expand its targeted group from minors with permanent residence permits to include children with varying formal status and a much greater spectrum of psychosocial needs. At the time of evaluation, the partnership was too young to be expected to have had any substantial, or cumulative, effects. The assessment of partnership services during the larger part of 2016 should be seen as indicative of the partnership's abilities to contribute to unaccompanied minors' well-being and integration, and achieve its objectives under still fairly favourable circumstances.

Housing and care services

One of the partnership's aims was to offer 'good and professional care' and a 'safe homelike environment' (IOP Göteborg, 2016: 2). Interestingly, while the municipal partner aimed for all youth housing under its supervision to provide a similar basic service quality, the complementary partnership services broke this rule of thumb. CSOs utilised the partnership platform to preserve their specificity and values, such as commitment, sensitivity to needs and flexibility in attending to urgent needs, in all services, including housing (see Box 4.1 regarding language training). One example of a housing service tailored to achieve a common standard was partnership-organised complementary staff trainings aimed to close evident knowledge gaps remaining after basic municipal trainings, and to compensate for variations in CSO organisational capacities. Additionally, even though the immigration wave and protracted asylum procedures forced the partner organisations to abandon the initial idea of more homogeneous housing based on children's formal status, housing staff nevertheless attempted to differentiate children according to their perceived needs. In line with this, another outstanding example of how CSOs utilised novel thinking and service tailoring was by introducing an innovative, alternative form of housing for children with support needs, where fewer children than usual were housed with a higher density of professional staff.

At their residential homes, children's major needs were safety, including clear rules, adult presence as well as their respect and continuous contact, help with their daily needs, and integration. The interviewed children were overall satisfied with their 'homes' and with housing staff, although with some reservations for insufficient attention or strict rules (Narbutaité Aflaki, 2016; Schneider, 2016). Housing staff were an important link to Swedish society. In addition, children particularly appreciated being offered platforms, such as the regular house meetings and the reference group, as this allowed them to influence the choice and planning of joint activities.

In sum, the front-line staff at CSOs showed commitment and undertook actions to create qualitative and home-like care. While partnership with a local authority seemed to benefit CSO innovation, service tailoring and personalisation potential, it did not, however, save CSOs from the unfavourable consequences of some local and especially national political decisions that curbed CSOs' capacity to provide the intended quality housing and care. The housing staff thus conveyed a mixed picture of endeavouring to do their best to cater to children's needs while coping with a much greater diversity than envisioned, as well as with unexpected shifts in government reception policies that threatened service continuity and forced frequent organisational adjustments.

Integration services

Turning to the additional integration services, we find that sponsor families and crisis counselling were among the most frequently used and appreciated partnership services in the studied period. Early in the partnership, Göteborgs Räddningsmission identified children's needs for social ties with established Swedes, and in response, recruited, trained and matched interested families with children as their long-term private contact with Swedish society. By the end of 2016 (Bräcke diakoni, 2017), 150 children residing in partnership housing had successfully been matched with a voluntary Swedish sponsor family. This innovative service covered a systemic approach with co-production elements, where matchmaking needs were supported by start-up evenings, regular sponsor family consultations, written or oral follow-up assessments, and face-to-face meetings incorporating experiences of both sponsor families and young newcomers in service development.

   One way of measuring *sponsor family service* achievement is looking at whether a private relationship has been established, based on frequency and duration. A yet more ambitious assessment can address the quality of the relationship. The latter refers to several social inclusion dimensions, such as social bonding, children's knowledge of society, language and the sense of belonging to the social context. The study shows that most of the contacts were ongoing, with varying frequency – from monthly to weekly or occasionally even more frequent contacts. For many children, the relationship continued even after leaving partnership housing, which allows for the conclusion that the services have, in most cases, succeeded in extending children's social network through a private relationship with a Swedish family. The majority of the children appreciated the quality of these relationships (see Box 4.1). Given that they had not met their own family for a long time, some children especially valued the social aspects of having a 'supplementary family' and taking part in family activities such as a picnic, going fishing, playing games or simply talking, enjoying attentiveness and human kindness. As one child put it: "I have two families, one in my heart and one here, I feel safe with them". Other children indicated more instrumental reasons, such as being able to practise their language or playing their favourite or new sports. Some were offered an opportunity to contribute to family gardening and allocated their own gardening plot. Yet another got help with lessons for a driver's licence (Sverker, 2016). Others felt that they could call and ask about things or just get some support in their lives. In general, the quality of the relationships contributed to children's empowerment, increased their self-confidence and gave them valuable tools to increase the chance of inclusion. The sponsor families also indicated their satisfaction in giving youngsters some meaningful activities and relationships, and they also received counselling in handling their role in relational challenges. The service model was so attractive that it was up-scaled to at least one neighbouring municipality (Uddevalla) and several more initiated partnership negotiations with Göteborgs Räddningsmission.

Crisis counselling needs were also captured early by housing staff, and transmitted to a partner organisation, Skyddsvärnet, eager to offer support. The 12 volunteering psychologists observed major post-trauma syndromes among nearly a third of the children (Narbutaité Aflaki, 2016) and offered systematic help as an important precondition for the children's well-being and integration. The 500 counselling sessions held with the children, during a total of 75 counselling periods in 2016 (Bräcke diakoni, 2017), testify to a high service relevance that was successfully implemented, except for the involuntary closures. Some of the cases had to be cancelled because painful traumatic memories surfaced and the time for treatment was not right. In other cases, treatment was involuntarily cancelled when children were moved to housing units outside the partnership, especially after asylum application rejections or age upgrading. When possible, the psychologists offered support even in such cases to prevent children from suicide or injuring themselves. Judging by the information received from the service coordinator and the interviews, the impact on the absolute majority of children was positive, at least in short- and mid-term perspectives (Göransson, 2016).

Work experience services during the summer vacation were organised by another CSO partner, Bräcke diakoni, on very short notice for the (40) minors who showed an interest. Although there was significant drop-out for various reasons, the training opportunities were appreciated by most participants in the activities. Among the 22 who completed on-the-job training, 93% had a more positive approach to their chances of finding a job in Sweden, and 75% appreciated the chance to practise the Swedish language and meet Swedish people (Narbutaité Aflaki, 2016). Generally speaking, this service made a significant contribution to achieving the partnership goal to increase children's chances of integration. As CSOs chose to adhere to municipal policy, they could only offer a very symbolic compensation for on-the-job training, which could partly explain unexpected drop-outs, while other reasons were the negative impact of protracted asylum processes, insufficient coordination with municipal service counterparts and lack of time to co-design services by better matching the offers with newcomers' interests. The service co-creation lesson has been learned, and given a sustained interest in labour market issues, the services were further developed during the autumn of 2016 into an even closer collaboration with other partnership service coordinators and the children's reference group. The resulting thematic instruction on ways into education and jobs in Sweden, and workshops on CV writing, have been broadly appreciated (Bräcke diakoni, 2017) as children felt more empowered to take the next steps.

The *leisure-time services* coordinated by Individuell Människohjälp gave all interested partnership children access to cultural events, sports and other activities as a way to increase their chances for meaningful leisure and integration. Together with children and a voluntary reference group, the coordinator identified and offered 25 activities, mostly organised by voluntary associations, during five summer weeks. Despite the language barrier or lack of social ties, children could partake in activities ranging from testing new sports and games or learning new skills (such as bicycling, photography, writing hip-hop music), to exploring their physical surroundings and the new culture. The overall impact increased children's chances for meaningful, rewarding leisure and their knowledge of the country. In some instances, it facilitated new social contacts (see Box 4.1). Nevertheless, as participation was rather meagre and uneven, for reasons of overlaps with municipal activities, the Islamic Ramadan period and general passivity among the children, the effect on the children's empowerment was not as substantial as expected, only resulting in short-term energy boosts. However, evidence indicates a great potential for a positive cumulative effect of complementary partnership services.

In sum, the analysis clearly indicates that the partnership has achieved positive impact in increasing unaccompanied children's chances of integration and well-being. The partnership has enabled the more effective use of resources, better coordination and higher service quality (see Box 4.1) and innovativeness through resource pooling and collaborative processes.

Overcoming challenges and learning points

The initiation of this innovative partnership has been facilitated by several circumstances: (1) a local political climate supportive of collaboration and Social Investment in unaccompanied children; (2) mission-driven policy entrepreneurs (Petridou et al, 2015) among CSO leaders and municipal administrators that promoted the partnership idea; (3) municipal administrators' knowledge and trust in the CSOs' capacities based on experiences of other collaboration forms; and (4) a positive mutual experience among several partners of an earlier IOP on EU migrants. An additional contributing factor was partner commitment to the same social values, which eased agreement on the policy problem and joint action. Altogether, these circumstances strengthened the trust between the actors, prompting this experimental collaboration model. As the partnership kept pursuing its goals at least until 2017, it is of interest to identify a few major supportive factors in its implementation and adaptation.

Balanced collaborative partnership

First, one of the most distinctive characteristics of the Gothenburg partnership was its openness to dialogue and *mutual influence* in both designing and implementing partnership goals. What is more, the CSOs were allowed *great influence* on the partnership guiding principles (such as dialogue, respect for CSO specificity), financial mechanisms and processes, thus creating relatively balanced power relations on shared issues. Such influence was enabled through initial dialogue processes and later through partnership joint decision-making and discussion structures.

It is interesting to note that CSOs took advantage of the collaborative partnership spirit and structures to balance the stronger municipal SRD power, thus acting as one united actor in strategic partnership decisions and strengthening their power vis-à-vis the municipality. The mutual involvement contributed to greater knowledge of each other and the target group, which created trust and smoother communication, all of which helped in dealing with complex policy problems (Narbutaité Aflaki et al, 2017).

Second, an additional factor that sustained partnership legitimacy in the eyes of CSOs was their *possibility to retain an independent voice*, both within the partnership structures and in national and local policy debates, especially on formal policies that obstructed the achievement of the partnership's aims. The parties were able to critically and openly reflect on partnership strengths and weaknesses (including two seminars with evaluating researchers) on several occasions. Interestingly, partnership and collaboration with other CSOs sometimes even prompted service organisations to undertake a government critique (Göransson, 2016).

Third, the collaborative partnership spirit has also rubbed off on the relations between the municipality and individual CSOs in the regulatory housing and care services. CSOs had great freedom in the design and implementation of complementary integration services but also retained some discretion and specificity in the highly regulated housing services. Instead of treating and controlling CSOs as ordinary subcontracted service actors, reflecting a mistrust-based steering (Montin, 2016), local government adopted a different attitude, helping organisations to develop their services through supportive dialogue and *steering based on trust* in CSO capacities. These three characteristics helped to create a fairly 'balanced partnership', confirming earlier claims (Salamon and Toepler, 2015) about sustainable state–third sector relations.

Policy entrepreneurs and supportive leadership

Besides partnership relations, it was the actors closest to the target group who played a decisive role in service development and implementation, and the achievement of partnership goals. These street-level professionals acted as service entrepreneurs and intermediaries. Having discovered new needs, those actors, often service coordinators, pushed forward service and service delivery innovations. At other times, housing staff especially acted as intermediaries between the perceived children's needs and partnership added-value services. Overall, partnership relations and structures facilitated service innovation through knowledge exchange, pooled resources and common capacity building.

An important contributor to partnership sustainability and capacity was the collective leadership representing both sides and all partner organisations and exercised primarily but not exclusively through the Steering Board. Both parties on the Board had a major role in developing a shared perspective on the target group, partnership aims and methods, both at the early partnership stages and in the face of later unexpected challenges. The Board also prioritised and coordinated the contributions of individual organisations based on insights from operative collaboration groups. Acting as both strategic and facilitative leader, the Steering Board was able to direct and orchestrate the innovative Social Investment in unaccompanied minors and facilitate service implementation and the first partnership adjustment agreements. These findings support previous arguments about the importance of collective leadership (Ansell and Gash, 2008) and collaborative management (Salamon and Toepler, 2015) in innovative policies.

Partnership challenges and achievements in a turbulent political context

Implementation of public service (Windrum, 2008) and social innovations is a complex topic marked by risk, uncertainty and embeddedness in political contexts (Brandsen et al, 2016). In the Gothenburg case, even if the partnership initiation phase, starting with dialogues and ending with signing the agreement, proceeded relatively smoothly, there were some initial challenges that grew in importance (especially due to insecure status, see Box 4.1), affecting service development and implementation. The complexity and unpredictability of minors' needs, which gave the impetus for the partnership in the first place, became major challenges. In addition, the partnership had to deal with unexpected changes in national immigration and regulatory policies announced in late 2016 (Regeringskansliet, 2016; SFS, 2016), which dramatically decreased the inflow of minors and lowered the demand for housing and care services. On top of that, the government has circumscribed its budget for newcomer minors' housing, forcing Gothenburg municipality to take on a significant financial burden and to lower payments to the CSOs. An additional government strategy was to make housing providers turn to forms of housing that demand fewer staff for minors aged 15 and above. All these changes forced the partnership into an *adaptation* phase, curtailing its original quality ambitions. The 'real' implementation phase of the original partnership intention was thus rather short, starting with housing and care service development, which were new to all CSOs, and experimental design and implementation of the first set of partnership integration services. In order to keep to its Social Investment aims, the Gothenburg partnership was forced to constantly adapt to major contextual changes.

The construction of the partnership funding model, including the common resource pool, was vulnerable to drastic changes in the inflow of asylum-seeking minors and to shifts in government compensation policies, requiring a special adaptation solution to prevent partnership cessation. The partnership model could only continue based on trust in a common cause, increased responsibility and economic burden sharing, especially on the part of the municipal partner. The apparent clash between national policies and partnership goals was at least temporarily solved to the advantage of the partnership thanks to the commitment of the collective leadership. The adjusted partnership agreement required the commitment of both parties, especially the SRD, to accept increased costs to sustain an acceptable service quality. The adaptation phase was also complicated by the remaining ambiguities about the IOP's judicial status (Narbutaité Aflaki et al, 2017) and lack of political recognition of its expanding institutionalisation in the country. Against this background, the partnership's existence risked being interpreted and assessed on the basis of other known legal models, primarily commissioned services, thus undermining its specific purpose, means and popular legitimacy.

Policy implications

The Gothenburg example provides many policy lessons regarding promoting and sustaining IOPs as a tool for innovative Social Investment. This chapter highlights three of them specifically. First, if successful state–third sector partnership *relations* are to be entered into to address wicked social issues, it is important to have a joint collaborative partnership management and institutional structure based on political will, mutual trust, influence and continuous dialogue, both at the partnership outset and during its later stages. When Social Investment is undertaken in regulated policy areas, the partnership collaboration will be more legitimate and effective if public authorities modify and adjust their steering from formal and control-based to flexible and trust-based while retaining a supportive leadership role.

Second, the strategic and supportive role of the *partnership leadership* is essential in finding fruitful ways to organise the partnership and communicate its commitment to participant organisations, as well as in exploring street-level actors' abilities to make use of partnership advantages in demanding service development, coordination and integration tasks. It is essential that collective leadership facilitates each organisation's unique role and added value in this kind of collective Social Investment.

Third, in the context of welfare policy 'juridification', normalising market-based contracts rather than collaborative agreements, the mutual trust created in the implementation phase proved to be very important in the face of national policy changes. Trust helped to prevent ending the partnership prematurely and instead prompted negotiations on a politically rather than legally settled solution. In Gothenburg, where only a fraction of local government took part in the partnership, a collective municipal commitment to the partnership's goals would have enabled a better way to exploit the partnership's potential.

Conclusion

One of the themes of this volume is the relationship between the state as Social Investment actor and local social innovations. The bold step to start a second IOP (followed by several more) in Gothenburg signals both a major shift in the Gothenburg municipal minor reception policy and in its overall approach to the governance of wicked social issues. This also indicates local government awareness of IOPs as prominent, democratically legitimate and relevant alternative forms of Social Investment in crisis contexts. The major conclusion of this chapter is that IOPs carry a real potential for collaborative organisational resilience and innovativeness in addressing wicked social needs in local crisis contexts. Supported by favourable political and institutional contexts, IOPs may pave the way for a more integrative and qualitative approach to Social Investment. The Gothenburg IOP, at least under initial circumstances, showed itself to be a successful policy alternative to state monopoly and market-based contracts by outperforming singular service providers regarding service flexibility, innovation, variety, coordination, integration and a cumulative positive impact on targeted children. IOPs may thus not only be a tool for social innovations, but, as in Gothenburg and as argued in this volume, should also be seen as an integral part of social innovation (Brandsen et al, 2016).

Box 4.1: Partnership impact in the words of interviewees

The ability of Civil Society Organisations (CSOs) to create added value for children at the same cost is the major advantage of the partnership.

"For us it has been important to have partnership relations and this kind of relationship with the municipality ... where we can show that if you give us good preconditions, we can do good things with high added value." (CSO representative, Collaboration Group)

"This is what holds the partnership together – giving young people more quality for the money, and not starting a youth housing to earn money by minimising personnel." (CSO representative)

For children, the partnership offered much more than housing.
Sponsor family:
"Before, I did not know how a Swedish home or a family look like, beyond what I could see in the streets... But now they send me text messages and I visit them ... and we do various activities. I meet them about three times a month. We cook, see films, talk, it is the best thing with all this." (Child 1)

Summer activities:
"[I appreciate] that you can get to know the city, get new friends, socialise with Swedes."

"It matters less what you do as long as you get a chance to talk about the game and other things in Swedish and learn more about the country."

"All these activities gave me much more than just learning about the city." (Children 1–5)

Youth housing organised through partnership provided added value to the children:
"The strength of our housing form is all volunteers [our own and sent by partner organisations IM] who regularly visit our children and study Swedish with them. The children appreciate it very much. Two different teachers have called me during the autumn wondering what do we do with our children who speak so much better Swedish than the rest of the class. ... This is integration for real!" (Housing Director)

Note

[1] See Statistiska Centralbyrån (CSB). Available at: http://www.scb.se/sv_/Hitta-statistik/Statistik-efter-amne/Befolkning/Befolkningens-sammansattning/Befolkningsstatistik/25788/25795/Behallare-for-Press/386883/ (accessed 2 February 2017).

References

Ansell, C. and Gash, A. (2008) 'Collaborative governance in theory and practice', *Journal of Public Administration Research*, 18: 543–71.

Bräcke diakoni (2017) 'Årsredovisning av mervärdesinstaser 2016'. Available at: www.mynewsdesk.com/se/brackediakoni/documents/aarsredovisning-av-mervaerdesinsatser-2016-66551 (accessed 26 January 2019)..

Bransden, T., Evers, A., Cattacin, S. and Zimmer, A. (2016) 'Social innovation: a sympathetic and critical interpretation', in T. Bransden, A. Cattacin, S. Evers and A. Zimmer (eds) *Social innovations in the urban context*, London: Springer International Publishing, pp 3–20.

Evers, A. and Brandsen, T. (2016) 'Social innovations as messages: democratic experimentation in local welfare systems', in T. Bransden, A. Cattacin, S. Evers and A. Zimmer (eds) *Social innovations in the urban context*, London: Springer International Publishing, pp 161–80.

Göransson, B. (2016) 'Utvisade unga ställs på gatan', *Dagens Nyheter*, 20 June.

IOP Göteborg (2016) *Överenskommelse om Idéburet offentligt partnerskap. Mottagande av ensamkommande barn och ungdomar i Göteborg*, Göteborg: Göteborgs stad. Available at: https://socialutveckling.goteborg.se/uploads/IOP-mottagande-av-ensamkommande-barn.pdf (accessed 10 February 2018).

Montin, S. (2016) 'En moderniserad kommunallag i spänningsfältet mellan politik och marknad', *Statsvetenskaplig tidskrift*, 118(3): 339–57.

Narbutaité Aflaki, I. (2016) 'Exploring how the civil society public partnership matters for social impact: a case of unaccompanied asylum-seeking children reception and integration in Gothenburg, Sweden', Case Study Briefing, H2020 Innovative Social Investment: Strengthening Societies in Europe, InnoSI.

Narbutaité Aflaki, I., Eriksson, H. and Schneider, T. (2017) 'Utmaningar och framgångsfaktorer för att initiera, genomföra och anpassa ett idéburet-offentligt partnerskap', Karlstads universitet, Chalmers and Jonkoping Academy.

Petridou, E., Narbutaité Aflaki, I. and Miles, L. (2015) 'Unpacking the theoretical boxes of political entrepreneurship', in I. Narbutaité Aflaki, E. Petridou and L. Miles (eds) *Entrepreneurship in the polis: Understanding political entrepreneurship*, Farnham: Ashgate.

Regeringskansliet (2009) *Regeringens skrivelse 2008/09:2007. Överenskommelsen mellan regeringen, idéburna organisationer inom det sociala området och Sveriges kommuner oh landsting*, Stockholm: Integrations- och jämställdhetsdepartementet (accessed 30 May 2017).

Regeringskansliet (2010) *Bemyndigande att underteckna en överenskommelse mellan regeringen, idéburna organisationer inom integrationsområdet och Sveriges Kommuner och Landsting.* Protokoll vid regeringssammanträde 2010-04-14. Integrations- och jämställdhetsdepartementet. IJ2009/2235/UF (accessed 31 May 2017).

Regeringskansliet (2016) 'Ett nytt ersättningssystem för mottagandet av ensamkommande barn och unga' Stockholm, Regeringskansliet, Promemoria, 21 June. Available at: www.regeringen.se/49e724/contentassets/200774d5e2de4a3e8c7ca8ec00ff1c20/ett-nytt-ersattningssystem-for-mottagandet-av-ensamkommande-barn-och-unga (accessed 15 November 2017).

Salamon, L.M. and Toepler, S. (2015) 'Government–nonprofit cooperation: anomaly or necessity?', *Voluntas*, 26(6): 2155–77.

Schneider, L. (2016) 'Vi vill lära känna ett land', En kvalitativ studie om idéburna organisationers betydelse för ensamkommande barns integration, Göteborgs universitet.

SFS (2016) 'Lag (2016: 752) om tillfälliga begränsningar av möjligheten att få uppehållstillstånd i Sverige'. Available at: www.riksdagen.se/sv/dokument-lagar/dokument/svensk-forfattningssamling/lag-2016752-om-tillfalliga-begransningar-av_sfs-2016-752 (accessed 15 November 2017).

Sverker, J. (2016) 'Unikt partnerskap för att ge flyktingbarn tryghet', *Dagen*, 10 June. Available at: www.dagen.se/unikt-partnerskap-for-att-ge-flyktingbarn-trygghet-1.736920 (accessed 10 February 2018).

Windrum, P. (2008) 'Innovation and entrepreneurship in public services', in P. Windrum and P. Koch (eds) *Innovation in the public sector services: Entrepreneurship, creativity and management*, Cheltenham: Edward Elgar, pp 3–20.

Part B: From a caring state to an investing state: labour market activation

Judit Csoba and Susan Baines

Discussions on Social Investment have focused strongly on employment policy and especially on active labour markets. The four chapters in this section are about new needs-based and person-centred interventions with labour market activation as a primary aim, sometimes in association with aspects of solidarity and social cohesion.

Productive social policy and the notion of the activating welfare state have become dominant topics of debates in the field of welfare during the past decades (Kluve, 2007; Bonoli, 2012; Morel et al, 2012; Nolan, 2013). Active labour market (ALM) initiatives are intended to ensure that citizens become productive and self-reliant, and they are strongly associated with the Social Investment paradigm (Bonoli, 2012; Hemerijck, 2013; Kuitto, 2016). There are many questions, critiques and debates in the literature related to the tools and effects of labour market activation (Lodemel and Trickey, 2000; Trube, 2003; Kluve, 2007; Rueda, 2007; Hemerijck and Eichhorst, 2009; Cantillion, 2011; Butterwegge, 2015). Whereas early interventions and maximising the educational attainment of children contribute to the 'stock' of human capital, ALMs ease its flows with varied actions to overcome barriers to employment.

The emphasis on economic returns from activating those furthest from the labour market has been a powerful argument for 'selling' Social Investment (Morel and Palme, 2017). As previously discussed in Chapter One, it is possible to take a more holistic view of human capital than the purely productivist version. Such a view values interventions in employment not only for economic inclusion, but also for increasing 'human flourishing' (Morel and Palme, 2017, citing Sen, 2001). This is consistent with the way in which Bourdieu theorised work as 'neither an end, nor a virtue in itself'; in his analysis, 'what is to be appreciated is not the activity aiming at an economic objective, but the activity itself, irrespective of its economic function' (Bourdieu, 1978: 328).

Reflecting on the 10 case studies that feature in this book, almost all of them included some elements of ALM intervention, sometimes as a secondary focus. The four chapters in this section analyse programmes where labour market activation is a primary aim, although not necessarily the only one. Chapter Five (the Youth Guarantee, Finland) and Chapter Six (connecting vocational school graduates with the labour market in Greece) are about improving young adults' prospects for employment and increasing their future productivity. Two of the programmes – the action programme for the labour market integration of migrants (MAMBA) in Germany (Chapter Seven) and Assistance from A to Z in Poland (Chapter Eight) – target vulnerable, stigmatised groups and have strong social as well as economic rationales. Both these interventions also promote social solidarity and social cohesion. In MAMBA, in particular, some service providers and stakeholders consider these to be equally important, or even more so, than securing jobs.

The programmes were quite complex, combining the use of a wide range of social, psychological and professional support, and vocational and social activation. They created multifaceted services, including counselling, mentoring, vocational training, work experience, time placement and supported employment. All four programmes received European Structural and Investment Funds; all activated existing resources to create new services; and all included innovations in governance. Table B.1 highlights the special features of each of the labour market activation case studies in each chapter along the dimensions of resources, services and governance.

Table B.1: Elements and specificities of the case studies in Chapters Five to Eight

	Resources	New services	Governance
Youth Guarantee Finland (Chapter Five)	Agencies from the top of the governance hierarchy to the local level, as well as professionals from various fields	Improved access to education and jobs for young adults with One-Stop-Guidance Centres bringing resources under one roof	Public–private–people partnership, with young people shaping their own future Freedom of municipalities to organise local services
Connecting vocational school graduates with the labour market Greece (Chapter Six)	Institution of systematic transition-to-work programmes Motivated partners (trainers and entrepreneurs)	Education, vocational counselling and acquisition of work experience to make transition to the labour market easier	New links and networks between businesses and vocational education

(continued)

Table B.1: Elements and specificities of the case studies in Chapters Five to Eight (continued)

	Resources	New services	Governance
MAMBA (action programme for the labour market integration of migrants) Germany (Chapter Seven)	Actors with extensive and varied experience Valuable connections to companies and good reputation in negotiations with public authorities	Low threshold of access to services, comprehensive case management system, mentoring	Inter-sectoral collaboration between organisations with very different priorities
Assistance from A to Z ('Accompaniment' of homeless people) Poland (Chapter Eight)	Led by an experienced non-governmental organisation close to the beneficiary group	Social and vocational activation of homeless people for labour market inclusion	Informal support from various stakeholders, including public services and businesses

References

Bonoli, G. (2012) 'Active labour market policy and social investment: changing relationship', in N. Morel, B. Palier and J. Palme (eds) *Towards a social investment welfare state*, Bristol: The Policy Press, pp 181–204.

Bourdieu, P. (1978) *A társadalmi egyenlőtlenségek újratermelődése*, Budapest: Gondolat Kiadó.

Butterwegge, Ch. (2015) *Hartz IV und die Folgen Auf dem Weg in eine andere Republik?*, Weinheim and Basel: Belitz Juventa.

Cantillion, B. (2011) 'The paradox of the social investment state: growth, employment and poverty in the Lisbon era', *Journal of European Social Policy*, 21(5): 432–49.

Hemerijck, A. (2013) *Changing welfare states*, Oxford: Oxford University Press.

Hemerijck, A. and Eichhorst, W. (2009) *Whatever happened to the Bismarckian welfare state? From labor shedding to employment-friendly reforms*, Bonn: Forschungsinstitut zur Zukunft der Arbeit [Institute for the Study of Labor].

Kluve, J. (2007) *Active labor market policies in Europe: Performance and perspectives*, Wiesbaden: Springer.

Kuitto, K. (2016) 'From social security to social investment? Compensating and social investment welfare policies in a life–course perspective', *Journal of European Social Policy*, 26(5): 442– 59.

Lodemel, I. and Trickey, H. (2000) *An offer you can't refuse*, Bristol: The Policy Press.

Morel, N. and Palme, J. (2017) 'A normative foundation for the social investment approach?', in A. Hemerijck (ed) *The uses of social investment*, Oxford: Oxford University Press.

Morel, N., Palier, B. and Palme, J. (eds) (2012) *Towards a social investment welfare state: Ideas, policies and challenges*, Bristol: The Policy Press.

Nolan, B. (2013) 'What use is "social investment"?', *Journal of European Social Policy*, 23(5): 459–68.

Rueda, D. (2007) *Social democracy inside out. Partisanship and labor market policy in industralised democracies*, Oxford: Oxford University Press.

Sen, A. (2001) *Development as freedom*, Oxford: Oxford Paperbacks.

Trube, A. (2003) 'Vom Wohlfahrtsstaat zum Workfarestate – Sozialpolitik zwischen Neujustierung und Umstrukturierung', in: H.-J. Dahme, H.-U. Otto, A. Trube and N. Wohlfahrt (eds) *Soziale Arbeit für den aktivierenden Sozialstaat*, Opladen: Leske+Budrich, pp 177–203.

FIVE

The Youth Guarantee and One-Stop Guidance Centres as a social innovation and a policy implementation tool in Finland

Kaisa Sorsa

Introduction

The Youth Guarantee programme in Finland is designed to prevent the social exclusion of young people by promoting access to education and employment after basic education. The main objective is to ensure that all young people aged under 25 (and recent graduates aged between 25 to 29) will be offered employment, continued education, a traineeship, an apprenticeship, a place in a workshop or a place in rehabilitation within three months of leaving school or of unemployment. By preventing the social exclusion of young people, the overall aim is to increase their welfare and involvement in society, as well as ensuring that Finland will have a qualified workforce in the future (Työ- ja elinkeinoministeriö, 2013).

One-Stop Guidance Centres (OSGCs) ('Ohjaamo' in Finnish) are an implementation tool of the Youth Guarantee. They provide low-threshold support for young people (below the age of 30), offering personal and electronic services relevant to their individual life path. The operating model of OSGCs is based on the cooperation of several public sector service providers offering information, advisory and guidance services to young people. It is a joint venture between the Ministry of Employment and the Economy, the Ministry of Education and Culture, and the Ministry of Social Affairs and Health. The services of the Employment and Economic Development Office are available at all centres. In addition, wider collaborative networks include third sector organisations, voluntary organisations and other bodies that work with young people. The OSGC model creates a new form of public–private–people partnership, with young people actively shaping their own future.

This chapter addresses the interaction between the Youth Guarantee and the Finnish OSGCs, referring to the contexts of regulatory tools, institutional arrangements and governmental decision processes. It reports research undertaken with service providers and young people involved with the OSGC in Turku, a city of 184,000 inhabitants on the south-west coast of Finland.

The Youth Guarantee and OSGCs as an innovative implementation tool in Finland

The social problem that is the focus of the Youth Guarantee programme is youth unemployment, which has been consistently higher than that of the adult population over decades (Reilly, 2013). One factor is that young people often lack the skills to easily find a job. Another has been the increasing deregulation of the labour market over the past 20 years, which has made the transition from education to full-time employment even more difficult. Even when young people do manage to find a job, they are often stuck in a cycle of temporary contracts and poorly paid work. According to statistics from the Ministry of Employment and the Economy of Finland, the number of structural unemployed in October 2015 was 217,000, which was 16,000 people more than a year earlier. Long-term unemployment has increased in recent years in all age groups but most of all among 25–34 year olds (Ministry of Finance, 2016).

Youth unemployment has been and continues to be a significant problem in Europe. The introduction of active youth labour market policies through the European Employment Strategy has been adopted on the political level as a change instrument. Another instrument is extra funding. The umbrella European-level strategy combines several aims to support national Youth Guarantee programmes, which already existed in some member states. The challenge on the European Union (EU) level, as well as on the national level, is that tackling youth unemployment issues crosses administrative boundaries and local contexts.

The Youth Guarantee is a national and regional policy related to EU policies. It is implemented by authorities on national, regional and local levels. The implementation of the Youth Guarantee in Finland has taken place since 2005, before the EU umbrella programme, with improvements conducted in 2013. After the 'new stage' of the Youth Guarantee programme supported by EU legislation, several impact analyses and evaluations have been conducted by public sector institutions, as well as by research organisations. The earlier evaluations focused on the impact of the Youth Guarantee, based on the aims set, for example, in legislation and parliamentary programmes. These evaluations also cover different stakeholders' perspectives, including those of the target group, that is, young people not in employment, education or training (NEETs) (Määttä and Määttä, 2015), as well as the public sector implementation authorities' perspectives (Tuusa et al, 2014). The Finnish Auditing Office evaluation concerned the effectiveness and efficiency of the Youth Guarantee programme (Valtiontalouden tarkastusvirasto, 2014).

In the report 'On the society's edge' (Määttä and Määttä, 2015), Youth Guarantee problems were described from the service providers' viewpoint. According to Määttä and Määttä, there exist several barriers to the use of the employment and education services, and also barriers to the reconciliation of the services. There are many reports about youth unemployment but the knowledge does not contribute to change. Määttä and Määttä found that one of the obstacles for young unemployed people is the difficulty of getting services. Another bottleneck is that young people are guided from one service provider to the other. Young people are in a 'jungle' of services (Määttä and Määttä, 2015). Other obstacles are that no one on the service providers' side has an overall picture, and continuity from service to service does not work fluently, which causes volatility (Määttä and Määttä, 2015). A need to re-evaluate the legislative framework was recommended as the unforeseeable impacts of legislation have created bottlenecks for change, as well as different kinds of administrative instructions and courses of action. Yet another challenge is created as a consequence of the financing structure of the public services, especially sectoral budgeting (Määttä and Määttä, 2015).

In order to improve the implementation of the Youth Guarantee programmes, the Finnish government created a national service model called the 'One-Stop Guidance Centre', supported by the European Social Fund (ESF). The objective of the OSGC service model was to become a low-threshold service point for young people under 30 years of age that takes the individual circumstances of young people into account. In addition, it was intended to offer multidisciplinary information, guidance and support with the aid of the basic public services of various administrative branches and a cooperation network, all under the same roof.

The first OSGCs were established in early 2010 before the current national project. By November 2015, there were 30 regional pilot

OSGCs in places where around 60% of Finland's 16–30 year olds live. The OSGCs currently employ around 300 people, of which one quarter are supported by ESF funding. The OSGC initiative is 75% funded by the ESF. The Central Finland Centre for Economic Development, Transport and the Environment (Keski-Suomen ELY-keskus) is responsible for the Youth Guarantee's national ESF project.

The Youth Guarantee programme in Finland had already elaborated a Theory of Change during its 10-year existence. In the case of the Youth Guarantee, there are multiple interventions in different parts of the network – on the local level and on the national level – that should help young people. The Theory of Change in our case study is a system-level perspective. It means that OSGCs are part of the national-level Youth Guarantee network, and the governance is dependent, on the one hand, on the local-level contextual situation and instruments and, on the other hand, on the framework created at the national level in the context of the Finnish government ministries. The multi-level governance calls for the need to orchestrate the whole system. The key issue is: how does the service network look from the customer point of view at the moment when the service is used?

Another issue is the extra funding that plays a crucial role for the implementation and for embedding the model in the long run. As part of the funding of the Youth Guarantee and the implementation of OSGCs is based on project funding from different EU funding sources or local foundations, the continuation of the projects is always insecure. This problem was mentioned in the OSGC interviews in the City of Turku for this case study, as well as in other evaluation reports.

The Youth Guarantee is both a structural reform to drastically improve school-to-work transitions and a measure to immediately support jobs for young people. The Finnish Ministry of Education and Culture is responsible for the guarantee of education and training, the young adults' skills programme, the youth workshop, and outreach youth work. The Youth Guarantee project is being implemented in collaboration with the Ministry of Employment and the Economy and the Ministry of Social Affairs and Health. Local authorities are responsible for student counselling during basic education. Youth Guarantee does not have any special legislation. Cooperation is based on voluntary agreements. However, in order to ease the multi-sectoral cooperation, the Act on multi-sectoral service cooperation was adopted in 2014 and it tried to create one-stop shops by obliging the Social Insurance Institution, municipalities and employment and economic administration offices, together with job-seekers, to draft a 'multi-sectoral' plan for employment.

OSGC as an implementation tool represents pioneering practice, which demonstrates a new way of doing things in the public–private– people partnership. OSGCs have a versatile set of services, for example, guidance to the right service, personal guidance, educational and work counselling, outreach youth service, services of the Employment and Economic Development Office, economic and development services, Social Insurance Institution's services, mental health care and crisis services, multicultural youth services, workshop services, and entrepreneurship services.

During the first trials, it was found that OSGCs needed to improve cooperation between actors and levels. That would make the service experience more integrated from the young person's point of view. The Employment and Economic Development Office services should become more individual. Also, the information flow in multi-sector cooperation was supposed to be improved. The role of employers should be enhanced by offering more information on the Youth Guarantee and by making the support for employers easier to get. The role of different associations should be developed in tackling the unemployment of young people. The Youth Guarantee contributes to the aim of introducing early intervention, low–threshold, single-point, integrated youth services, which have turned out to be successful.

Implementation and impact of OSGCs on the national and local levels

According to the final evaluation report (Tuusa et al, 2014), the Youth Guarantee programme on the national level has had an effect on the operations of organisations providing youth services, but further adjustments of the operating models were required. Youth participation in planning the services had not increased to any notable degree. The effects of the programme were expected to become stronger in the future. In implementing the programme, focus should be placed on coordinated, mutually agreed and adaptable region- specific models for cooperation. The financial evaluation of the programme did not provide a comprehensive view of the economic effects since the existing statistics and monitoring of grants, resources and services did not provide sufficient information. In order to evaluate the economic effects, a revised method of statistical analysis and access to information is required. The OSGC service model was meant to respond to these criticisms. Reports of Ervamaa (2014) and Aaltonen et al (2015) raised the following issues, which should be improved in the near future:

- low-threshold services should be gathered in OSGCs;
- the information flow in multi-sector cooperation should be improved;
- cooperation should be improved between actors and levels;
- the role of employers should be improved by offering more information on the Youth Guarantee and by making the support for employers easier to get; and
- the Employment and Economic Development Office services (TE offices) should be improved to become more individual.

All these issues focus on the structural organisation of the Youth Guarantee and on the implementation of the political programme at the local level. The OSGCs typically have institutional representation from municipal, education, social and health authorities, so that young people can find the services or combination of services that they need in one physical location. In the OSGC model, young people are active participants in shaping their own future. A customer perspective is at the core of the OSGC's operative model as all the public authorities' services are offered from the same place and the services are individualised.

Local-level implementation

Our case study focused on the local OSGC in the City of Turku. The OSGC service model was still developing during the Innovative Social Investment: Strengthening Communities in Europe (InnoSI) project. The City of Turku management is based on the City of Turku Strategy 2029, which was accepted on 23 June 2014. The strategy is divided into programmes, and the welfare and activity programme defines the goals for the Youth Guarantee. Collaboration inside the city organisation was not working well in the beginning of the evaluation period of our case study. The sharing of comprehensive responsibility for employment-related tasks had not been defined unambiguously in 2014. There were plans to reorganise them as there were several groups in the city that took care of part of the employment management tasks (Turun kaupungin tarkastuslautakunta, 2014). In May 2015, the problem was partially solved as the Employment Services Centre was established under the supervision of the City of Turku's Development Group. The town board had also named an Employment Issue Committee, which deals with and takes a stand on employment management (Turun kaupungin tarkastuslautakunta, 2016). However, transition towards co-produced services for young unemployed people was troublesome.

The managerial roles between the Employment and Economic Development Office, Social Insurance Institution and City of Turku employment services have been under a three-year reorganisation. The Youth Guarantee had goals for 2017 in the welfare and activity programme. The theme 2.2.7 defines the goal of the Youth Guarantee and methods for it: 'Youth guarantee materializes as an outcome of broad, multi-sectoral co-operation'. Methods to reach that goal will be: (1) sufficient individual guidance to young people for moving to secondary education; and (2) multi-sectoral cooperation. Additional strategic goals for the Youth Guarantee were that 45% of under 30-year-old young people will be in work-oriented vocational upper-secondary education and 18% in general upper-secondary education.

The City of Turku OSGC's main aim was to build a very low-level threshold for young people to come to the OSGC. In practice, this means that the aim was to create a bureaucracy-free atmosphere in which a young person can find all the services in the same place. It should be easy to find the place both mentally and physically. There is, for example, no need to book an appointment – sometimes, even the need to book an appointment can be an obstacle for a young person who has mental problems. OSGC service providers do not force young people to make decisions, which can be a relief for some young people. Young people may find a job in companies in Turku, or vacant posts of the Employment and Economic Development Office. There are subsidies for companies to hire young people. As an example of a new activity, the OSGC organised young persons' job-search speed-date events.

The implementation of the strategy started slowly. The OSGC's core principle, multi-sectoral cooperation, did not come true in May 2015 as the employees of the Employment and Economic Development office, the Social Insurance Institution and the City of Turku employment office were in different places. In May 2015, it was promised to the auditing office that the reorganisation of the physical places of these two offices would be confirmed later in 2015 (Turun kaupungin tarkastuslautakunta, 2016). According to an internal report in 2016, the Employment Services Centre had started, but in the spring of 2016, the Social Insurance Institution and other employment services were still in different facilities. It was estimated that they could move under the same roof later in the autumn of 2016 (Turun kaupungin tarkastuslautakunta, 2016).

Activities in Turku's OSGC started on 1 March 2015. During the first months, the activities were focused on organising the project team and marketing the OSGC to the potential customers and cooperation organisations. There were one project coordinator and three customer coordinators. In the same facilities, there were four career planners in Turku Employment Service Centre and two workers in the 'NuortenTurku' information centre. A health services representative was available for appointments on Fridays and a sexual advisor once a week. In the same facility, there is one expert for young people's services from the Employment and Economy Office of South-West Finland. From the Social Insurance Institution, there was no representative, but availability using a 'lync' connection was under development. New customers of OSGC Turku reached 540 between 1 March and 30 November 2015. During the same period, 119 young people were employed either by the City of Turku or by local companies. There were 1,000 visitors. According to the OSGC's project manager, the quantitative goals had been positively exceeded during 2015.

Impact for beneficiaries and services

Young people visiting the OSGC have given very positive feedback about how they were received, how their needs were taken comprehensively into account and how many of their problems were solved and information needed was given in an understandable way during the one visit. From the young customer's perspective, according to the OSGC project coordinator, they feel very confident as the customer is not being shunted between different service providers. This was evidenced from interviews with young service users. An interesting comment from one young person illustrates the difference between the 'old' and 'new' service models' mentality: "I did not feel guilty when I visited OSG centre … [whereas] in the employment office, this was a normal feeling, as well as when visiting the Social Insurance Office". Young people using the services of the Turku OSGC told their stories to students from Turku University of Applied Science, who were trained as community reporters (for some of these young people's experiences, see Box 5.1). According to OSGC employees, cooperation in service delivery has been changed compared to how it used to be when different organisations were on their own. Now, the OSGC employee moves with the young person from one service provider to another. In that way, the information gap between service providers is overcome. Staff give their time to the young person in order to understand his or her situation as a whole, not only in terms of unemployment.

Box 5.1: Young people's stories about the Turku OSGC

Students at Turku University of Applied Sciences were trained community reporters and used these skills to collate stories relating to the Youth Guarantee from other young people in the city. The stories from Turku illustrate the diversity of ways in which young people in Finland are being included into the labour market, and the multiplicity of actors involved in providing this support. They confirm that the OSGC meets their needs as intended because multiple workers and services are available under the same roof. One young woman talked about the support that she has benefited from in a range of ways. She wanted to gain an internship in a kindergarten, and once she had located a suitable one, the paperwork was "all worked out very fast". She was also offered a work-preparation course that paid her additional money, which she needed as she was not living with her parents any more. The Turku young people also convey in their stories a strong sense that the way in which the OSGC works with the individual and understands their circumstances is key to providing meaningful support. This approach is particularly important when working with young people with complex needs. The stories of a young woman with disabilities and a young woman recovering from a mental health condition are exemplars of this. Both have received support tailored to their needs, including group workshops, educational programmes and internships. These personalised interventions have "brought meaning" to their lives and "helped a lot".

Barriers between different public sector actors and private sector actors have been removed, and cooperation between them is improved. Service delivery has improved as all service providers are in the same place. The fundamental idea of the operation of the OSGC is that the professionals working there work as employees of their host organisations (eg municipality, career and education guidance, educational institution, the Social Insurance Institution, etc) but are based at the OSGC premises. The professionals' input into the OSGC's operation can vary from full-time to collaborative periodic on-duty sessions. The different partnership actors' cooperation in the OSGC is very easily organised as they all are in the same place and knowledge sharing takes place daily. The OSGC has weekly meetings and every employee bears responsibility for the functioning of the centre. Employees reported that one need not think about the administrative boundaries during the day.

Staff working in the OSGC explained that they always listen to the needs and opinions of the young clients when it comes to their services and the ways in which they could be improved. Participation by the young people is a key theme in the OSGC. Young people contributed by decorating the facilities in Turku, for example. Also, together with the broadcasting company Yleisradio, they have planned the Raiteille Festival. Together with the Humanistic University of Applied Sciences, the project started the productising of the OSGC's services.

In Finland, the state has increased the freedom of municipalities to organise the implementation of local services for unemployed youth. In the Youth Guarantee programme, costs of the subsidy are transferred from the state to municipalities for multi-sectoral service cooperation. Project-based funding from the ESF continues until 2020. During the period of this case study, economic impact was not possible to evaluate as the OSGC process was just beginning.

Lessons learned in the Social Investment context

Every young person has individual needs and challenges that should be taken care of. Communication between different administrative organisations is still a challenge because of regulatory bottlenecks such as personal data protection. Officials in different administrative branches were used to interpreting the problem of the social exclusion of a young person in different ways. They also had different understandings of how that exclusion could be prevented and what kind of interventions should be used. Lifelong guidance is a shared policy and the administrative responsibility of several ministries at national and regional levels. The challenge is how to establish a consistent cooperation model with other sectors and service providers. We learned in the Youth Guarantee case study that regulatory barriers can hinder the successful implementation of the programme. Therefore, more enabling regulation is needed.

The OSGC service model has shown that with multi-sector cooperation, it is possible to take into account a young person's individual circumstances and offer services tailored accordingly. The Turku OSGC has achieved its goal of empowering the young people by encouraging them to cooperate from the very beginning of the OSGC project. This has been taken into account by giving each young person an individual service and by giving preference to the young person's needs. Cooperation between services has become easier than before as they are in the same building. On the national level, young people's feedback on OSGCs' service content and quality was graded at 9.16 (on a 4–10 scale) and their service experiences were very positive. OSGCs have succeeded in being easily accessible places. As an integrated model with face-to-face and online services, the OSGCs strengthen and simplify services for young people and eliminate the duplication of activities.

The main commonality in governmental discussions on the Youth Guarantee five years ago was the framing of youth unemployment from a supply-side perspective. At the national and European levels, youth unemployment was framed not as a structural problem, but as an individual one, affecting those young people who lack employability, persistence and competitiveness. Thus, unemployed young people were stigmatised as having personal and/or moral shortcomings (Besamusca et al, 2012). Similarly, many recent studies and reports on youth exclusion neglect or completely ignore the social position of young people, their perspectives and their experiences of the welfare service system (Aaltonen et al, 2015). As a result, the area in need of intervention is presumed to be a lack of skills or a mismatch between the skills that such individuals have and market needs. According to this kind of argument, the upgrading of young people's skills should be an important medium- and long-term measure to address youth unemployment and the skills mismatch in Europe (Higgins, 2012). This supply-side narrative also features a tougher stance on unemployment benefits, informal work and collective bargaining rights. Against this background, the OSGC model is pioneering in that it 'mobilises each citizen to become an active part of the innovation process'.

Social Investment in Finland occurs against a background of the Finnish national government extending the roles and responsibilities of municipalities or subregions. The deployment of the OSGC service model promotes the building of human capital through integrated approaches to social services provision. However, the project-based funding, which has become the main source for the Youth Guarantee programme and OSGCs' operations, throws a dark shadow. It does not support the long-term outcomes of the Youth Guarantee. Sponsors from the political level are needed to ensure continuity and funding. Political decision-makers are also the key actors in developing the enabling regulatory environment that allows cooperation between different administrative levels. The OSGC delivery model has proved to be an innovative and effective way of responding to social challenges by activating people's creativity to develop solutions and make better use of scarce resources. However, the reorganisation of the tasks and facilities, and amalgamating the different working cultures of cooperating organisations, takes time, as was evidenced in the Turku OSGC. This case study is consistent with evidence that social innovations are strongly context-driven and institutional embeddedness is decisive.

References

Aaltonen, S., Berg, P. and Ikäheimo, S. (2015) *Nuoret luukulla. Kolme näkökulmaa syrjäytymiseen ja nuorten asemaan palvelujärjestelmässä* [*Young people in social services. Three perspectives on exclusion and status of young people in the service system*], Helsinki: Finnish Youth Research Network/Finnish Youth Research Society. Available at: http://www.nuorisotutkimusseura.fi/julkaisuja/nuoretluukulla.pdf

Besamusca, J., Stănescu, I. and Vauhkonen, J. (2012) 'The European youth guarantee: a reality check', Renner Institute. Available at: http://adapt.it/adapt-indice-a-z/wp-content/uploads/2013/08/FEPS_YG-a-reality-Check.pdf

Ervamaa, S. (2014) *Kohti onnistunutta nuorisotakuuta? Nuorten ja ammattilaisten näkemyksiä nuorisotakuun toteutuksesta ja kehittämisestä. Onnistunut nuorisotakuu –loppuraportti*, Helsinki: Sälekarin Kirjapaino Oy.

Higgins, J. (2012) *A youth guarantee for Europe. Towards a rights-based approach to youth employment policy*, Brussels: European Youth Forum. Available at: www.projects.aegee.org/yue/files/youth_guarantee_for_europe_YFJ_2012.pdf

Määttä, M. and Määttä, A. (eds) (2015) 'Parempia ratkaisuja koulutuksen ja työn ulkopuolella olevien nuorten tukemiseen', Valtioneuvoston selvitys- ja tutkimustoiminnan julkaisusarja 16/2015.

Ministry of Finance (2016) 'Europe 2020 Strategy. Finland's national reform programme'. Available at: http://ec.europa.eu/europe2020/pdf/csr2016/nrp2016_finland_en.pdf

Reilly, K. (2013) 'Guaranteeing our future: a report on the need for a youth guarantee'. Available at: https://www.oireachtas.ie/parliament/media/committees/euaffairs/Youth-Guarantee-Report.pdf

Turun kaupungin tarkastuslautakunta (2014) 'Työtä ja leipää – Turun työllisyysasioiden arviointi'. Available at: http://www.turku.fi/sites/default/files/atoms/files/2013_tyollisyysasioiden_arviointi_tlk_6.6.2014_pdf_0.pdf

Turun kaupungin tarkastuslautakunta (2016) 'Vuoden 2015 arviointi'. Available at: www.turku.fi/sites/default/files/atoms/files//vuoden_2015_arviointi_tarkastuslautakunta_26_5_2016.pdf

Tuusa, M., Pitkänen, S., Shemeikka, R., Korkeamäki, J., Harju, H., Saares, A., Pulliainen, M., Kettunen, A. and Piirainen, R. (2014) *Yhdessä tekeminen tuottaa tuloksia: Nuorisotakuun tutkimuksellisen tuen loppuraportti*. Ministry of Employment and the Economy. Employment and Entrepreneurship 15/2014. Helsinki: Edita Publishing Oy. Available at: https://tem.fi/documents/1410877/2859687/Yhdess%C3%A4+tekeminen+tuottaa+tuloksia+14052014.pdf

Työ- ja elinkeinoministeriö (2013) 'Nuorisotakuun tavoitteet ja sisältö'. Kirje nuorisotakuun alueellisille ja paikallisille toimijoille. Valtakunnallinen nuorten yhteiskuntatakuu -työryhmä Muistio 12.3.2013. Dnro TEM066:00/2011. Available at: www.eduskunta.fi/FI/tietoaeduskunnasta/kirjasto/aineistot/kotimainen_oikeus/LATI/Sivut/nuorisotakuu.aspx

Valtiontalouden tarkastusvirasto (2014) 'Nuorisotyöttömyyden hoito', Valtiontalouden tarkastusviraston tarkastuskertomukset 8/2014.

SIX

Acquiring work experience for vocational education graduates in Greece

Alexandra Koronaiou, George Alexias,
Alexandros Sakellariou and George Vayias

Introduction

The social, economic and working environment in Greece is defined by volatility and insecurity. The programme 'An Integrated Intervention for Connecting Vocational Schools Graduates with the Labour Market' was a cooperative action for addressing the issue of youth unemployment. The initiative was deployed in the eight Convergence Regions of Greece: Eastern Macedonia and Thrace; Epirus; Western Greece; Thessaly; Peloponnesus; Crete; Ionian Islands; and Northern Aegean. They were hit by a large increase of unemployment rates between 2010 and 2014, for example, from 11.9% to 28.7% in Western Greece, from 9.6% to 23.4% in Peloponnesus, from 9.4% to 22.3% in North Aegean, and from 12.0% to 24.0% in Crete (ELSTAT, 2015). The beneficiary group of the intervention was 7,000 graduates of vocational training institutes (IEK), apprenticeship schools (EPAS) and vocational upper-secondary schools (EPAL), aged up to 29 years old and unemployed when the programme took place. A large number of participating enterprises were included as part of an integrated project that aimed at providing: (1) theoretical education; (2) vocational counselling; and (3) the acquisition of work experience (internships) as a means of tackling the adverse impact of unemployment.

The programme had both investive and innovative dimensions. More than being a means of transferring knowledge and expertise to a large number of participants, it particularly tried to empower them to become active agents of change in their own lives. Further to that, and related to previous similar projects, individualised vocational counselling sessions and quality-controlled internships combined with theoretical education were types of services introduced to beneficiaries for the first time (Evers et al, 2014). In that respect, the programme aimed to forge prospects for vocational training graduates, functioning as a tipping point in their life course and their connection with the labour market.

Connecting unemployed vocational education graduates with the labour market

During 2010–14, the age group of young people up to 29 years old was at the centre of the adverse impact on the labour market of the economic crisis in Greece that commenced in 2009. This was in particular evident in exceedingly high rates of unemployment in 2014: at 51.5% of 15–24 year olds and 41.1% of 25–29 year olds (ELSTAT, 2014). In addition, there was underemployment and part-time employment, social insecurity and instability, lack of trust in political and democratic institutions, along with continuous cuts in income, wages and pensions (Matsaganis, 2013; Cedefop, 2014). Such a worrying state of society, education and the economy, along with its effects on this specific age group, was followed by heightened concern about youth unemployment and the disadvantages that young people face in their attempt to enter the labour market.

In response to that situation, and following a series of regulatory and legislative incentives regarding vocational education and training, the Greek Ministry of Labour, in collaboration with the Ministries of Education, Culture and Development, drew up a unified operational action plan of targeted interventions to boost youth employment and entrepreneurship in the context of the National Strategic Reference Framework (NSRF) 2007–2013 Operational Programme. Under this action plan, a number of vocational training-related initiatives were implemented to foster employment and entrepreneurship for persons aged 15 to 35 years old (Cedefop, 2014). Objectives of these initiatives included, but were not limited to:

- Strengthening vocational training and apprenticeship systems, particularly via the combination of training and work experience programmes that subsidise job placements for young people and practical training in workplace settings (voucher for vocational training), either during education or later.
- The institution of systematic transition-to-work programmes to help students gain initial work experience. These would need to

be adapted to the needs and profiles of young job-seekers through a combination of guidance, counselling, training and employment (eg job voucher schemes for young job-seekers).
• Providing more counselling and vocational guidance, especially for young job-seekers, through supporting vocational guidance in schools, career orientation and entrepreneurship counselling (such as through vocational education career offices and actions promoting youth entrepreneurship).
• Measures aimed at reducing early school leaving (Cedefop, 2014).

The programme was implemented in the context of the EU Youth Employment Initiative (YEI), which was the source of funding. The YEI intended to provide financial support to the member states worst hit by youth unemployment. It was allocated to regions with youth unemployment rates (YURs) of more than 25% in 2012 and, for member states where YURs had increased by more than 30% in 2012, Nomenclature of Territorial Units for Statistics (NUTS) level 2 regions that had YURs of more than 20% in 2012 (EC and ESF, 2014). In general, on the EU level, the YEI typically supported the provision of: (1) apprenticeships; (2) traineeships; (3) job placements; and (4) further education leading to a qualification. The programme's design and implementation were primarily grounded and dictated by the YEI rationale, principles and guidelines (EC and ESF, 2013, 2014). More specifically, in the case of Greece some worrying figures that supported the implementation of the specific programme were are follows:

• unemployment rate in December 2014 of 25%;
• youth (under 25) unemployment rate in December 2014 of 50.6%; and
• young people not in employment, education or training (NEETs) rate in 2013 of 20.4%.

In this respect, tackling youth unemployment was expected to be achieved primarily through actions oriented to the direct link between vocational education and training with employment and the labour market. This was the idea for principally addressing the programme 'An Integrated Intervention for Connecting Vocational Schools Graduates with the Labour Market' to vocational schools and institute graduates (IEK, EPAS and EPAL). For its design and implementation, a consortium was assembled. The Labour Institute of Greek General Confederation of Labour (INE/GSEE) was the coordinator of the programme, supplemented by the following social partners:

- Centre for the Development of Educational Policy (KANEP/GSEE);
- Hellenic Confederation of Professionals, Craftsmen & Merchants (GSEVEE/IME & KEK);
- National Confederation of Hellenic Commerce (ESEE/KAELE & INEMY); and
- Hellenic Management Association (EEDE).

The composition of the consortium reflected the will and the ambition of the leading social partners engaged in active employment practices and policies in Greece to join forces and bring about maximum effectiveness of this specialised intervention (INE/GSEE, 2015a). The programme was implemented in 2015 (January to November). The call for proposals was issued by the Ministry of Education in July 2014. The joint ministerial decision was issued in December 2014 and the programme was publicly announced on the coordinator's and social partners' web sites in January 2015. By December 2015, most of the programme's actions were completed.

The programme's objectives can be outlined as follows:

- increase of youth employability;
- development of professional as well as horizontal ('soft') skills for the beneficiaries (communication, team-working capability, etc);
- establishment of a professional/working culture for the beneficiaries; and
- personal development of the beneficiaries – increase of their self-esteem, expansion of their personal and professional networks, enhancement of job satisfaction, and widening of their chances to be integrated into the labour market (INE/GSEE, 2015a).

These objectives were expected to be achieved via a combined scheme of well-designed activities that included:

- Theoretical education for cultivating and fostering a set of horizontal ('soft') skills so as to match the career needs of all professional and business sectors. This comprised 80 hours of theoretical training in four modules – (1) Informatics, (2) Administrative and Organisational Skills, (3) Entrepreneurship and Innovation, and (4) Conflict Management and Communication.
- Vocational counselling sessions oriented to the establishment of employability, professional adjustment and professional resilience, that is, factors that help the individual become accustomed to the

labour market and recognise potential job opportunities. This comprised of four vocational counselling sessions.

• Acquisition of work experience (up to six months of internship) in enterprises by developing an efficient system of 'coupling' the graduates' specialties with the area in which each enterprise trades.

The programme was implemented at a time when Greece was undergoing, as it still is, a severe economic crisis, with immense repercussions on social and cultural levels, seriously affecting young persons' employability and access to the labour market, physical and mental health, and sense of social inclusion (Papadakis, 2013). If times of crisis are typically times of change, then this is paralleled by the fact that a (or any) programme's 'wish' or 'ambition' to provoke some kind of change is, or should be, considered as an inseparable aspect of an intervention aiming at social profit. That given, research conducted for the evaluation purposes of the Innovative Social Investment: Strengthening Communities in Europe (InnoSI) project indicated that the main change that the consortium aspired to attain was to establish and broaden the access of vocational (IEK, EPAS and EPAL) graduates to the labour market. It should be noted here that after holding meetings with the programme's stakeholders, it was concluded that there was no explicit Theory of Change developed while designing, preparing and implementing the programme. Yet, according to the implementation guides of the programme (INE/GSEE, 2015a) and vocational counselling (INE/GSEE, 2015b), it can be argued that the intervention wanted to: (1) improve the beneficiaries' body of knowledge and skills; (2) provide professional/work experience of high quality and profitability; and (3) offer vocational/career empowerment and support. In that respect, the programme's short- or mid-term objective was to bring change via an orchestrated and well-planned series of actions on two axes. One of these was giving the vocational graduates as profound and rich as possible horizontal skills and work experience, which can be capitalised in the future by helping them either to find a permanent job or to 'create' a new job by innovatively combining their vocational specialty with the skills/knowledge and experience collected via the programme. The other was to enhance and broaden the professional prospects of unemployed young people so that their active participation in the labour market is promoted and ensured as much as possible.

However, after completing our research, it turned out that there was actually an underlying long-term objective. In other words, the impact that the programme was aiming at was broader. Apart from equipping the beneficiaries with a common set of skills that will be more or less useful in almost any type of future working environment, and giving them the chance to familiarise themselves with real-time working conditions, the programme's vocational counselling and guidance would, on a mid- and, most importantly, long-term basis, help them:

- create awareness of career options through assessment of interests, values and ambitions;
- make the right choice regarding the type of job they want to do;
- understand the conditions, demands and necessities of the labour market;
- receive support, motivation and a boost to their morale as employable persons, which is necessary for long-term success, especially in times of crisis; and
- feel more confident and realise the practicality of expanding their interpersonal and professional networks.

This can be considered as an innovative feature of the programme given that it had not been implemented in previous interventions. It was a service provided to a large number of people who resided in problematic environments in terms of working prospects that affect their personal and social life. At the same time, another innovative service was introduced. This was a system for continuously monitoring the quality of the programme's internship phase, securing the expected results and preventing possible abusive behaviours or other non-expected results. The consortium's intention was not just to place the beneficiaries in enterprises as interns. Most importantly, it was to deploy an active mechanism for observing the work-experience acquisition stage via regular communication of the quality-control inspectors with the beneficiaries and onsite meetings at the enterprises so that they can intervene in cases if needed. Emphasis was given on the compliance with the legal framework on labour issues and on ensuring that the beneficiaries are placed in the enterprises as interns who are there to learn and familiarise themselves with the conditions of the workplace.

In summary, the programme intended to empower and make more confident a significant number of young adults, and to motivate them to meet new people and create networks, in order to change their self-perception, as well as their place in the family, workplace and society in general. At the same time, the programme was thought of as a 'prototype' or a 'model' than can be adopted when designing and implementing similar interventions in the future.

Key findings: implementation and impact

As part of the evaluation conducted for the purposes of the InnoSI project, the programme was assessed in terms of implementation and impact. In this section, findings regarding these two aspects are presented.

Findings on implementation

The programme was addressed to unemployed vocational graduates, aged up to 29 years. It was designed and managed by a consortium of social partners established for that purpose. While the original composition of the consortium was slightly modified, this change did not practically affect the regular flow of the programme. The vast majority of the actions and subprojects included in the bid documents of the programme were eventually implemented as initially planned. Activities oriented to publicising and communicating the programme to the general population, and, specifically, its target group, were designed centrally but were implemented in close cooperation with the participating social partners in all regions around the country. Despite delays in disbursement that led to some publicity arrangements being cancelled, the programme was well communicated. Moreover, all staff and personnel of participating social partners were keen and willing to support the programme on every possible level as responses to incoming questions, feedback to messages and information on various issues were admittedly immediate.

The part of the programme related to the theoretical education of the beneficiaries ran without difficulties or any other complexities. Altogether, the educators proved to be quite competent and highly qualified. On the other hand, the beneficiaries also responded well to the modules that they were taught. Finally, the total number of educators contracted with the consortium was sufficient as each educator was assigned approximately 20 beneficiaries. The part of the programme concerned with the vocational counselling of the beneficiaries was also implemented satisfactorily. There occurred some complexities in the beginning that mainly pertained to: (1) delays in starting the counselling sessions due to the overall delay of the programme; (2) some minor organisational complexities while 'matching' the beneficiaries with the enterprises; and (3) the fact that vocational counselling was something absolutely brand new to most of the beneficiaries. These complexities were quickly resolved as the rationale, the objectives, the usefulness and the feasibility of vocational counselling were communicated to the beneficiaries more efficiently and in detail.

A substantial drawback of the programme's implementation was the delay in the disbursement of the funds. This can be explained by, or attributed to, the instability of the political and economic conditions at the time in Greece. The truth is that this troubled situation did not generally affect the programme's implementation. However, it caused the side effect of making the beneficiaries feel distressed and uncertain about whether they would eventually get the scholarship (money) for participating or not. Further to that, many beneficiaries received the full amount of the scholarship just one or two months before the programme's establishment.

The part of the programme that related to the acquisition of work experience by the beneficiaries was also well implemented. The quality and level of cooperation and communication between the interns and the enterprises was positively evaluated by both sides, without reporting or identifying any extreme problems or difficulties, except for a few isolated cases. Finally, a major feature of the programme's implementation was that the money that the beneficiaries received for participating was given in the form of a scholarship. This served two significant purposes. On the one hand, it reflected the consortium's intention to provide the beneficiaries with the highest financial benefit possible as scholarships were tax-free. On the other, it aimed to be some kind of incentive for the vocational graduates as an award for continuing their training efforts after the programme.

In summary, given that the programme was implemented on a pilot-scale basis, as most of the stakeholders' staff and members of project teams asserted, it could be argued that it was altogether well and competently implemented. It combined innovative elements and activities in terms of lifelong and adult-learning processes, and of introducing and applying vocational counselling. It successfully established new practices and mechanisms such as the internship quality control in the enterprises, and it enabled vocational graduates to become acquainted with the demands and conditions of the labour market.

What would have happened if all actions and subprojects initially intended had been implemented is open to debate. However, this does not imply that the programme was mis-implemented. On the contrary, secondary dysfunctions, minor organisational flaws, technical problems (eg with filing applications to become beneficiaries) and the major issue of the short amount of time available for implementing all the programme's actions were all overcome successfully. This is credited to the exceptional cooperation of the consortium that skilfully 'invested' a great deal of human resources, time, infrastructure, knowledge and expertise.

Findings on impact

The programme aimed to support young people who, although they were vocational education graduates, were not in education, employment or training. Enterprises were given the opportunity to employ – as interns, not as regular employees – a large number of graduates to extend their workforce and to benefit from fresh new ideas. The partners successfully designed and deployed an innovative system for ensuring the internships' quality standards. The programme was quite a complex one, with very limited time available (just under one year) for communicating the programme, recruiting educators, counsellors and quality inspectors, and developing a wide network of enterprises for the beneficiaries' internships.

In identifying and describing the impact that the programme had on the beneficiaries, the team of educators reported that the overall activities of the programme succeeded in attracting the beneficiaries' participation. Their exceptional rate of response and engagement with the demands and the requirements of the intervention reflect a positive outcome considering that the beneficiaries were carefully targeted by the consortium. The programme provoked the interest of the beneficiaries, which allows us to assume that the theoretical training, the vocational counselling and the internship stage were appealing to them. Positive effects of the programme can, in particular, be detected through the individualised counselling sessions, whereby the young people's morale was uplifted and their self-confidence was strengthened. Contact with the environment of the workplace and the actual prerequisites and conditions produced essential impacts as most of the beneficiaries participated in 'on-the-job' training for the first time in their lives. Familiarisation, also for the first time in their lives, with the methods and techniques of adult and lifelong learning was illuminating to almost all beneficiaries as the vast majority experienced the transition from school to vocational education. The purely experiential acquaintance of the beneficiaries with the enterprises and the labour market, by extension, largely contributed to the empowerment of their ability to correspond successfully and, above that, to fully comprehend expectations on the enterprise's side. Internships provided the beneficiaries with the opportunity to establish, to cultivate and to extend as much as possible a network of acquaintances that might be useful in the future while searching for a job or starting up their own enterprise. Alongside this, it prompted them to move themselves from passivity and to feel that solutions are more likely to show up via an energetic attitude. Finally, the programme specifically motivated those beneficiaries who reside in rural areas by actively incorporating and 'persuading' them to show more zeal given that programmes and initiatives such as the one discussed here are rarely implemented in the places where they live.

As far as the team of counsellors is concerned with regards to the impact of the programme, it is concluded that their viewpoints are pretty much identical to that of the educators. They argued, in particular, that via the individualised counselling sessions, the beneficiaries acquired general as well as specific information on the labour market and, also noticeably, on issues and matters of rather personal interest. The counsellors also argued that the programme had positive aspects in that counselling sessions and interventions were individualised and appropriately adjusted to the necessities of each beneficiary. Beneficiaries: learned and worked with tools that can potentially be useful in job searching, for example, preparing their résumé, preparing for a job interview and so on; became acquainted with utilising the internet, and social media in particular, as a means to search for a job and establish networks; and developed a more critical viewpoint towards their position in the workplace, their rights and their cooperation with the employer. Further to that, motivation enhancement, an increase of self-esteem and a boost to self-confidence in relation to the beneficiaries' personal and social prospects can be factored into the impact of the programme.

The viewpoints of the quality inspectors were on the same wavelength as those of the educators and counsellors. Given their specialised role in the programme, they argued that the intervention provoked impact on all beneficiaries without almost any exception, that is, those employed, those unemployed and those who had worked before acquired work experience that is not only valuable per se, but can be included in their résumé. Apart from the horizontal skills gained, the beneficiaries had the chance to explore and develop general as well as personal working traits. The programme also had an impact on quality inspectors as it enabled them to advance specialised working skills given that this particular 'task' was somehow completely new. The participating enterprises had the opportunity to work and collaborate with young graduates, who brought new ideas to the workplace in quite a few cases. Through (internship) time, relationships of trust between the beneficiaries and the employers came to light, which could possibly produce permanent working positions in the future.

In summary, the vast majority of supervisors firmly believe that the internship phase of the programme had noteworthy impact on the beneficiaries' professional prospects, work culture and efficiency in working as part of a team. On the other side, the beneficiaries' rating of the modules taught, the effectiveness of the theoretical education and the time duration of the overall programme was quite high. The vast majority of them hold the strong conviction that the knowledge and skills that they acquired were usefully deployed in the enterprise during their internships. In the internships, they also had the opportunity to obtain extra skills, mostly related to the area of activity of the enterprise. Relevance between the beneficiaries' specialty and the area of the enterprise, as well as levels of satisfaction in the guidance and support that they received in the workplace by the supervisors, was high. Lastly, the programme enhanced not just their work culture, but also their employability and their professional prospects. This is evidently reflected in the notable percentage of those who highly and very highly stress that the expectations they had in the beginning of the programme were ultimately met to a large extent.

While trying to assess the impact of the programme, it was evident that what our findings showed cannot actually be considered as impact in the strict sense of the term. As concluded from the existing evaluations' findings, the programme produced positive effects on various levels. However, the absence of a follow-up survey of the impact is an obstacle in that it does not allow us to have a clear picture of the present situation of the beneficiaries and the status of the enterprises affected, or not, through the programme. In particular, a survey of the current conditions of the beneficiaries' social, economic and professional status, including quantitative as well as qualitative indicators, would be revealing of the programme's impact almost two years after its establishment.

Learning points and policy implications

The evaluation of the programme revealed that its strong features were the high degree of fund absorption, the achievement of quantitative targets and the sufficiency of the available funds. In addition, there was increased participation and positive feedback from the beneficiaries and their involvement in the programme's activities. There occurred a positive impact on the beneficiaries, notably, through the individualised counselling sessions, the increase of young people's morale and the enhancement of their self-confidence, which led to the development of new horizontal and specialised skills. The programme's publicity and implementation was, in general, evaluated positively by the beneficiaries and also by the participating enterprises.

Findings deriving from both the qualitative and quantitative evaluation showed particularly encouraging results in terms of both the means chosen and the effectiveness of the initiative. The overall stages of application filing and personnel recruitment were positively assessed. All target groups that participated in quantitative and qualitative research highly rated the programme's e-platform efficiency and the support provided by all participating social partners' staff. With regards to the theoretical education: the modules taught were considered satisfactorily; the training material was rich and comprehensible; the educators were appropriately trained and communicative; while the time duration of the training stage was, for the most part, sufficient. The professional-experience acquisition stage (internship) was one of the most successful parts of the project. The high quality and level of cooperation between interns and enterprises was very positively assessed, despite minor occurrences and difficulties. Both sides expressed a high level of satisfaction, a good level of collaboration and a spirit of mutual understanding. It was underlined that the beneficiaries developed or improved a series of horizontal ('soft') skills: organisational capabilities, personal time management, consistency, team-working spirit, professionalism, flexibility and adaptability. The programme's infrastructure and organisation favoured a systematic cultivation of professional attitudes and values that were certainly strengthened by the interns' daily contact with the workplace. At the same time, relationships of trust between beneficiaries and fellows and employers were developed over time, which can potentially transform into professional ones. The number of beneficiaries who would be willing to continue working in the host enterprise, as well as the amount of enterprises that would be positive about continuing their cooperation with them, was impressive. The 'weak' features of the programme, related to limited time available for implementation, delays in fund disbursement, the short duration of internships and minor organisational issues, do not override the 'strong' ones.

The programme's main objective was to enhance potential access to the labour market for a social group that is at risk. Yet, an underlying objective came to light, which was to map and explore the effectiveness of various strategies for investment in human capital and the degree to which these are consistent with the development of innovations that meet urgent social needs. In that respect, it could be argued that the programme has successfully highlighted some points that require improvement.

Future similar programmes should last longer so as to give the beneficiaries sufficient time to acquire more professional experience in enterprises. This would also allow for more resources to be allocated and utilised by organisers and coordinators, and would maximise chances for employment after the programme's establishment. In particular, initiatives for tackling sensitive social problems could be implemented in cycles provided that the beneficiaries are able to complete the entire five-month internship in each cycle. Internships should have an institutional dimension in terms of continuity and time planning, and provide some kind of certification from the enterprises. A more careful preparation is also needed in terms of the regional distribution of the beneficiaries, as well as organisational arrangements and open communication channels during implementation. This will allow for problems that arise to be solved in time and improve the interconnection between operators. A coherent administration structure is also important, especially in large-scale projects, for the proper coordination of various programme stages in that it will ensure proper guidance for beneficiaries in their regions and will achieve greater homogeneity in the provision of (social) services. Employers should be given incentives, or be somehow prompted, to hire the interns in their enterprise – for a certain period of time or permanently – after the completion of the programmes via an employment contract. It may even be useful for enterprises to retain job offerings and get a bonus/reward for participating in Social Investment initiatives.

One of the elements to be highlighted is that of bureaucratic procedures, which could be reduced. Administrative and secretarial procedures and services should ideally be processed electronically/digitally so that fewer working hours are needed and easier management is achieved. Furthermore, key management issues that need to be simplified are the finances, the contracts and the repayments. Future (social) interventions should establish closer cooperation with business representational bodies (associations, chambers, etc) so as to inform all sectors of a country's economy (public, private, third sector). An extensive mapping of labour market needs is strongly advised on both a central and regional level for two principal reasons. One is defining the specialties offered/taught by vocational institutions so that they most accurately match each region's labour needs. The other is to more efficiently meet the needs of local/regional enterprises. This is essential to help the absorption and integration of unemployed beneficiaries, preventing them from social pathologies and/or leaving the country in search of a better future. Finally, follow-up surveys should also be an inseparable feature of programmes. These should include, but not be limited to: the type of long-term change(s) that the programme provoked; possible implications, outcomes and effects on local/regional societies and/or local labour markets; policy reforms instigated; and the feasibility of implementing a similar programme in the future.

The creation and implementation of breakthrough ideas on how people should pursue their interpersonal activities and social interactions so as to meet one or more life objectives can be accomplished via social innovation interventions. Analysis and discussion of the programme presented in this chapter showed that there is an apparent need for new social services, not as expenditure, but as investment, which through bringing up or enhancing people's skills, will increase well-being, cohesion, inclusion and participation on both individual and social levels.

References

Cedefop (2014) *Vocational education and training in Greece. A short description.* Luxembourg: Publications Office of the European Union.

EC (European Commission) and ESF (European Social Fund) (2013) *Youth Employment Initiative. Fiche no 34*, draft working paper, Brussels: European Commission. Available at: http://www.mmr.cz/getmedia/8606d095-0421-4014-bf10-4a92c25c500e-/Explanatory-fiche-to-SAWP-on-YEI.pdf?ext=.pdf (accessed 21 November 2016).

EC and ESF (2014) *Guidance on implementing the Youth Employment Initiative*, September, Luxembourg: European Commission, Directorate-General for Employment, Social Affairs and Inclusion, Unit E1.

ELSTAT (Hellenic Statistical Authority) (2014) 'Press release on labour force survey' (4th Quarter 2014), p 2. Available at: https://www.statistics.gr/en/statistics/-/publication/SJO01/2014-Q4 (accessed 1 November 2017).

ELSTAT (2015) *Greece in figures (July–September 2015)*, Athens: Hellenic Statistics Authority (ELSTAT).

Evers, A., Ewert, B. and Brandsen, T. (eds) (2014) 'Social innovations for social cohesion. Transnational patterns and approaches from 20 European cities', WILCO project.

INE/GSEE (Labour Institute of Greek General Confederation of Labour) (2015a) *Implementation and management guide for the project 'Access to labour market: Acquiring work experience for Vocational Training Institutes (IEK), Apprenticeship Schools (EPAS) and Vocational Upper Secondary Schools (EPAL) graduates*, Athens: INE and GSEE.

INE/GSEE (2015b) *Vocational counselling guide*, Subproject 14, Athens: INE and GSEE.

Matsaganis, M. (2013) *The Greek crisis: Social impact and policy responses*, Berlin: Friedrich Ebert Foundation, Department of Western Europe/ North America (Study/Friedrich-Ebert-Stiftung). Available at: http://library.fes.de/pdf-files/id/10314.pdf

Papadakis, N. (ed) (2013) *Barometer of the absents: NEETs (young people not in education, employment or training) in Greece*, research report, Athens: I. Sideris Publications.

SEVEN

Network for the labour market integration of migrants and refugees in Münster, Germany (MAMBA)

Nikola Borosch, Danielle Gluns and Annette Zimmer

Introduction

The acronym MAMBA[1] stands for a networking approach to labour market integration earmarked for migrants and asylum seekers in the city and region of Münster in the state of North Rhine-Westphalia, Germany. In the late 2000s, MAMBA was put in place by a non-profit organisation called GGUA (Gemeinnützige Gesellschaft zur Unterstützung Asylsuchender e.V.) located in Münster, which looks back upon a long tradition of providing support and counselling for migrants and asylum seekers. From an organisational point of view, MAMBA translates into an institutionalised cooperation of public, semi-public, commercial and non-profit organisations entrusted with tasks connected to integration and labour market policies. Today, the non-profit organisation that started MAMBA still serves as the key administrative unit of the network, as well as a hotspot for refugees and migrants in search of support such as legal advice or help with administrative paperwork. Since access to the German labour market is highly regulated and many professions require documentary evidence of formal qualifications, migrants, including refugees, are faced with significant difficulties. Moreover, residence laws make the granting of a long-term residence status conditional on employment for some groups of migrants. In order to support these different groups, MAMBA takes an encompassing approach that consists of both individual counselling and legal advice, as well as of active support services with respect to labour market integration in terms of education, apprenticeships, job search and placement. Specifically tailored to migrants and refugees with difficulties in accessing the labour market in Germany, MAMBA is placed at a crossroads of integration and labour market policies and stands out for its innovativeness and sustainable Social Investment in both fields. MAMBA takes an innovative approach to labour market integration by building on a close network of public, business and non-profit actors that are working in the field of labour market and employment policies to best address the needs of the target groups (BEPA, 2010). This creates synergies and builds on the resources of the clients to enhance their access to and participation in the German labour market and society.

MAMBA as a reaction to policy change

Background

Balancing and counteracting the deficiencies of German integration policy constitutes the 'raison d'être' of MAMBA as a locally embedded network supporting migrants and refugees in their efforts to feel at home in Germany. The country looks back upon a long policy tradition of non-integration of migrants, for example, 'guest workers' since the 1950s, whose stay was assumed to be temporary. Although there were many voices criticising the non-existence of a policy supporting the integration of migrants into the German labour market and society, there was no policy change until the late 1990s, when key German politicians started to question the leitmotiv of 'Germany is not a country of immigration' (Geissler, 2014; Hoesch, 2017). Previously, the European Union (EU) had passed a directive in favour of facilitating the labour market integration of refugees. Also, the EU had launched a programme providing grants for initiatives and networks that aimed at supporting needs-oriented local assistance for refugees and migrants. The German federal government finally opted in favour of setting up a funding stream with the goal of facilitating integration into the labour market for those migrants and refugees enjoying the right of residence by drawing on funding from the European Social Fund (ESF) (BMAS, 2008a, 2008b).

As soon as the German government had launched the new programme, the chairman of Münster's non-profit organisation assisting migrants took the initiative to set up a network of locally active organisations. After a period of intense consultation with the goal of finding common ground on how to cooperate best for the sake of integrating migrants into the regional labour market, MAMBA was created in 2008 and made possible with the financial support of the programme (Borosch and Klein, 2017). Since then, MAMBA's key objective is to enable migrants, including refugees with subordinate access to the labour market, to become sustainably employed in the regional labour market. Accordingly, MAMBA strongly builds on the assumption that labour market integration constitutes a key prerequisite of overall or societal integration. However, Germany's highly regulated market for qualified jobs impedes access for migrants, in particular, for refugees and persons without a long-term residence permit. According to German law, there is a close nexus between employment and residence permits (Bertelsmann Stiftung, 2015). MAMBA is set up as a network of five organisations, each of which is active in the city and region of Münster. Each member of the network contributes specifically to MAMBA's overall goal of making refugees and migrants fit for the German labour market through a variety of support measures, ranging from training, especially vocational education, to the counselling of vulnerable individuals, to arranging contacts with companies and other possible employers.

Profile of the network

The organisations working together under the umbrella of MAMBA are well-known local actors; each of them stands out for its long-term expertise in a particular area and policy field. What makes MAMBA innovative is the joint effort of these 'local players' to cooperate for the benefit of a distinctive and vulnerable group trying to find a new home in Münster. The cooperating organisations do not focus exclusively on MAMBA; instead, the project constitutes just one aspect of their multifaceted profiles. After a brief characterisation of each member of the MAMBA network, we will focus on the implementation of the programme and specifically on the topic of synergetic cooperation. Moreover, we will cover the funding of MAMBA, which, unsurprisingly, turns out to be the 'Achilles heel' or weak spot of the network.

The organisations involved in MAMBA are:

- GGUA, a non-profit refugee support organisation with a long tradition in counselling as well as lobbying activities on behalf of asylum seekers;
- The Jugendausbildungszentrum (JAZ), a tax-exempt limited liability company affiliated with the German welfare association Caritas that offers vocational training, low-threshold job opportunities and counselling, in particular, for youngsters and young adults facing difficulties accessing the labour market;
- GEBA (Gesellschaft für Berufsbildung und Ausbildung mbH), a for-profit organisation offering training and vocational education;

- HBZ (Handwerkskammer Bildungszentrum), the educational and training centre of the Chamber of Crafts in Münster; and
- the Jobcentre, that is, the local public employment agency.

As the initiator of MAMBA as well as its central administrative unit, the non-profit refugee support organisation GGUA constitutes the 'spider in the web' that is responsible for a variety of tasks within the network. Among those, safeguarding smooth cooperation among the cooperating partners, public relations and lobbying on behalf of MAMBA count most prominently. From an organisational point of view, the GGUA is legally organised as a membership-based voluntary association with a participatory governance structure. Besides MAMBA, the GGUA is the host of various independently managed projects or programmes for improving the living conditions of refugees and migrants.

Founded in 1979, the GGUA has a long tradition of support for asylum seekers and refugees. Its key objective is to provide advice regarding their legal status and German residence law. Furthermore, the GGUA tries to support Münster's migrant population with issues such as accommodation or communication with local authorities. Moreover, the GGUA perceives itself only partly as a service provider; it is also significantly engaged in advocacy and provides a forum for the citizens of Münster to actively support refugees and migrants through donations of time (volunteering) and money. The labour force of the GGUA thus comprises employees (25 full time), interns and more than 200 volunteers. One GGUA project, for example, matches volunteer learning mentors and suitable migrants. Similar to other non-profit organisations, funding constitutes a difficult issue for the GGUA. It is financed through membership fees, donations and public grants, which cover the greatest share of its costs, particularly staff expenditures. By and large, public grants are contract-based, earmarked for specific activities and limited in scope and duration. Financing and funding continue to cause problems, endangering the sustainability of the organisation, even though the GGUA enjoys a fine reputation of solid expertise.

The second non-profit organisation of the MAMBA network is the JAZ, that is, the centre for vocational training of young people. In contrast to the GGUA, the JAZ is not a standalone non-profit; instead, it is an adjunct of Caritas, Germany's largest welfare association, which is closely affiliated with the Catholic Church in Germany (Boesenberg and Vilain, 2013). For various reasons, the JAZ is a very valuable member of the MAMBA network. First, the JAZ, founded in 1982, is thoroughly embedded in the Catholic milieu of Münster, which has always been very influential. Hence, cooperation with the JAZ constitutes a source of legitimacy for the network. Second, the JAZ also looks back upon a long tradition of cooperation with public and private partners – specifically the local government – and the business community of Münster in the area of vocational education and training, particularly for young people who face difficulties in getting access to the labour market. The JAZ is primarily active in three key areas:

- individual counselling for school graduates in order to facilitate their transition to employment or apprenticeship;
- provision of education and training specifically tailored to the needs of young people who lack the requirements to start a job or an apprenticeship; and
- training on the job in facilities and organisations either affiliated with Caritas or the Catholic Church in Münster.

The workforce of the JAZ encompasses counsellors, coaches and social workers, whose prime task is to improve the employability of young people. The JAZ offers assistance in finding a job or apprenticeship, and, if necessary, there are intensive programmes of crisis intervention with the goal of preventing youngsters from dropping out of employment or apprenticeships. There are various public funding streams that are earmarked for programmes working with this target group. As a non-profit organisation, the JAZ is thoroughly financed through government grants and contracts.

Similar to the JAZ, the GEBA – a for-profit company with the goal of enhancing the employability and career prospects of various groups – offers a broad range of courses and counselling programmes. The company is based in Münster and has worked closely together with public institutions and private businesses since 1991. With 11 branches all over the region and 18 full-time professionals, the GEBA is a well-established provider of services in the region. One of its prime fields of activity is the provision of German-language courses, which are very well suited for the constituency of the MAMBA network. The GEBA also works closely together with companies providing programmes for the needs of professionals and employees in management positions. However, in particular, its engagement in the area of vocational education, language and preparation courses commissioned by public bodies makes the GEBA a very valuable partner of the MAMBA network. The GEBA programmes that are of prime relevance for the

MAMBA network are either financed through programme lines of the German federal government or the ESF, and encompass language courses that are specifically tailored either to the needs of migrants or refugees who have just arrived in the country, or to those who are already in a position to enter the job market.

A partner with a semi-public status is the HBZ, a sophisticated training facility operating as a branch of the Chamber of Crafts in Münster. In Germany, the Chambers of Crafts are follow-up organisations of the former guilds and fraternities; founded in the late 19th century by the government, they operate under public law. Membership is compulsory for companies and family businesses working in the so-called craft sector, which covers a wide range of vocational activities ranging from the tiling of roofs to metal working or cooking. The German craft sector is highly regulated. Vocational training is supervised by the Chamber of Crafts, which also award certificates of apprenticeship and master craftsman's diplomas. All over Germany, there is a decisive need for well-trained craftsmen and craftswomen. The reasons for the scarcity of trained labour in this area are at least twofold: first, working in the craft sector is less prestigious than other professional activities; and, second, due to the booming German economy, there are many open positions and possibilities for gainful employment but hardly any applicants. The HBZ in Münster, founded in 1978, counts among the largest and most diversified vocational training facilities in the country. With a capacity of about 2,000 places for vocational training and apprenticeships, the HBZ is without any doubt an important player within the MAMBA network. Furthermore, being a department of the Chamber of Crafts guarantees the HBZ easy access to the local and regional business community of the crafts sector. Moreover, the Chamber is traditionally in close contact with local and regional politicians and therefore has a strong voice in politics. Besides providing access to training possibilities, the integration of the HBZ into the MAMBA network increases the legitimacy and reputation of the network.

Finally, the Münster Jobcentre – the local branch of the public employment agency – constitutes the public partner within MAMBA. Germany has a long tradition of employment policies that aim at improving the employability of citizens by initiatives such as continuing education programmes, retraining and counselling and coaching. The Jobcentres also cover particular expenses linked to the attainment of sustainable employment, such as the costs for a driver's licence or for relocation. For many years, the prime target group of the Jobcentres has been the long-term unemployed, who very often live in difficult circumstances and need assistance in terms of counselling and personal coaching in order to find their way back into the labour market. Also, the Jobcentres administer a variety of government-funded programmes, for example, providing low-threshold working opportunities within non-profit or public organisations. However, access to these programmes is highly regulated. Therefore, the role of the Jobcentre within the MAMBA network is restricted to those migrants and refugees in possession of a working permit. Nevertheless, the Münster Jobcentre, as the key public agency in the area of labour market policy, constitutes a valuable partner of the network, which provides legitimacy and raises the reputation of MAMBA in local and regional politics. Moreover, MAMBA also works for the benefit of the Jobcentre in Münster by raising awareness of the specific situation of refugees and asylum seekers and providing better access to these target groups. For example, due to the cooperation within MAMBA, the Münster Jobcentre has access to the expertise of the GGUA, whose professionals might recommend professional interpreters and give advice with respect to particular problems. As such, MAMBA translates into a win–win situation for each member of the network.

Beside the operative partners, there is a Steering Committee in charge of strategic decisions, representation and the supervision of the network's activities. It consists of high-level representatives of the participating organisations and the network coordinator, who is a full-time professional employed by the GGUA.

Key findings: implementation and impact

Implementation – cooperation as the underlying rationale

The GGUA, JAZ, GEBA, HBZ and Münster Jobcentre work together under the umbrella of MAMBA with the aim of supporting refugees and migrants effectively and efficiently on their way to becoming integrated into the German labour market and society. Since the start of the project in 2008, the MAMBA partners have developed a division of labour that serves this purpose best. First, migrants and refugees become aware of the network through the GGUA, which acts as the first point of contact, establishes a trustful relationship and provides first-hand support, in particular, regarding the status of residence. Access of the GGUA to the target groups is easy as it is a well-established actor that is often recommended by volunteers, social workers, local authorities and, notably, the group of asylum seekers themselves. Right from this early stage, the professionals at the GGUA are careful to respect the competences of the network partners. Whereas the GGUA is responsible for further counselling adult refugees and migrants, the JAZ is the core organisation for taking care of members of the younger generation. This division of competences also mirrors the complexity of the legal environment for migrants and the various funding streams and government-supported programmes that often differ according to the respective age groups.

Each partner strives to use the most appropriate approach to best serve the needs of its clients. The key holders of earmarked programmes and courses with the aim of labour market integration are the GEBA and the HBZ. Their tasks encompass the assessment of the personal background and professional profile of the client, and determining his or her career perspectives and support needs. Due to their excellent connections to the local and regional business community, these two MAMBA partners operate as intermediaries by organising internships and low-threshold job opportunities that fit the qualifications and current needs of the migrants. Apprenticeships can be a crucial stepping stone for future paid, long-term employment as most employers strive to retain employees that they have prior work experience with. Again, the partners have agreed on a division of labour: the HBZ, as an affiliate of the Chamber of Crafts, takes care of those migrants and refugees interested in handwork; and the GEBA primarily supports those clients interested in making a living by employment in other skilled and semi-skilled professions.

Finally, the Münster Jobcentre, due to its in-depth knowledge of government-funded support and counselling programmes, provides assistance to refugees and migrants who are eligible for further support and access to specific sources of funding. Moreover, the Jobcentre supports the migrant and refugee participants enrolled in the MAMBA programme by helping them with minor problems, such as the need to cover travel expenses. In sum, the highly trained personal coaches of the Jobcentre, the HBZ and the GEBA are very engaged to help their clients to enhance their careers with the aim of becoming financially independent members of the Münster community.

Within the MAMBA network, the GGUA is in charge of the *central coordination*. The coordinator is the representative of the entire MAMBA network and responsible for public relation activities. Beside this, he is engaged in the Steering Committee of the National Thematic Network of work integration networks on the federal level and in the Steering Committee of the local MAMBA network, and acts as an interface for exchange and coordination between the levels. The coordinator is also responsible for the reporting obligations and other programme requirements. What is more, the coordinator is even involved in substantive tasks, such as staff training, which raise awareness of the legal constraints regarding labour market access, as well as the preconditions of different groups of migrants. Training is also offered to the staff of other refugee aid organisations and to their volunteers, as well as to public administrators and employers. In addition, the structural activities of the coordinator include communication with institutions and public bodies to achieve a common interpretation of legal and administrative regulations, as well as margins of discretion.

Very different priorities and ideas of the network members led to occasional disputes regarding strategies, measures and priorities early in the programme. The interviews with MAMBA workers undertaken for the Innovative Social Investment: Strengthening Communities in Europe (InnoSI) project indicate that although some differences remain, they have learned to manage the institutional diversity. The MAMBA network was able to establish mutual respect between the members through regular meetings, short communication channels and an open-door approach.

Achievements, hurdles and setbacks

The MAMBA network enjoys a very good reputation among policy experts. It is perceived as a fine example of a successful investment in a difficult policy field. Since being set up in 2008, more than 1,700 people – migrants, refugees and asylum seekers – have participated in MAMBA. Due to data protection issues as well as problems of registration, it is difficult to provide exact figures on how many participants of MAMBA have been successfully integrated into the labour market. According to the representative of MAMBA and to an official evaluation (MAMBA, 2015), approximately 34% of those having had contact with the programme in its second period of funding were either placed in a programme of qualification, such as an apprenticeship, or have even managed to sign a working contract for long-term employment. Currently, it is estimated that the success rate will increase to 40% of those who join the programme. For the year 2019, it is forecasted that MAMBA will be in touch with about 800 migrants.

It is noteworthy to keep in mind that the majority of the programmes and courses provided by the MAMBA network constitute a long-term investment in the development of human capital since the programmes are linked to training, counselling and even schooling, which are likely to provide further pay-offs in the long run. It will take some time to be able to calculate the social returns on investment. However, even a conservative estimation of the programme's results demonstrates that investing in the MAMBA network is doubtlessly worth the effort. If just 10 migrants successfully integrate into the labour market thanks to the MAMBA network, enabling them to make a living and to contribute to social insurances, the social return in terms of savings of public assistance that would otherwise have to be spent as subsistence allowances outweighs public expenses earmarked for the MAMBA network. Successful placements by MAMBA have surpassed this number by far.

In addition, the impact of MAMBA is not limited to fiscal savings. By matching open job offers with skilled refugees and migrants seeking work, the network contributes to local economic performance and thereby further increases public benefits. In doing so, MAMBA helps migrants as well as employers to overcome the bureaucratic hurdles established by German law regarding the employment of refugees and persons without a permanent residence permit (cf Dopheide, 2016). Moreover, participating refugees and migrants are empowered to become financially independent, to work in skilled jobs – including the professions they have exercised in their countries of origin – and thereby to regain some autonomy in their lives. This is particularly relevant for refugees who leave their countries of origin involuntarily, have often suffered traumatising experiences and are forced into a state of legal instability and passiveness by the asylum procedure (Frings, 2017; Krause, 2017).

In the meantime, the MAMBA network is no longer a standalone initiative. Around the country since the late 2000s, similar networks have been established that partly refer to MAMBA as an example of best practice and partly follow a slightly different approach. These networks are working together at the federal and regional levels of governance through regular cooperation meetings, in particular, the National Thematic Network (Das Nationale Thematische Netzwerk, 2015). The cooperation on the federal and state levels enhances the cooperation of all organisations involved and enables the development of common instruments, positions and strategies.

Nevertheless and despite its good reputation and obvious success, MAMBA still rests upon a rather fragile funding structure. The key player that set MAMBA in place, that is, the GGUA, is a typical hybrid non-profit organisation that combines service provision with community engagement and advocacy on behalf of the growing population of migrants in Germany. The 'spider in the web' is also the most vulnerable organisation of the MAMBA network in terms of funding because the GGUA is neither a public entity like the Münster Jobcentre, nor a social enterprise with a defined target market like the GEBA, nor an adjunct to a powerful, prestigious or semi-public organisation, as is the case with the JAZ, which is affiliated with Caritas, or the HZB, being the training centre of the Chamber of Crafts in Münster. Furthermore, the GGUA was among the very first organisations in Germany to raise their voice against a government policy that was obviously not in tune with reality. Therefore, it has been perceived as somehow leftist and progressive ever since. Against this background, funding of the MAMBA network that contributes to the overall funding scheme of the GGUA turned out to be highly dependent on the so-called political climate. In other words, the availability of and access to government support for the MAMBA network has been dependent on the left- or right-wing party affiliation of the government in power at the local, regional and federal levels of the German governance structure.

Starting from its initiation in 2008, MAMBA was funded by the federal programme *Bleiberechtsprogramm* (Programme Regarding the Right to Remain), which was part of the superordinate 'XENOS – Integration and Diversity' in the ESF grant period of 2007–13 (BMAS, 2008a). The *Bleiberechtsprogramm* was subdivided into funding phase I (2008–10) and funding phase II (2010–end of 2013), with MAMBA being awarded funding in both rounds. The fate of MAMBA was in jeopardy in 2012 when the federal government communicated its plan to cut funding and discontinue the programme. During debates in Parliament and the public sector, the majority of actors expressed their support for the continuation of the *Bleiberechtsprogramm* (cf Deutscher Bundestag, 2013). Possibly in response to this vocal criticism, the federal government initiated the follow-up programme, ESF-Integrationsrichtlinie Bund, with a guaranteed funding period from 2014 to 2020, building on the 'lessons learned' from the previous funding period (BMAS, 2014).

Conclusion: lessons learned and policy implications

MAMBA demonstrates the different strengths of the partner organisations and how these can be combined in a network to build on their respective resources and create synergies. The particular situation of migrants – and refugees in particular – creates a gap in the coverage of traditional employment policies. This is not only due to language barriers, but also because of a lack of information on the side of public employees, employers and the refugees themselves, as well as the precarious living conditions of persons without a permanent residence permit. MAMBA helps to bridge these gaps. In particular, non-profit organisations can provide access to the target groups, public actors can provide legitimacy and funding, and actors linked to the business world can provide contacts to potential employers and thereby reduce reservations on their side regarding the employment of persons with an insecure residence status or foreign qualifications. Close collaboration between the network partners, together with in-depth case management for each participant, enhances the tailoring of the programme's offers to the needs and resources of each individual, and reduces the risk of dropouts. In addition to working intensively with individuals to improve their job prospects, MAMBA attempts to address structural barriers to labour market integration by raising awareness with employers and providing training for Jobcentre staff.

MAMBA stands out as a success story mainly as a result of intensive, time-consuming personal assistance achieved through the fruitful cooperation of organisations with very different priorities. It aligns well with the Social Investment approach to labour market activation, although the main goal of the lead organisation is more about social justice. Most refugees and migrants who participate strive to become active members of local society and to make an independent living by participating in the local labour market. Many have qualifications that are sorely needed in the German labour market. The fictional case of Leyla (see Box 7.1) illustrates the contribution of the MAMBA network.

Box 7.1: Achieving new language skills and financial independence

Leyla is a 37-year-old nurse who participated in MAMBA. When she reached Münster after fleeing from Damascus, she lacked the language skills and knowledge to immediately gain paid employment in a hospital, although nurses are desperately needed in Germany (cf Biermann, 2017). She made contact with the GGUA, which supported her in becoming an official participant in the MAMBA programme. Subsequently, she received counselling on legal issues from GGUA staff and took a course on work-related German-language skills. Her case manager at the GEBA arranged an internship at a local hospital for her to prove her qualifications and language skills. After six months, Leyla was offered half-time employment as an assistant nurse. When she was granted a residence permit, she was entitled to take up offers from the Jobcentre, to gain official recognition of her qualifications obtained in Syria and to access further vocational training. Four years after her arrival in Germany, Leyla received her certificate as a qualified nurse for paediatrics. She continues to work at the clinic in a skilled position and has achieved financial independence.

Note: Leyla's story is fictional but realistic, being based on in-depth interviews with partners and participants of the MAMBA network.

At the same time, MAMBA shows how insecure funding – resulting from, among other things, the development of political majorities – can threaten the success of a highly successful intervention. Public funding is usually granted on a project basis, that is, for a limited period of time and often at short notice. One of the strengths of MAMBA is its collaboration with well-established actors and the contacts and trust that have been generated by repeated interaction throughout the different phases of the programme. They have helped to bridge the different organisational 'cultures' and views on the topic that existed prior to the programme, although this was not easy and required time and effort to be devoted to communication and coordination between the network members. Endangering these achievements through the discontinuation of the programme would create costs for the public purse, as well as hamper the overall goals of refugee integration and a thriving local and regional economy.

Note
[1] MAMBA stands for **M**ünsters **A**ktionsprogramm für **M**igrantInnen & **B**leiberechtigte zur **A**rbeitsmarkintegration in Münster & im Münsterland.

References

BEPA (Bureau of European Policy Advisers) (2010) *Empowering people, driving change: Social innovation in the European Union*, Luxembourg: Publications Office of the European Union.

Bertelsmann Stiftung (2015) *Die Arbeitsintegration von Flüchtlingen in Deutschland. Humanität, Effektivität, Selbstbestimmung*, Gütersloh: Bertelsmann Stiftung.

Biermann, K. (2017) 'Krank gespart', *Die Zeit*, 28 November. Available at: http://www.zeit.de/arbeit/2017-11/pflege-krankenhaus-pflegekraefte-mangel

BMAS (Bundesministerium für Arbeit und Soziales) (2008a) *Programmbeschreibung 'XENOS – Integration und Vielfalt'*, Bonn: BMAS.

BMAS (2008b) *Bekanntmachung der Förderrichtlinie 'ESF-Bundesprogramm zur arbeitsmarktlichen Unterstützung für Bleibeberechtigte und Flüchtlinge mit Zugang zum Arbeitsmarkt'*, Bonn: BMAS.

BMAS (2014) *Funding Guidelines – ESF Integration Guidelines of the Federal Government*, Berlin.

Boeßenecker, K. and Vilain, M. (2013) *Spitzenverbände der Freien Wohlfahrtspflege*, Weinheim: Juventus.

Borosch, N. and Klein, A. (2017) 'MAMBA – labour market integration for refugees and asylum seekers in the city of Muenster (NRW)', InnoSI WP4 Case studies, D4.2, Evaluation report on each case study. Available at: https://www.uni-muenster.de/imperia/md/content/ifpol/innosi/germany_mamba.pdf

Das Nationale Thematische Netzwerk (Das Nationale Thematische Netzwerk im ESF-Bundesprogramm zur arbeitsmarktlichen Unterstützung für Bleibeberechtigte und Flüchtlinge mit Zugang zum Arbeitsmarkt) (2015) *Flüchtlinge in Arbeit und Ausbildung. Potenziale für Wirtschaft und Gesellschaft*, Berlin: Das Nationale Thematische Netzwerk.

Deutscher Bundestag (2013) *Kleine Anfrage der Abgeordneten Ulla Jelpke, Heidrun Dittrich, Petra Pau, Frank Tempel, Jörn Wunderlich und der Fraktion DIE LINKE. Integrationsperspektiven von geduldeten und bleibeberechtigten Flüchtlingen*, Drucksache 17/13608, Berlin: Deutscher Bundestag.

Dopheide, D. (2016) 'Integration durch Ausbildung und Arbeit', *Wirtschaftsspiegel*, 4: 12–15.

Frings, D. (2017) 'Flüchtlinge als Rechtssubjekte oder als Objekte gesonderter Rechte', in C. Ghaderi and T. Eppenstein (eds) *Flüchtlinge*, Wiesbaden: Springer Fachmedien, pp 95–111.

Geissler, R. (2014) 'Migration und Integration' in *Sozialer Wandel in Deutschland*, Berlin: Bundeszentrale für politische Bildung, pp 40–53.

Hoesch, K. (2017) *Migration und Integration*, Wiesbaden: Springer Fachmedien.

Krause, U. (2017) 'Die Flüchtling – der Flüchtling als Frau. Genderreflexiver Zugang', in C. Ghaderi and T. Eppenstein (eds) *Flüchtlinge*, Wiesbaden: Springer Fachmedien Wiesbaden, pp 79–93.

MAMBA (Münsters Aktionsprogramm für MigrantInnen & Bleibeberechtigte zur Arbeitsmarktintegration in Münster & im Münsterland) (2015) 'Antrag auf Fördermittel aus dem Europäischen Sozialfonds und auf Fördermittel des BMAS. ESF-Integrationsrichtlinie Bund mit dem Handlungsschwerpunkt Integration von Asylbewerber/-innen und Flüchtlingen (IvAF)'.

EIGHT

Labour market activation and empowerment of the homeless in Poland

Aldona Wiktorska-Święcka and Dorota Moroń

Introduction

The subject of this chapter is 'Assistance from A to Z: Professional Activation of Homeless People from Wroclaw Circle St. Brother Albert Aid Socicty', hereafter referred to as 'Assistance from A to Z'. It applies to a specific group of people at risk of exclusion – the homeless – and is an investment in their activation for the labour market and social empowerment. 'Assistance from A to Z' was implemented between 2012 and 2015 in Wroclaw by the non-profit organisation Koło Wrocławskie Towarzystwa Pomocy im. św. Brata Alberta (Wroclaw Circle St. Brother Albert Aid Society). It involved interventions to promote the social and labour market integration of homeless people who were out of work and at risk of social exclusion, in three annual cohorts. 'Assistance from A to Z' was implemented under the Operational Programme Human Capital and was financed by the European Social Fund (ESF). It received funding of PLN3,230,097 (amounting to €773,695 at the average euro rate used in public procurement in 2016).

'Assistance from A to Z' is an example of investment in homeless people who, thanks to intensive actions for social inclusion, overcame their difficult life situation, returned to the labour market and even became self-reliant. The innovative solutions contributed to the project's success. The key innovative element of 'Assistance from A to Z' was the use of 'accompaniment', a method of working with homeless people based on the support of an 'accompanist', who is an individual adviser, mentor and assistant providing comprehensive help in solving the problems of the project participant. In the Polish context, another innovative aspect was the joint implementation of a wide range of support, especially the combination of social and professional support with psychological, motivational and legal assistance.

'Assistance from A to Z': innovative homeless support

'Assistance from A to Z' concerns the area of social inclusion, which is important in Polish social policy. Active inclusion focuses on the fight against unemployment and for labour market inclusion (through social and vocational activation). It also refers to the fight against poverty (especially among children), support for families, the development of activities for young people (including training and support for entering the labour market), safety and the activation of seniors and people with disabilities. An important, though underestimated, policy area is housing and homelessness. This area is marginalised for two reasons. First, homelessness is not perceived by the public as a key social problem. A national survey of homeless people conducted in 2015 found 36,100 homeless people in Poland, of whom approximately 25,600 were in institutions for the homeless, and approximately 10,500 were outside the institutions (MPiPS, 2015: 9). The homeless are therefore only 0.09% of the population. Poverty and unemployment are much more prevalent and hence are seen as more important problems. At the same time, the unemployment rate was 9.7%, and the percentage of people below the official poverty line was 12.2% (GUS, 2015: 6; 2017). The second reason is the significant cost of housing policy and the lack of funds. Since the early 1990s in Poland, there has been no professional housing policy, especially in support of social housing. Limited financial resources and the lack of available public housing (including social and protected) at the disposal of municipalities do not allow for housing support to help people in need.

Policy towards people in difficult life situations (eg homelessness and unemployment) focuses on support through the social assistance system. The main role is played by social assistance centres operating in each municipality. In the case of unemployed people, these actions are complemented by the activities of labour market institutions. The main objective of these institutions is social inclusion, the empowerment of individuals and families, overcoming difficult life situations, and the preservation of human dignity. Social assistance centres focus mainly on assistance and shielding activities. They offer financial assistance in the form of grants (ensuring a minimum income) and material help in the form of accommodation, meals or clothes.

The implementation of material support is often outsourced to non-governmental organisations (NGOs), which in the case for homeless support in Wrocław, where it is realised by the Wroclaw Circle St. Brother Albert Aid Society. In the case of the homeless, social assistance centres offer activation support under individual programmes. The homeless can take advantage of addiction treatment, obtaining employment, legal and psychological consultation, and solving family and housing problems, but NGOs believe that they do not bring satisfactory results. Moreover, there is no information about their effectiveness published by the public sector. The weakness of these programmes mainly concerns the insufficient scope of support and the lack of adaptation to the real needs of the homeless. It should be emphasised that this is the only form of multifaceted activation for homeless people implemented by public institutions. Hence, there is a need to undertake various activities and search for innovative ways of supporting homeless people that will lead to social inclusion.

Support addressed to homeless people is supplemented by the activities of NGOs, the largest of which is the St. Brother Albert Aid Society. NGOs help the homeless through the establishment and operation of shelters, night shelters and houses for homeless people. They also provide other assistance such as charity kitchens and baths, and they issue food, clothing, cleaning products and medicines. In addition, they offer social work, legal and psychological assistance, and religious services. Most often, in the implementation of these activities, they cooperate with local governments. The Wroclaw Circle is part of the St. Brother Albert Aid Society, which has been operating since 1981 and was the first Polish NGO to provide help to the homeless. At the end of 2015, the Wroclaw Circle had 131 members, including 119 ordinary members and 12 supporter members. The organisation employed 84 people (Wroclaw Circle St. Brother Albert Aid Society, 2016a). It helps almost 3,000 people every year (Wroclaw Circle St. Brother Albert Aid Society, 2016a) and also implements many projects of support and activation for the homeless (Wroclaw Circle St. Brother Albert Aid Society, 2016b). The 'Assistance from A to Z' project is one such project distinguished by its innovative character.

'Assistance from A to Z' was designed to take into account the identified needs of homeless people, as follows:

• Personal needs: psychological support, support in solving health problems and obtaining a disability certificate, and support with the renewal of contacts with the family.

- Economic needs: supplementing the skills needed for functioning on the labour market (preparation of application documents, interviews with employers, etc), supplementing vocational qualifications and experience, support in looking for a job, support in remaining in employment through motivational support and assistance in contacts with employers, and economic and living needs associated with satisfying the basic life needs, including food, tickets for public transport and accommodation in a night shelter, shelter or housing for homeless persons.
- Legal needs: support in solving legal problems related to debt, especially alimony.
- Socio-vocational needs: social activation and motivational support in the whole process of social and professional activation.

Needs assessments emphasised the coexistence of various problems of the homeless. It was pointed out that homelessness is most often the result of the coexistence of many social problems, including addiction, unemployment, housing problems, family conflicts and so on. Homelessness is also the cause of other problems (psychological, health, etc), which makes it difficult to take up employment and causes exclusion from social life.

The main aim of the 'Assistance from A to Z' project was improving the acquisition of social and work-related skills and competences by the homeless. Objectives included a reduction or limitation of the negative social impact of homelessness, the acquisition of competences enabling homeless people to navigate the labour market, the acquisition or improvement of vocational skills, and the acquisition of vocational experience. Adopted goals were in line with the main assumptions of the Operational Programme Human Capital, under which the project was implemented. An important diagnosed need that could not be directly met in the framework of the 'Assistance from A to Z' project was the need for housing support towards housing independence and leaving the institutions for the homeless. However, the Wroclaw Circle St. Brother Albert Aid Society also helped the homeless to achieve this goal – as far as possible.

The insight into the particular field of public intervention that was the social and vocational activation of homeless people was part of the new Theory of Change developed within the case study. The defined long-term outcome was the following: 'Homeless people who are under the care of Wroclaw Circle St. Brother Albert Aid Society become independent. They have a permanent job that allows them to move out of shelters/hostels, as well as being able to cope with social and vocational challenges'. This long-term outcome assumed positive changes for both beneficiaries and the local community, as well as for the public sector. Based on several preconditions, intermediate outcomes within the Theory of Change were also formulated:

• Homeless people know how to get help and to deal with everyday problems: they know who the accompanist is; they know what kind of support they need; they know who can offer support, where and when; and they participate in meetings with a therapist and psychologist. If necessary, they make use of the services of a lawyer.
• Homeless people cope with challenges in the labour market. They actively look for work, improve their skills and monitor conditions on the local labour market.
• Homeless people cope with independent living in supported conditions; they are aware of their obligations and rights and they know where, if necessary, they can get support.

Expected outcomes, both those that should ultimately be achieved within the 'Assistance from A to Z' project and those indirect ones, resulted from certain assumptions. Those generally referred to the occurrence of complex interdependent psychological, social, legal and institutional problems, which relate to the functioning of a homeless person in society.

Based on this, designing the project intervention incorporated various actions and activities. Beneficiaries of the project could benefit from, among other things, classes encouraging social competences and activation (eg sports, arts), information technology (IT) training, work training, vocational training, meetings with entrepreneurs, and vocational internships. The project provided psychological support, support in solving legal problems and accompanist support.

The key innovative element of the 'Assistance from A to Z' project was the use of the 'accompaniment' method. This is a form of working with people who are in crisis and are threatened by many social problems. Its essence is an individual approach to the beneficiaries' situation and the complex nature of the aid, aimed at supporting the development of the beneficiary. This is a 'customer-focused' help strategy where support and advice are tailored to the client's needs. 'Accompaniment' is an emotional aid aimed at reducing stress and activating individual strategies for coping with stress. It is also valuable help by giving the person a sense of acceptance and security, restoring faith in their own abilities, and providing assistance on partnership terms. The accompaniment method is focused on the individual needs and expectations of the beneficiary (Kot, 2008). An 'accompanist' is an individual assistant for the homeless person who adapts to their individual needs, supporting and motivating them to action.

Since the accompanist is key to good project implementation, an important aspect is the selection of candidates for this position. There are no predetermined requirements regarding the education or qualifications of the accompanist. Due to the scope of tasks, the Wroclaw Circle St. Brother Albert Aid Society expected that the candidates would have a university degree, preferably with a social profile. It was also necessary to know about issues related to social work, psychology, law, solving social problems and contacts with public and private institutions, as well as having excellent computer skills. Extremely important was the ability to work with people in difficult situations. The Wroclaw Circle St. Brother Albert Aid Society sought candidates for accompanists from mainly among its employees, members and volunteers. People who became accompanists met the requirements, and the work as an accompanist was an additional gainful job for them. Most of the accompanists worked for the Wroclaw Circle St. Brother Albert Aid Society as employees of the night shelter or shelter. It was advantageous because they had extensive experience in working with homeless people. Additionally, they had opportunities for more frequent contacts with the participants of the project due to meeting them in their main job as well. The accompanists received a salary for work in the project. However, the majority of them reported spending much more time on working with the homeless than planned in the project. Thus, they did part of their work as volunteers.

This solution was invented and implemented in France by Caritas France as a support for the activation of the unemployed (Vigneau-Cazalaa, 2008a, 2008b). It has been adapted to Polish conditions for working with the unemployed and the homeless by Caritas Poland and St. Brother Albert Aid Society (Kot, 2008; Słowik, 2008; Wilczek, 2008; Wiktorska-Święcka, 2015; Wiktorska-Święcka et al, 2015; Czochara, 2012/13). So far, several projects have been implemented in Poland using this method, each time adapting it to the needs of the beneficiaries (Wiktorska-Święcka, 2015; Wiktorska-Święcka et al, 2015). In each of these cases, it brought very good results and was a key factor for the success of the project. In the context of Poland, the use of such a wide range of support was innovative, especially combining social and vocational support with psychological, motivational and legal assistance. Public institutions usually limit the support (due to limited financial resources allocated to social assistance), which prevents the active inclusion of homeless people who require a comprehensive approach. The flexibility of the forms of support offered was also extremely important.

Key findings: implementation and impact

The scope of the 'Assistance from A to Z' project was the dissemination of the idea of social integration. It was implemented in the field of social inclusion and one of its assumptions was to strengthen the social economy sector. It took into account the issues of the economic and social activation of people at risk of social exclusion. The target group were socially excluded people, that is, homeless people aged 50–64. Additionally, among 136 project participants, 54 (eight females and 46 males) were people with disabilities who received benefits because of it. The participants were also, in varying degrees, lonely and unable to make social contacts, to function in society or to cope with the labour market. Many had not maintained contact with family members or were in other ways socially excluded, sometimes suffering from symptoms of disease and addiction, or subject to legal sanctions (primarily maintenance obligations).

'Assistance from A to Z' was a local project but it was related to the national and European Union (EU) active inclusion policy. The project was implemented under the regional component of 'Priority VII: Promotion of Social Integration' of the Operational Programme Human Capital (which was financed at 85% by EU funds through the ESF and at 15% by the national budget). The financial expenditures for the project amounted of PLN3,230,097 (€773,695). The Wroclaw Circle St. Brother Albert Aid Society did not contribute financially to the project; however, its employees and members were responsible for the preparation of the project and then for its implementation. There was no formal cooperation with the public sector. Although public institutions, such as the Municipal Social Assistance Centre in Wroclaw and District Labour Office in Wroclaw, performed tasks of social and professional activation of the homeless, including with beneficiaries of the Wroclaw Circle St. Brother Albert Aid Society, they did not participate in this project, although they supported its implementation unofficially.

The Wroclaw Circle St. Brother Albert Aid Society, as an NGO, carried out the project entirely alone. However, the social assistance centre informally supported the Wroclaw Circle during the recruitment of beneficiaries. On a small scale, the project was also supported by employers representing the public and private sector. They offered directional advice and internships for beneficiaries. The involvement of employers in the project helped to find internships and even employment for homeless people. Importantly, it also changed the attitudes of employed people to the homeless. Very often, homeless people were stereotypically seen as people who live on the streets, are dirty, are addicted, have no education, do not want to work, steal and are dangerous. Including homeless people in workplaces allowed for a change in the attitude of the rest of the staff. The homeless have established new contacts, acquaintances and even friendships. This additional value of the project should be recognised.

'Assistance from A to Z' has been effective for the beneficiaries of the project. Indirect (unintended but desirable) effects for external stakeholders have also been seen to some extent. There were no unplanned negative effects. The Wroclaw Circle St. Brother Albert Aid Society treated the funding application as a kind of 'road map' and scrupulously complied with its provisions. Interviewed front-line workers and managers appreciated the changed (improved) situation of the beneficiaries in social activation, as well as on the vocational dimension.

Referring to Dane and Schneider (1998), it is possible to identify the following aspects of the fidelity of the intervention within the 'Assistance from A to Z' project:

- Adherence (project components are delivered as prescribed): based on available resources and context, the project identified a set of activities addressed to beneficiaries, focusing on both individual and team competences, as well as their social and labour market integration.
- Exposure (amount of project content received by participants): participants had access to a wide range of activities, including individual psychological coaching, group activities, therapeutic treatments and vocational training, in addition to the support offered by an accompanist.
- Quality of the delivery (theory-based ideal in terms of processes and content): accomplishing coherent action and delivering the amount of products and services that were intended.
- Participant responsiveness (engagement of the participants): due to the completion of activities as intended, beneficiaries benefited from the intervention in various ways (eg by new knowledge and skills, new competences, and new experiences).
- Project differentiation (unique features of the intervention are distinguishable from other programmes/projects): what distinguishes the 'Assistance from A to Z' project is the method of activation

used, the so-called accompaniment method. This has not been widely disseminated in Poland yet, but it is expected to support changes in organisations, communities and systems.

The quality of the intervention (the amount, frequency and duration with which the treatment is given to produce changes in outcomes) within the project 'Assistance from A to Z' had multiple dimensions. It was generally developed to improve beneficiaries' outcomes by changing their behaviour (measured by being on time, to appear well-clothed, etc). The implication was that the 'dose' had to be considered at two distinct levels. These were the individual(s) who learned new skills and other stakeholders (families, community members, social workers, local institutions, local entrepreneurs). One of the components of quality referred to the implementation of activities necessary for the intervention to be carried out with fidelity. This included the amount of training that participants receive in preparation for them to deliver the intervention, or the amount of time that accompanists spent working with beneficiaries on an intervention. Another equally important component, 'intervention dosage', referred to the amount of an intervention that was provided to beneficiaries or others (eg family members and social care providers) in order to change their behaviour. That is why questions about how much of an intervention was necessary to achieve positive outcomes were relevant for practitioners, researchers and policymakers. 'Dosage' affects not only outcomes, but also many other features of social integration projects, such as cost, staffing, replication and scale-up.

The project intervention impacted on other stakeholder groups, as indicated earlier. Indirect audiences of the project were the municipality of Wroclaw, other public entities (Lower Silesia Region) and local entrepreneurs. In this way, the reach of the intervention cannot be measured in numbers, but is indicated from what stakeholders reported.

An important issue in the case of social interventions is their effectiveness, including cost-effectiveness. Investment should bring benefits in the future. The economic analysis of the project was carried out using Social Return on Investment (SROI) analysis. Selecting the SROI analysis is connected with the fact that it combines the advantages of cost–benefit analysis with a social audit. What makes it unique is the monetary presentation of all relevant investments and the effects of the activity, converting social impacts into monetary terms. SROI analysis focuses on impacts, including long-term impact, which in the case of the target group of the 'Assistance from A to Z' project, is of great importance. Of particular significance is the fact that SROI takes into account the perspective of the stakeholders, which promotes objectivity (SROI Network, 2012). Conducting an economic evaluation of the 'Assistance from A to Z' project using the SROI method allowed the identification of the estimated cost of the project, the inputs, activities, outputs and impact.

Analyses indicate that 'Assistance from A to Z' brought economic benefits exceeding the expenditure for the project, which makes the activation of the homeless economically viable. Applying a standard SROI methodology estimated a 1.2 positive ratio, which helps to legitimate the expenditure on the implementation of the project. The SROI ratio of 1.2 means that for every PLN1.00 invested in the 'Assistance from A to Z' project, we obtain PLN1.20 in return. So, for every PLN1.00 invested, we get PLN0.20 of benefit in five years.

The main economic benefits of the project were achieved for its homeless participants. However, the public sector (the state and the municipality of Wroclaw) also achieved some economic benefits from the project associated with smaller expenses for homeless assistance, as well as higher tax revenues and insurance contributions from those who gained employment. This indicates that it was a successful use of ESF money. It was a 'Social Investment' in the sense of the Social Investment Package (SIP) because people who suffered from poor life chances were supported to access the labour market.

Learning points and policy implications

The project evaluation showed the effectiveness and economic efficiency of the new tools applied to supporting homeless people. The evaluation demonstrated that the main factors of the project's success were:

- reliable diagnosis of the needs of homeless people;
- adapting support to the diagnosed needs;
- application of the wide range of support, combining social and vocational support with psychological, motivational and legal assistance;
- using the accompaniment method as a key way of supporting and motivating homeless people; and
- involvement of the employees in the project, with additional support from members and employees of Wroclaw Circle St. Brother Albert Aid Society.

The project's success is an exemplar of how activities carried out by an NGO, with financial support from the public sector, can bring good results. The example of the Wroclaw Circle St. Brother Albert Aid Society is consistent with claims that NGOs are closer to people (than public services) and have more knowledge about their problems and needs. Additionally, they have workers composed of dedicated employees, members and volunteers. As an NGO, the Wroclaw Circle operates in a less standard manner than public institutions, looking for better and more effective ways of achieving goals. It reaches for innovative solutions and tests them. This case study contributes to a wider set of research results which indicate that Polish NGOs – independently and in cooperation with the public sector – implement social projects effectively and efficiently (Rymsza, 2004; Moroń, 2012; Iwankiewicz-Rak, 2014; Oliński 2015; Szymańska et al, 2016).

Both the representatives of the Wroclaw Circle St. Brother Albert Aid Society and indirect stakeholders appreciated the activities carried out. They positively assessed their sequence (from social activation, to support to acquire individual skills, to internship opportunities), content (the accompaniment method) and the scope (the amount of the support). Similarly, they assessed acquired work-related skills. Also, desirable changes in social behaviour were observed (eg punctuality, taking care of appearance, new hobbies of beneficiaries).

A key facilitator in the implementation of the project was the motivation of beneficiaries. This was maintained by incentives both of a material kind (eg free public transportation) and of a less tangible nature. The latter included the opportunity to meet representatives of other social groups, training that was located in various parts of Wroclaw, the opportunity to spend time in an interesting way and awareness that they could learn something and improve their image (eg make-up classes were offered during the project). The 'Assistance from A to Z' project also showed that the innovative accompaniment method is a very efficient solution for supporting homeless people and has the potential to be adopted as a tool for working with homeless people both in public institutions and NGOs.

The project showed that in the case of homeless people, it is very important to provide comprehensive support to solving the various problems that they have, and that activation for work alone is not enough for homeless people to take up a job. Experiences from the implementation of the project also show a great need for housing support, in particular, the need to provide homeless people with the opportunity to obtain flats with a low rent from communal municipal resources (see Box 8.1).

Box 8.1: 'Assistance from A to Z' from the perspective of end users

All homeless participants perceived considerable benefits associated with the completion of the project. Among these, they mentioned enriching experiences, motivation to change the situation, the ability to look for work, and legal advice, which was helpful in regulating life situations (eg maintenance obligations). Benefits could also include: "find a job, new knowledge, advice from professionals" (Beneficiary 1), "a job every day, no boredom, the opportunity to meet new people, material benefits" (Beneficiary 2) and new competences and skills, for example, from a training course as a warehouse forklift driver (Beneficiary 1). They also stressed intangible benefits, especially social ones: "People looked at me differently" and "meeting new people" (Beneficiary 1); and "being among the people" (Beneficiary 2).

To remain in the project, beneficiaries were usually motivated with a paid 'scholarship' – "I could buy medicine, I had the money for my own needs" (Beneficiary 2) – and the vision of finding a job. There were individuals who "did not need any motivation" and one person whose motivation gradually increased with subsequent project activities from initial scepticism: "sports and artistic activity were completely pointless, I wanted to give up" (Beneficiary 1). There was evidence of increasing awareness of others – "I did not want to disappoint the manager" (Beneficiary 2) – as well as of internal motivation – "I realised that this is important to me" (Beneficiary 3).

When asked about the role of the accompanist, beneficiaries generally positively evaluated the support given to them by persons performing this role. They followed the recommendations of the accompanist and reported that during the meetings with the accompanist, in their opinion, there was an atmosphere that was conducive to good communication and cooperation. In assessing the issues discussed during the meetings with the accompanist, opinions were divided. Some of the beneficiaries thought that the most useful were related to "focus on contact with the family" (Beneficiary 3), while others thought "employment". At the same time, there were opinions that "any" (Beneficiary 1) or "all" (Beneficiary 3) issues had to be considered as useful. Regardless of this, they were of the view that participation in meetings with the accompanist increased the chance of finding a job.

'Assistance from A to Z' has demonstrated the great importance of the human factor for the success of the implementation of activities. The employees involved, especially accompanists, are an extremely important element of the activities. This speaks for the implementation of this type of project by NGOs or other social-economy entities.

The project showed that although the state is considered to be the main 'social investor', other sectors play a significant role in this respect. In 'Assistance from A to Z' the role of the public sector was to invest, both through the implementation of activities and through support for the social-economy sector and private entities. In Polish conditions, NGOs' resources are usually not sufficient for the independent implementation of activities, hence the need to obtain them from the public sector. However, NGOs can be effective performers of activities consistent with the Social Investment welfare paradigm.

There is a need to include the private and informal sectors (families, citizens) in the implementation of social interventions. In Polish conditions, multi-sectoral cooperation (public, non-governmental and private sectors at the same time) and more complex cooperation, for example, the co-production of services, is underdeveloped. Yet, its usage – as the project's experience shows – can be an important factor for the effectiveness of actions.

It is also important to show the effectiveness and economic efficiency of the investments carried out. In Polish social policy, such activities are generally not carried out. For the implementation of investments, it is necessary to support both politicians and voters. In public opinion, activities in the field of social policy are perceived as a cost rather than an investment, hence the need to promote an investment approach and to demonstrate the effectiveness of such actions.

In the implementation, 'Assistance from A to Z' social innovations significantly contributed to effectiveness. In particular, the accompaniment method has been verified and should be further disseminated. There is potential for it to be included in the activities implemented by other aid institutions.

References

Czochara, M. (2012/13) 'Praca socjalna z osobami bezdomnymi w Polsce – rozwiązania modelowe stosowane w organizacjach trzeciego sektora', *Trzeci Sektor*, Special Issue, pp 32–42.

Dane, A.V. and Schneider, B.H. (1998) 'Program integrity in primary and early secondary prevention: are implementation effects out of control?', *Clinical Psychology Review*, 18: 23–45.

GUS (Główny Urząd Statystyczny) (2015) *Zasięg ubóstwa ekonomicznego w Polsce w 2015 r.*, Warszawa: Główny Urząd Statystyczny.

GUS (2017) *Bank Danych Lokalnych GUS*, Warszawa: Główny Urząd Statystyczny. Available at: https://bdl.stat.gov.pl/

Iwankiewicz-Rak, B. (2014) 'Organizacje pozarządowe w Polsce – działalność usługowa na rzecz społeczeństwa', *Prace Naukowe Uniwersytetu Ekonomicznego we Wrocławiu*, 355: 23–33.

Kot, J. (2008) 'Kompleksowy system wsparcia na podłożu metody towarzyszenia', in A. Wiktorska-Święcka (ed) *Wyprowadzić na prostą. Innowacyjne metody aktywizacji społecznej i zawodowej na przykładzie wdrażania modelu lokalnej sieci wsparcia osób bezdomnych i zagrożonych bezdomnością*, Wrocław: Oficyna Wydawnicza ATUT, pp 149–67.

Moroń, D. (2012) *Organizacje pozarządowe – fundament społeczeństwa obywatelskiego*, Wrocław: Wydawnictwo Uniwersytetu Wrocławskiego.

MPiPS (Ministerstwo Pracy i Polityki Społecznej) (2015) *Sprawozdanie z realizacji działań na rzecz ludzi bezdomnych w województwach w roku 2014 oraz wyniki Ogólnopolskiego badania liczby osób bezdomnych (21/22 styczeń 2015)*, Warszawa: Ministerstwo Pracy i Polityki Społecznej.

Oliński, M. (2015) 'Efektywność społeczna kontraktowanych zadań publicznych', *Optimum: studia ekonomiczne*, 4(76): 135–52.

Rymsza, M. (ed) (2004) *Współpraca sektora obywatelskiego z administracją publiczną*, Warszawa: Fundacja Instytut Spraw Publicznych.

Słowik, S. (2008) 'Rozwój metody towarzyszenia w Polsce', in A. Wiktorska-Święcka (ed) *Wyprowadzić na prostą. Innowacyjne metody aktywizacji społecznej i zawodowej na przykładzie wdrażania modelu lokalnej sieci wsparcia osób bezdomnych i zagrożonych bezdomnością*, Wrocław: Oficyna Wydawnicza ATUT, pp 141–4.

SROI Network (2012) 'A guide to social return on investment'. Available at: www.thesroinetwork.org

Szymańska, U., Majer, P. and Falej, M. (2016) *Organizacje pozarządowe a samorząd – 25 lat doświadczeń*, Olsztyn: Wydział Prawa i Administracji Uniwersytetu Warmińsko-Mazurskiego.

Vigneau-Cazalaa, M. (2008a) 'Wprowadzenie do metody towarzyszenia: źródła metody towarzyszenia wielowymiarowego i zindywidualizowanego we Francji', in A. Wiktorska-Święcka (ed) *Wyprowadzić na prostą. Innowacyjne metody aktywizacji społecznej i zawodowej na przykładzie wdrażania modelu lokalnej sieci wsparcia osób bezdomnych i zagrożonych bezdomnością*, Wrocław: Oficyna Wydawnicza ATUT, pp 133–40.

Vigneau-Cazalaa, M. (2008b) 'Praktyczne aspekty wdrażania metody towarzyszenia we Francji', in A. Wiktorska-Święcka (ed) *Wyprowadzić na prostą. Innowacyjne metody aktywizacji społecznej i zawodowej na przykładzie wdrażania modelu lokalnej sieci wsparcia osób bezdomnych i zagrożonych bezdomnością*, Wrocław: Oficyna Wydawnicza ATUT, pp 209–26.

Wiktorska-Święcka, A. (2015) *Od towarzyszenia do włączenia. Praktyczne aspekty wdrażania innowacji społecznych na przykładzie metody towarzyszenia*, Kielce: Caritas Diecezji Kieleckiej.

Wiktorska-Święcka, A., Moroń, D. and Klimowicz, M. (2015) *Zarządzanie innowacjami społecznymi. Trendy, perspektywy, wyzwania*, Warszawa: Difin.

Wilczek, J. (2008) 'Model lokalnej sieci wsparcia osób bezdomnych i zagrożonych bezdomnością wdrażany w ramach projektu IW EQUAL "Wyprowadzić na prostą"', in A. Wiktorska-Święcka (ed) *Wyprowadzić na prostą. Innowacyjne metody aktywizacji społecznej i zawodowej na przykładzie wdrażania modelu lokalnej sieci wsparcia osób bezdomnych i zagrożonych bezdomnością*, Wrocław: Oficyna Wydawnicza ATUT, pp 145–8.

Wroclaw Circle St. Brother Albert Aid Society (2016a) *Sprawozdanie merytoryczne i finansowe za rok 2015 z działalności Wrocławskiego Koła Towarzystwa Pomocy im. św*, Wrocław: Brata Alberta, Towarzystwo Pomocy im. Św. Brata Alberta Koło Wrocławskie.

Wroclaw Circle St. Brother Albert Aid Society (2016b) 'Placówki'. Available at: http://www.bratalbert.wroc.pl/index.php?option=com_content&view=section&layout=blog&id=8&Itemid=57&lang=pl

Part C: Social solidarity and Social Investment

Flórián Sipos

The third and last section of the book is dedicated to the question of how social solidarities are present in programmes based on Social Investment and innovation. Social solidarity is undoubtedly a key notion in all forms of social policies since the welfare state itself can be regarded as an institutionalised form of solidarity to cope with the risks of an industrialised society (Van der Veen, 2012), albeit that not all forms of social policy promote solidarity. Horizontal solidarity within local societies also deserves special attention since globalisation processes and the transformation of the welfare state also mean challenges to local communities.

According to Durkheim (1984), solidarity is an inherent obligation of people, a part of the collective consciousness, the social bond that connects individuals with each other in mutual responsibility – as opposed to the maximisation of personal gain described by liberal economists of the age to describe contractual relationships. Durkheim did not regard solidarity as an unchanged reality; he described a transformation of solidarities from that of traditional societies (mechanic solidarity between similar individuals sharing the same norms) to that of modern societies (organic solidarity between individuals with different but complementing positions in society).

Solidarity is not the same as charity, or, at least, is not necessarily the same. Some scholars even contrast the two notions by stressing that solidarity is (or should be) a horizontal relation existing between equals that does not humiliate those who receive transfers in a certain situation and is (or should be) based on rights, participation and access (Filcak and Skobla, 2012). Lack of solidarity decreases cohesion and the sense of trust and reciprocity, and gives way to segregation and a hierarchical or 'us and them' way of thinking. Solidarity protects society from disintegration and anomie, and is regarded as an effective way of improving the social environment and the real quality of life (Filcak and Skobla, 2012).

Fenger and Van Paridon (2012) used two dimensions to distinguish between types of solidarities: motive (morality and reciprocity) and level (individual and institutional). Individual solidarity is based on the decision of a single person, while institutional solidarity refers to forms that are organised according to formal or informal rules. In the case of moral motivation, individuals (or groups) might contribute to the common good because of personal conviction or moral obligation – without expecting reward for this, just as in the case of charity. Others might perform acts of solidarity in order to improve their own situation – expecting that they will get something back immediately or in the future (reciprocal motivation). A typical example of this latter reciprocal solidarity is the modern welfare state.

Table C.1: Examples of four types of solidarity

Level	Motive	
	Morality	Reciprocity
Individual	Charity	Neighbourhood watch
Institutional	Development aid	Welfare state

Source: Fenger and Van Paridon (2012)

At present, another transformation is being observed by various scholars, a change that is related to the transition into 'late' or 'second' modernity. Individualisation and globalisation are the key elements that might cause challenges to traditional solidarities. Globalisation extends the potential community through class or national boundaries, while individualisation weakens the bonds between individuals. Thus, risk society erodes important aspects of solidarity (Taylor-Gooby, 2011; Deeming, 2017). However, not only the new risks, but also the changes in the perception of risks, have important impact on people's willingness to share risks. Nevertheless, old social risks and problems have not ceased to exist; they just need to be addressed in a different context and with new approaches (Deeming, 2017; Hemerijck, 2017).

The case studies of this section support these assumptions. They concern homelessness, rural poverty and energy poverty. These are not new problems, but they are addressed in innovative ways. The Green Sticht community in the Netherlands (Chapter Nine) creates a mixed, involved and tolerant neighbourhood that integrates vulnerable citizens with the support of other residents who sometimes choose to live there due to being inspired by ideals. Green Sticht prevents habitual neighbourhood resistance (NIMBYism) and increases the quality of life for all residents. The Social Land Programme in Hungary (Chapter Ten) aims at raising the living standards of poor Roma newly arrived in highly disadvantaged rural areas. Moreover, it also aims at diminishing social exclusion by empowering these incomers to undertake agricultural activities and thus become independent from state transfers, as well as more accepted by the 'original' inhabitants who have strong agricultural traditions. The programme thus facilitates the building of horizontal relationships and reciprocity, which are the main cornerstones of solidarity. The support that it provides is conditional and reciprocal, in that participants need to sign contracts and also return some part of their produce. Increased social cohesion in the communities is recognised as one of its main results.

Alginet Electric Cooperative in Spain (Chapter Eleven) – as expressed in its statutes – is inspired by the ideals of self-responsibility and solidarity. The forms of solidarity observed in Alginet are clearly institutionalised, but they are motivated not only by reciprocal, but also by moral, principles. By providing flexible solutions for payment and education in saving energy, it supports individual techniques for coping with problems related to energy poverty. The cooperative also contributes to solving other local problems in various ways, including food tokens, electricity discounts, donations to local charities and internet access at a reduced price.

In conclusion, solidarity is a central notion in such programmes, and is predominantly institutionalised and reciprocal, but not exclusively. It can also build on voluntary support from individuals (as seen in the case of Green Sticht) and might contain less obligatory and reciprocal elements (as seen in the case of Alginet Electric Cooperative). Our cases confirm that since the vertical structures of the welfare state are weakened with new risks – or rather new approaches to old risks – the reciprocity motivations of horizontal solidarity are strengthened.

References

Deeming, C. (2017) 'The politics of (fractured) solidarity: a cross-national analysis of the class bases of the welfare state', *Social Policy and Administration*, Early view DOI: 10.1111/spol.12323

Durkheim, E. (1984) *The division of labour in Society* (trans W.D. Halls), New York, NY: The Free Press.

Fenger, M. and Van Paridon, K. (2012) 'Towards a globalization of solidarity?', in M. Ellison (ed) *Reinventing social solidarity across Europe*, Bristol: The Policy Press, pp 49–71.

Filcak, R. and Skobla, D. (2012) 'Social solidarity, human rights and Roma: unequal access to basic resources in Central and Eastern Europe', in M. Ellison (ed) *Reinventing social solidarity across Europe*, Bristol: The Policy Press, pp 227–48.

Hemerijck, A. (2017) 'Social investment and its critics', in A. Hemerijck (ed) *The uses of social investment*, Oxford: Oxford University Press, pp 3–42.

Taylor-Gooby, P. (2011) 'Does risk society erode welfare state solidarity?', *Policy & Politics*, 39(2): 147–61.

Van der Veen, R. (2012) 'Risk and the welfare state – risk, risk perception and solidarity', in R. van der Veen, N. Yerkes and P. Achterberg (eds) *The transformation of solidarity – Changing risks and the future of the welfare state*, Amsterdam: Amsterdam University Press, pp 13–31.

NINE

The creation of a socially diverse neighbourhood in Utrecht, the Netherlands

Alfons Fermin, Sandra Geelhoed and Rob Gründemann

Introduction

The 'Green Sticht' project was developed between 1997 and 2002 in Utrecht, the fourth-largest city in the Netherlands. The small neighbourhood known as the Green Sticht was built in 2002/03 on a vacant lot of an old farm in the large new town extension of Leidsche Rijn before regular housing was constructed in the surrounding area. It combines a variety of residential and working functions, and mixes a group of people in a socially vulnerable position with people who want to live and work there out of idealism. The main objectives of the Green Sticht are to provide a safe haven and social support to homeless people in their process of reintegration, as well as a place to live for socially vulnerable people in general who are in need of a place in a neighbourhood where they are known, respected and actively involved in neighbourhood activities. In addition, the neighbourhood offers opportunities to work and meaningful daily activities for both local residents with a distance from the labour market and people with intellectual disabilities living elsewhere in the city.

The plans of the Green Sticht originate from the activities of the 'Fringe' (Rafelrand) civil society working group committed to realising concrete projects to help homeless people and those suffering from addiction. It is one of the projects that originated from a 1997 conference in Utrecht organised by the working group. Its charismatic chairman was Ab Harrewijn, a preacher and left-wing politician at that time, who died in 2002. He based his plans on insights from Emmaus Haarzuilens' 'living and working communities' in the Netherlands (part of a solidarity-based movement acting against poverty and exclusion) and from homeless people themselves. The latter were represented by NoiZ (a self-organised group of homeless people) and by a non-governmental organisation that offers shelter and support to the homeless in Utrecht called the 'Tussenvoorziening' (literally the 'In-between facility'). At this conference, various stakeholders committed themselves to support the development of the Green Sticht project. The directly involved organisations (the Tussenvoorziening, NoiZ and Emmaus Haarzuilens) were joined by a social housing corporation (Juliana, later merged into the national corporation Portaal), and some aldermen of the municipality of Utrecht. Plans were developed between 1997 and 2002 by the Foundation of the Green Sticht, in which the Tussenvoorziening, NoiZ, Emmaus Haarzuilens and the association of the future residents participated.

The term 'Sticht' denotes 'a convent community'. As in convent communities in the past, some people choose to live in the Green Sticht due to being inspired by ideals, while others have little choice because they are temporarily or permanently unable to live independently. In addition, the name also refers to the 'Sticht Utrecht', the territory in the centre of Utrecht ruled by the bishops of Utrecht in the Middle Ages. The Green Sticht is located along the medieval road to Utrecht. In addition, 'green' refers to the green character of the neighbourhood; as many trees as possible have been retained and ecological sustainability is an important value of the neighbourhood (eg expressed in the thrift shop).

The Social Investment elements of the Green Sticht relate to its approach of investing in both the capacities of vulnerable citizens to reintegrate and participate in society, and the capacities of a neighbourhood to realise a form of community spirit, as well as solidarity with the vulnerable neighbours, thus providing them with a basis for reintegration and participation. A highly innovative element of the Green Sticht project is that it intended to circumvent the habitual neighbourhood resistance against every plan for a homeless shelter in a specific neighbourhood ('not in my back yard' [NIMBY] syndrome). It did this by reversing the order, first establishing homeless facilities in a new housing estate, and only then building houses in the surrounding area. Of course, this is only possible in new construction projects. It has been innovative from the start, when it filled a gap in the range of services at the time. After 20 years, it is still innovative because of the way in which it creates a community of solidarity and informal support. Also, the type of organisation and method of financing are innovative: the project has been realised and maintained by a partnership of third sector organisations, with a central role for the residents' association, and it has been independent of structural public funding since the construction of the neighbourhood in 2003. This chapter will elaborate on these Social Investment and social innovation elements of the project.

Origins of the Green Sticht as a socially diverse neighbourhood

Background: combating homelessness in Dutch cities

The origin and development of the Green Sticht project closely reflect changes in the way of thinking about homelessness around the turn of the century. The project has its roots in the emancipatory movement of homeless people. In the mid–1990s, the situation of homeless people in Dutch cities became unsustainable: there was a chronic lack of (night) shelters for homeless people, the mere attempt to provide such a shelter led to fierce neighbourhood resistance and the government did not want to go ahead with and had no vision and policy for homeless people. For instance, in Utrecht, there lived around 800 rough sleepers in 1998 (at that time, Utrecht had a total population of 240,000). A substantial part of them were concentrated in a kind of 'tunnel' near the central train station and shopping centre of Utrecht (Van Scheppingen et al, 2013; interview with Jules van Dam).

Since the second half of the 1990s, societal and political awareness rose about a chronic lack of shelters for homeless people in the Dutch cities. Homelessness was increasingly perceived in relation to structural societal developments and risks, and not only as due to hopeless, incorrigible persons. The composition of the homeless population was also in the process of changing at that time: alongside the traditional category of homeless old men with alcohol problems, there were more and more youngsters, women, hard-drug addicts and rejected asylum seekers among them. Initially, mainly third sector organisations came into action. In addition, there was also a limited emancipation movement among homeless people themselves who no longer wanted to be patronised in night shelters. In Utrecht, a group of homeless people occupied a vacant building in order to set up a night shelter under self-management, and organised further (NoiZ). It was only after the turn of the century that the governments of the four major cities started to act, supported by an ambitious National Homeless Strategy from 2006.

Target groups and needs

Since its inception, the Green Sticht project has aimed at meeting the needs of various target groups: (1) a safe, tolerant and solidarity-based residential and working area for socially vulnerable citizens; (2) a temporary shelter for homeless people in a neighbourhood where they are accepted and that offers possibilities for meaningful daily activities and work; (3) a restaurant and thrift store that offers possibilities for meaningful daytime activities and work for people with intellectual disabilities; and (4) a neighbourhood that offers self-reliant and idealistic people the possibility to shape and to live their lives according to their ideals of solidarity and community spirit. The Green Sticht is set up as an integrative project, based on the insight that the integration of homeless people can only succeed if society and relevant people take their responsibility as well, and are willing to include them and offer opportunities to participate.

Homeless people in need of shelter and a place to recover and start their process of reintegration was the most urgent issue to be addressed. Thus, the needs addressed are:

- the lack of shelter and housing facilities for homeless people in Utrecht, especially for those prepared to reintegrate;
- a lack of provisions for the rehabilitation of homeless people, including opportunities to combine work or other meaningful daily activities with shelter, guidance and social support;
- overcoming strong neighbourhood resistance to the establishment of shelter facilities for homeless people;
- a lack of informal social support for socially vulnerable people who have problems living independently in an anonymous neighbourhood in a highly individualised society; and
- a lack of involvement of homeless people in the development and management of initiatives designed to improve their position.

These needs show a high degree of complexity. The problem of reintegrating into social life after a life on the street is particularly difficult for individuals because of a lack of self-confidence and lack of trust in other people and social structures. The project was conceived in order to be able to respond to both personal and community development needs. Reintegration into social life after homelessness – often combined with many other problems, including addiction, debts and loss of social networks – takes time and is also dependent on a safe and receptive social environment and the regularity of work. The needs were therefore defined in a multidimensional way, while, at the same time, the needs of other target groups were taken into account in the development of neighbourhood plans.

Theory of Change

The project was designed and realised by partner organisations, united in the Green Sticht Foundation since 1997 (for a timeline, see Table 9.1). A Theory of Change developed organically in the design phase of the project (1997–2002). The Green Sticht is a third sector project developed by organisations that share values and a mission, while the elaboration of the plans was also characterised by pragmatism. Thus, the Theory of Change that underpins the project plans aimed at supporting homeless people in their process of reintegration and the creation of a community of solidarity in the neighbourhood (Fermin et al, 2016). The Green Sticht Theory of Change is a combination of three distinct key assumptions:

1. It is possible to overcome neighbourhood resistance to the establishment of a homeless shelter by reversing the order: first constructing a shelter, and only then building houses in the surrounding neighbourhood. The working group thus utilised a specific momentum in the urban development of the new town extension.
2. Homeless people are able to recover and reintegrate through securing basic conditions of housing, work and social support, in combination with a limited degree of professional guidance. This involves the assumption that each person has the potential to recover him/herself (strengths-based approach).
3. It is possible to create and maintain a solidary, involved and tolerant neighbourhood by selecting and mixing appropriate categories of people, in combination with limited but appropriate (professional) support. This assumption was based upon the belief that alongside

Table 9.1: Green Sticht timeline

1997	Utrecht conference organised by the Fringe (Rafelrand) Working Group, chaired by Ab Harrewijn, various stakeholders committed themselves to support the development of the Green Sticht project.
1997–2003	The project organisation of Green Sticht – initially chaired by Ab Harrewijn, but soon replaced by Nico Ooms – elaborated the project plans within the wider Leidsche Rijn urban plans, developed a feasibility study, raised funds and so on.
2002–03	Building activities: the realisation of the Green Sticht.
2004–present	Process of implementation, adjustment and so on (2004–09 – the first five years of the Green Sticht; 2009–14 – a new multi-annual plan; 2015–20 – the current multi-annual plan).

the personalised approach, a community approach was also necessary for reintegration.

Thus, the project envisaged an integrated and multidimensional approach to the problem of the recovery of homeless people. Its personalised and community model offers homeless people opportunities and guidance to work on social reintegration step by step in the domains of working, living and housing. It permits them to work on their self-confidence, on the one hand, but also to gain social trust and exchange with others within a living community, neighbourhood and work environment, on the other. Today, especially the third element of the Theory of Change is still innovative, in combination with the integrated approach. The second assumption has become widely accepted (strengths-based approach) in the meantime. The first assumption is still innovative but is only applicable in specific circumstances, that is, in new housing estates.

Development and realisation of the project

In 2002, the foundation stone was laid and the first residents arrived in late 2003. Currently, it houses around 110 residents. It combines a variety of residential and working functions for a mixed group of people with and without a socially vulnerable position. The residential area combines various housing options: guest accommodation (shelter) for the homeless (G), a group home for a living and working community (Emmaus Parkwijk) (D), rooms for students, social housing for socially vulnerable people, the elderly and people who choose to live there due to their ideals (A/BC), and a few owner-occupied properties (I/K). The working functions include a thrift store (Emmaus Parkwijk) (C), a furniture workshop (for the recycling of furniture) (Fii) and a restaurant (De Hoge Weide), which employs people with intellectual disabilities (H) (see Image 9.1).

In order to create a sense of community, active participation in the neighbourhood and mutual support are promoted through the residents association, a newsletter and community activities. The different types of residency reflect the needs of homeless people, who need a step-by-step approach in getting used to living in their own place and environment. The self-organisation of the homeless (NoiZ) and the association of (future) residents of the Green Sticht were closely involved in the development of the project from the beginning. The residents association still plays a pivotal role in the project. In fact, the project has been developed from shared values, involving shared

Image 9.1: Plan of the Green Sticht

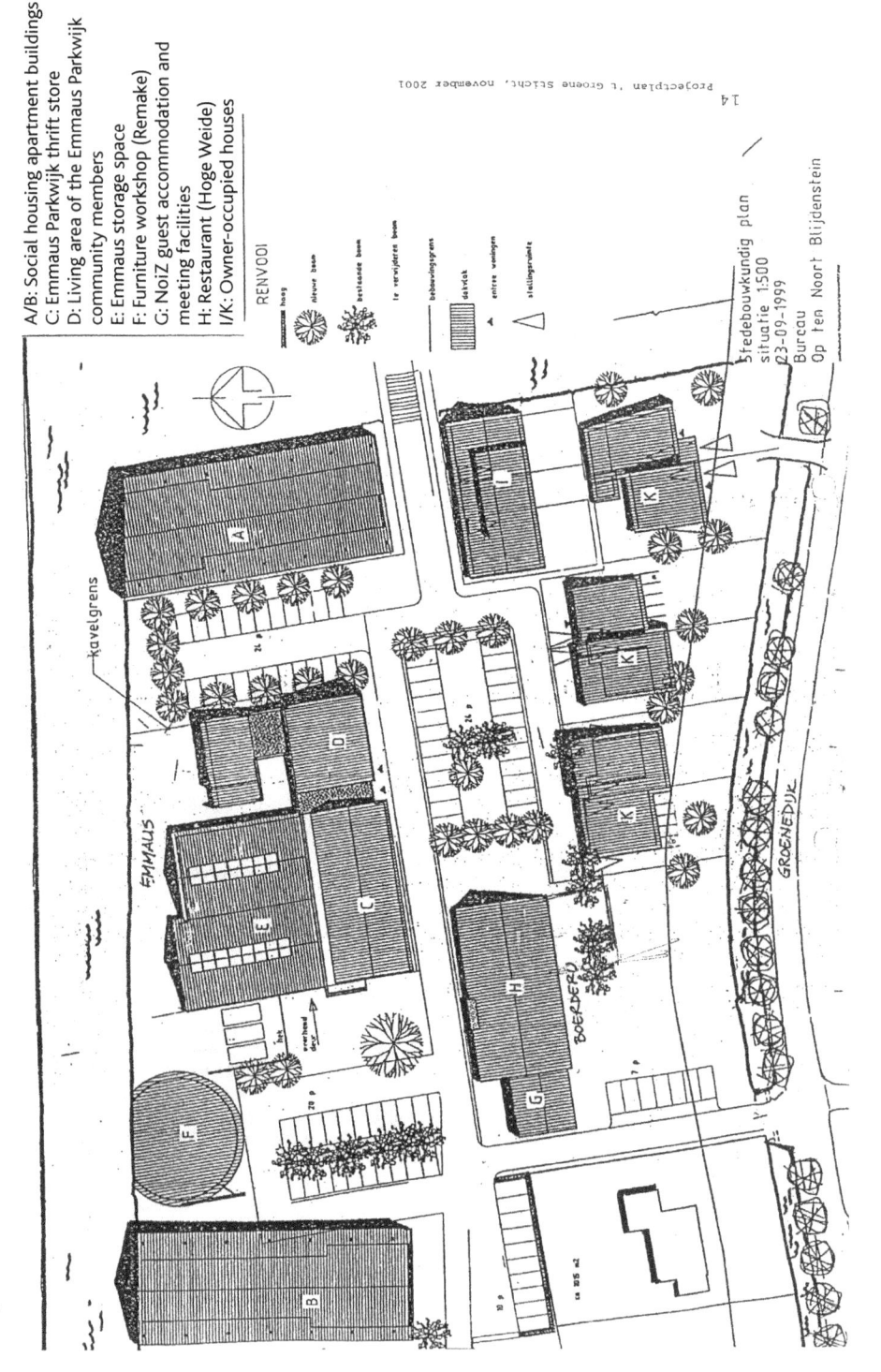

A/B: Social housing apartment buildings
C: Emmaus Parkwijk thrift store
D: Living area of the Emmaus Parkwijk community members
E: Emmaus storage space
F: Furniture workshop (Remake)
G: NoiZ guest accommodation and meeting facilities
H: Restaurant (Hoge Weide)
I/K: Owner-occupied houses

responsibility and shared power between (representatives of) service providers and service users. This is reflected in the structure of the Foundation that realised and manages the project.

Various organisations, public, private and philanthropic, contributed financially to the realisation of the Green Sticht. Emmaus Haarzuilens gave a substantial loan and the Foundation received a grant from the European Structural Fund. The municipality of Utrecht played an important supporting role. The land and farm for the new residential area were donated by the municipality. The construction of buildings for social housing was financed by the housing corporation Portaal, which has been renting out and maintaining the apartments since 2003.

Since the construction of the neighbourhood, the Foundation has not been dependent on structural subsidies for its operation. Renting out buildings to participating organisations (especially Emmaus, Reinaerde and the Tussenvoorziening) generates sufficient income to finance the core activities of the Foundation (see the circularity of financial flows in the organogram in Figure 9.1).

Innovation and implementation: the Green Sticht as a networked non-profit

One of the innovative elements of the Green Sticht is its organisational structure. This bears a close resemblance to a 'networked non-profit' organisation (Wei-Skillern and Marciano, 2008). A networked non-profit forges 'long-term partnerships with trusted peers to tackle their mission on multiple fronts' (Wei-Skillern and Marciano 2008). The Green Sticht is characterised by the three core elements of a networked non-profit: (1) putting their mission – a social goal – rather than their organisation (and its growth) at the centre of its activities; (2) the network is not governed by control, but based on mutual trust and shared responsibility – and, in this case, also shared power – made possible by shared core values and by investing in building with a shared vision as well as monitoring adherence; and (3) the Green Sticht Foundation sees itself not as a hub in the centre, but as a node in a constellation of equal, interconnected partners (Wei-Skillern and Marciano, 2008).

The Green Sticht's activities are focused on realising its mission. The objectives (or mission) of the Green Sticht Foundation are fixed in its statutes of 1997, which were updated in 2011 based on the results of a neighbourhood-wide consultation. The Green Sticht's long-term social objective (or mission) can be summarised as: to create and

Figure 9.1: The organisational structure of the Green Sticht

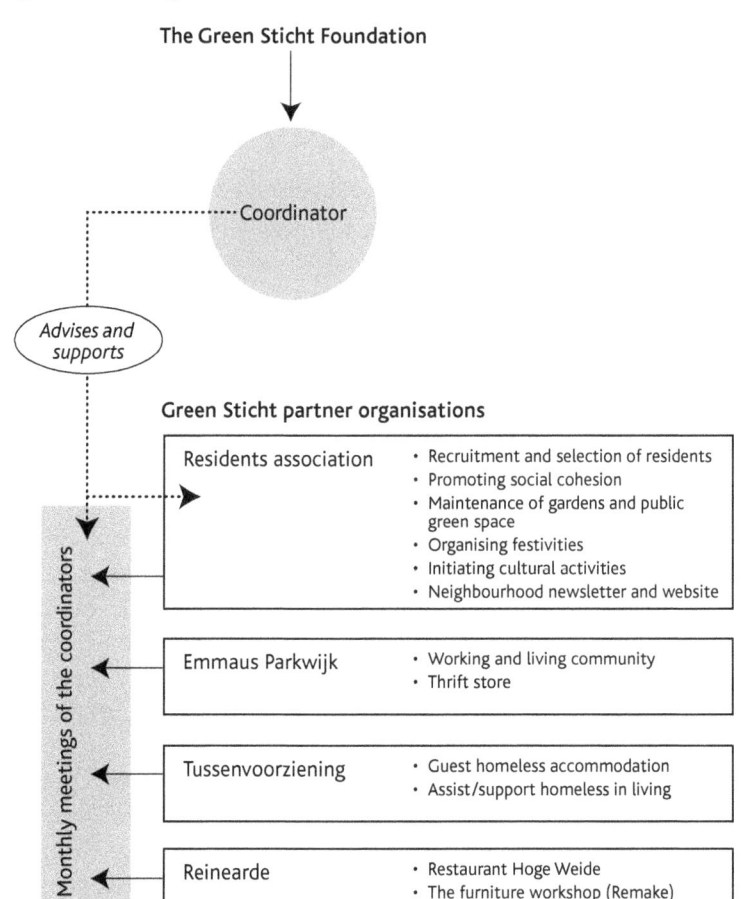

Source: Kluft and Metz (2010)

maintain a mixed neighbourhood in which people with different social backgrounds live and work together and support each other, while the neighbourhood also offers shelter to the homeless.

The Green Sticht has a layered organisational structure (Kluft and Metz, 2010). The Foundation is the formal initiator of the project. It owns the real estate (except the rental and owner-occupied houses) and rents them to the partner organisations. The advantage is that the Foundation has the choice to whom it rents the buildings in order to safeguard its key objectives. It also avoids the risk that the whole project fails because one of the organisations goes bankrupt or decides to change its policy so that it no longer fits within the

Green Sticht's mission (Kluft and Metz, 2010). Thus, it constitutes a basis for stability. The limited role of the overarching Foundation also relates to ideas of efficiency and trust in the professional competence of the partner organisations. The Foundation has mainly coordinating tasks and refrains from structural involvement in the management and implementation of care and welfare activities. In addition, this approach leaves room for the responsibility and diversity of the perspectives of the partner organisations, including the residents association (Kluft and Metz, 2010). The partners have to develop and execute their own programmes, and attract their own funding.

The central role of the Green Sticht residents association is quite innovative. The control over the development of the neighbourhood is shared – also legally – between the Foundation and the residents association. This is a result of Ab Harrewijns's Marxist idea 'that power should be divided so that the parties can constrain each other'. The residents association has the right to select residents and it has a seat and equal voice on the board of the Foundation. This reflects the confidence in a bottom-up approach to social change. However, the residents association can never decide to stop the homeless shelter. Such a decision would be blocked by the Foundation. The service users and providers have shared responsibility for developing and managing the Green Sticht. This reflects well the Green Sticht's value-driven approach based on democratic participation, equality, reciprocity and respect for all, taking into account relevant differences.

The organisational structure of the Green Sticht Foundation has remained the same over time, but some of the partners have changed. The main change was that Reinaerde has joined the Foundation. This is a non-profit care organisation in the Utrecht region that supports people with intellectual disabilities. In the absence of detailed goals and top-down management, there was and is plenty of room for customisation, flexibility, learning by doing and input from residents and clients. As is characteristic for a networked non-profit, self-evaluation and subsequent adjustments play a crucial role. Communication and coordination activities, as well as collective reflection and self-evaluations, have helped to update and keep alive the Green Sticht's mission and values.

There are various processes and procedures for coordination and alignment between the partners within the Foundation. The coordinator (and before 2003, the project leader) is appointed and paid by the Foundation for two days a week for day-to-day coordination activities. His main tasks are advising and supporting the partners. In addition, there are monthly meetings of the coordinators (or managers) of the activities of partner organisations in the neighbourhood. Here, again, equality is the point of departure: no one is the boss. Thus, the parties will try to find common ground and how to reinforce and complement each other (Kluft and Metz, 2010). The board of the Foundation meets three or four times a year to monitor and discuss the main lines of development and issues that cannot be solved at a lower level. Once a year, the board of the Foundation, the board of the residents association and the coordinators (managers) meet to evaluate the past year and to determine the annual plan for the next year. Periodically, dialogue evenings and other moments of reflection take place with all inhabitants, workers and professionals in the neighbourhood in order to keep the mission alive, to evaluate it and, if necessary, to renew it.

The target group of (formerly) homeless people was involved from the beginning (through NoiZ) in the development of the project and the realisation of the shelter facility. The shelter (called the 'guesthouse') is self-managed, until recently, with former homeless people as social managers. They have now disappeared because of strict requirements imposed by the Dutch Participation Act (of 2015) on working while receiving a benefit. The accommodation is now socially managed directly by the guests, in combination with limited professional support. This has inevitably led to a stricter selection of guests on their ability to become self-reliant.

The results and impact

In 2012, a questionnaire was drawn up in the neighbourhood for a study of the Netherlands Institute for Social Research (SCP) on social cohesion in Dutch neighbourhoods. This showed that in the Green Sticht, social cohesion is above the average of neighbourhoods in the Netherlands (Overburen, 2012). A number of internal evaluations have been carried out with a view to reassessing the objectives and drawing up new five-year plans for the Green Sticht. Residents, workers and professionals also entered into discussions with each other during the evaluations in 2008 and 2014. These evaluations indicated that the neighbourhood has largely achieved its objectives, but that continuous maintenance is required. Two external evaluations of the Green Sticht (Kluft and Metz, 2010; Fermin et al, 2016) confirmed the positive assessment of the internal evaluations.

Temporary and permanent residents with a social care background experience the neighbourhood as safe and tolerant. Informal support takes various forms, ranging from greeting each other to involving homeless people from the guesthouse in building up a biological market. A form of reciprocity and connection between the various groups of residents and workers (Kluft and Metz, 2010) has been constantly evolving since the start through joint living, working, decision-making and activities. Professionals of the social housing association Portaal and welfare organisation the Tussenvoorziening noted that homeless people in the Green Sticht cause less inconvenience and are less likely to suffer from a relapse than homeless people allocated housing in an anonymous neighbourhood. Also, the direct neighbours of the Green Sticht seldom or never complain about nuisance, and seem to be overall satisfied to live next to a neighbourhood with facilities such as a thrift store and a restaurant.

The elaboration and implementation of the mission of the Green Sticht have been adjusted over time. During various evaluations, including the neighbourhood-wide evaluations, successes as well as deficiencies were discussed, and adjustments were proposed. For example, the balloting procedure for new permanent residents has been tightened up over time. A socially active past appears to be a better predictor for neighbourhood activity than mere (declared) intentions. The neighbourhood runs on active residents, but residents 'with ideals' regularly turn out to be little active in the neighbourhood, while vulnerable residents sometimes develop into active residents. For this reason, a more flexible form of categorisation has been developed. Residents can evolve from 'active' to 'non-active' and vice versa. It also turned out to be quite a challenge to keep the enthusiasm and commitment alive throughout all those years. Enthusiasm and involvement of the local residents fluctuated over time but was kept alive because people regularly move and therefore new residents enter, because administrative tasks are rotated, and because local residents are taken seriously and participate in decision-making on the direction of the Foundation. Realising and maintaining the 'ideal mix' of one third socially vulnerable and two thirds resilient residents also had to be revised. It turned out that resilient residents move regularly – rental homes are too small for families – while vulnerable residents rarely move, which initially resulted in an increase of the share of vulnerable people in social housing apartments. The rules have been amended, and the turnover of residents is now taken into account in the balloting procedure. In the latest joint evaluation exercise, it turned out more professional support and guidance is needed for various neighbourhood activities. Maintenance of the social infrastructure has been added to the tasks of the Foundation (also legally in the statutes) since the coordinator also fulfils the role of social broker in the neighbourhood and the partner organisations now have obligations to be more actively involved in community activities. Furthermore, informal help is more often organised, such as in 'buddy' projects. Thus, the high expectations concerning community building and neighbourly support to socially vulnerable residents had to be tempered to more realistic ones, and required some more support by professionals.

The other element of the project where expectations appeared to be too high from the start was the realisation of work opportunities for homeless people in the neighbourhood. The Green Sticht Foundation aims at a multifaceted approach to reintegrating homeless people, with social guidance, work and acceptance by local residents. The integrated approach has been successful, except for the creation of job opportunities for people at a great distance from the labour market. The municipal requirements for tendering for reintegration projects constituted a barrier to the realisation of work opportunities in the neighbourhood for homeless people. In the opinion of reintegration enterprises, the risks were too high and the yields too small for this target group. Within the current social legislation, it was much easier and less risky to realise opportunities for work and meaningful activities for another target group, people with intellectual disabilities. Thus, an appropriate organisation (Reinaerde) for this target group became a partner in the Foundation. The homeless people in the guesthouse can still – but to a limited extent – carry out activities in the neighbourhood, such as work in the thrift store and cleaning the neighbourhood. Many find work activities outside the neighbourhood with the help of the Tussenvoorziening.

It was not possible to evaluate the reception of homeless people over time. The guesthouse of the Green Sticht seems to function properly, but there are no evaluations that confirm this. This is because it is one of the many facilities of the Tussenvoorziening, and has therefore never been evaluated separately. This facility has always been intended as an intermediate step in the process of reintegration. The duration of the stay of the 'guests', their through flow to other forms of housing and how often they relapse fluctuate over time, which is mainly due to changes in the target group – for example, more people with psychiatric problems due to extramuralisation in the care sector – and adjustments of selection criteria, which, in turn, are related to amended requirements and opportunities for subsidies because of changes in legislation and regulations (for examples of the experiences of guests, see Box 9.1).

Box 9.1: Experiences of Green Sticht residents

This is the story of A, a young woman who participated in a reintegration project for homeless people similar to the Green Sticht in Utrecht. She participated in the community reporters' training held at the Green Sticht:

> "Soon I will have my own house. After a very long time, I am very proud that I will finally have my own place. I have lived in a 24/7 shelter. Then I moved on to a flat with three other persons. And now it is really great to have my own place. I also know that I can enrol on an educational programme in September and I found a job at Majella Housing, the place where I will live. My children can stay over in my new house. Housemates will no longer disturb me. Yeah, it seems just wonderful. I've come a long way to get here. But it makes me really proud 'cause I know what I have done to achieve this. Eventually I did it."

In this 49-second audio story, A sketches what having a place of one's own means. Having her own house not only means having her own place; it is the start of a new phase in her life. Her voice is lively, happy and proud. The words on paper cannot transmit her joy about this achievement. Listening to or reading her story makes us a witness to her personal process; it gives her a voice. Self-confident and aware about herself and the process that she has gone through, she shares a story from the heart. Having her house, an education and a job also means independence and freedom and the joy of her children being able to stay over. She can move on with her life.

At the community reporters' training, she was eager to collect a story with D. He is an example to her. He works at the Green Sticht as an assistant coordinator and is the president of the residents association. A made a dialogue interview with him, which resulted in the following community reporting story:

> "As you know, I have worked here and lived here for a long time already, five years. I arrived here as the administrator of the guesthouse [shelter], in the administrators' building at number 20A. I worked also as an administrator, in the housing facility. Since May last year, I have my own apartment at 't Groene Sticht. I am also busy with an education called 'social work and expert by experience'. And now I am a trainee at 't Groene Sticht, as an assistant/coach. So, I switched again to a new role. I am also the president of the residents association at 't Groene Sticht. This is another role I have. Within this association, we would like to improve internal cohesion between the permanent residents and guests [short-term] residents. There are people from NoiZ, who use our guest house and also with Emmaus

and Reinaerde and the people with disabilities that work here. This is my
story at 't Groene Sticht."

D tells a story which shows the 'career steps' that can be taken within the Green
Sticht scheme. Only between the lines does it become clear that D has had a past
life as a homeless person. The role of coordinator of the guest house is always
occupied by one of the (former) homeless people. D draws on his experience to
contribute to the well-being of all Green Sticht residents.

The Green Sticht inspired three other Utrecht projects. In 2016,
Parana was realised (in the district of Overvecht) and in 2014 Majella
Wonen was realised. Both projects mix homeless people with regular
tenants: the former in a flat of five floors; the latter in two apartment
complexes in which the residents live permanently. They are not only
a variation, but also an improvement, on the starting points of the
Green Sticht. A new feature is that the coordinator conducts annual
'performance reviews' with the residents, in which they also express
their views on their activity plans for the coming year in the residential
complex. Moreover, self-reliant and homeless people are mixed in
different proportions, with comparatively more socially vulnerable
people than in the Green Sticht. In the summer of 2017, Place2BU
was realised, also in Leidsche Rijn (Utrecht), with 500 studios for
'regular' young people, young refugees with a residence permit and
youth from shelters (social care). Here, too, residents are selected and
mixed in certain proportions, activities are organised by the residents
association, and vulnerable residents receive support and guidance
from professionals. In all three projects – as well as in the Green Sticht
– the same organisations (social housing association Portaal and the
Tussenvoorziening) work together, with the same professional from
the Tussenvoorziening as a coordinator.

Learning points and policy implications

The Green Sticht and the other comparable projects in Utrecht show
that a contemporary model of solidarity can be created in residential
complexes or neighbourhoods by selecting and mixing resilient and
vulnerable residents, in combination with professional support and
guidance. The initiative is an example of how the principles of the
Social Investment paradigm can be realised locally through and in a
neighbourhood society, under specific conditions. Social Investment
requires social innovation (see Chapter One). Both the aim of realising

a solidary neighbourhood and the process of the implementation and organisation of the Green Sticht are socially innovative. It aims at creating a framework within which vulnerable people are able to work on their reintegration under favourable conditions. An important social innovative element of the project is that the Tussenvoorziening (and NoiZ), in their reception of homeless people in the Green Sticht, work on the basis of values of empowerment, self-management and the development of a social network. This creates self-confidence among the people themselves and trust between the supervisors and the 'clients', but also between the 'clients' and other workers and residents in the neighbourhood. One of the selection criteria for a shelter is that homeless people (want to) work at least 20 hours a week. Working provides regularity and contacts, and is one of the prerequisites for getting one's own life back on track, starting to function independently and achieving a goal in life. In addition, the Green Sticht aims at Social Investment in socially vulnerable people in general, as well as those living in social housing, by increasing their capacity to participate in society according to their ability. There is also a life-course perspective of vulnerability: everyone runs the risk of becoming homeless or vulnerable, but targeted and timely investments in their capacities can prevent these problems from arising or help individuals to recover by their own efforts.

The Green Sticht Foundation shows that new forms of cooperation based on trust, shared values and equality are important for achieving social innovation. The partner organisations work from a shared mission and shared values. The initiative is supported by a light organisational form, in which bureaucracy and administration are minimised. Due to its specific organisational structure and shared mission, the Green Sticht has been able to keep on developing and moving with the needs of residents, target groups and partner organisations.

The Green Sticht initiative is an example of how initiatives by third sector organisations and social entrepreneurs can fill gaps left by public organisations. In addition to a considerable measure of idealism, a pragmatic attitude is required in order to meet the requirements and opportunities offered by government policy and cooperation with other organisations. Although public sector support was essential for the realisation of the neighbourhood, since 2003, the local government has no longer been directly involved. This was made possible by the financial autonomy of the Foundation. However, two of the participating organisations (Reinaerde and the Tussenvoorziening) have been dependent on government policy and subsidies for financing their activities.

The initiative is still topical and offers lessons for other mixed housing projects. The central starting points or elements of the Green Sticht are the selection of permanent residents and 'guests', the search for an appropriate balance between resilient and vulnerable residents, the coordination of informal and formal networks and facilities, a central role for the residents (association), a shared vision or mission of all the organisations involved, a flexible organisational structure, and a limited but important role for the coordinator in the management of the social and physical infrastructure (see Fermin et al, 2016). These starting points have been adjusted over time and these experiences offer relevant insights for contemporary projects of mixed housing. Across the country, more and more mixed housing projects are emerging, regularly including socially vulnerable groups of residents.

The rise of mixed housing projects is encouraged by the current social and care policy context. In the retreating welfare state, the socially vulnerable should, in the first instance, rely on their social network and neighbours for social support. The involved and solidarity-based neighbourhood of the Green Sticht comes close to what the Dutch Social Support Act (Wmo) envisages as a caring society. However, it is precisely these demanding conditions which show that such a caring society will remain an ideal under 'normal' conditions, and is only possible in mixed housing projects with sufficient professional support and involvement of civil society organisations, in combination with space for social and physical engineering.

References

Fermin, A. (ed), Christiansson, M., van Doorn, L. and van Beek, G. (2016) *InnoSI WP4 case studies – The Netherlands: The Green Sticht*, chapter 1. Utrecht: Hogeschool Utrecht.

Kluft, M. and Metz, J. (2010) *'t Groene Sticht: Beschrijving van de good practice*, Utrecht: Movisie.

Overburen (2012) 'De gelukkigste plek van Nederland (resultaten SCP onderzoek) en kort verslag van de resultaten van het onderzoek naar beleving van de buurt door bewoners van 't Groene Sticht', Overburen, buurttijdschrift van 't Groene Sticht, ongepubliceerd document.

Van Scheppingen, M., Lap, S. Appelman, S. Hautvast, S., van Oosten, T. and Lammerink, W. (eds) (2013) *De straat is geen thuis: De canon van de Tussenvoorziening*, Utrecht: De Tussenvoorziening.

Wei-Skillern, J. and Marciano, S. (2008) 'The networked non-profit', *Stanford Social Innovation Review*, 6: 38–43.

TEN

Revitalising the self-sufficient household economy: the Social Land Programme in Hungary

Judit Csoba and Flórián Sipos

Introduction: the Social Land Programme

The Social Land Programme (hereafter, SLP) is an active social policy programme serving as an alternative to passive benefits. The SLP mainly targets socially disadvantaged persons and families who live in small, rural communities and who do not possess the capital needed for agricultural production. The objective of the programme is not employment, but the household economy, and beneficiaries participate as independent small-scale producers. The organisation of the SLP is the responsibility of municipalities. This case study comprised eight rural communities participating in the SLP.

The background to the SLP is increasing rural poverty following the fall of the communist regime. Hungarian governments sought local solutions for lost employment, combining the characteristics of the private and the state sectors. Household plots providing additional income had been well established in Hungary before the fall of communism. From the beginning of the 1990s, lagging agricultural regions started to become pauperised and reviving lost traditions of household farming and horticulture seemed to be an appropriate solution to rural poverty (Jász, 2003; Nagyné Varga, 2007; Rácz, 2009; Vida and Vidra, 2015; Csoba, 2017). An additional goal was to reinforce local communities and to reduce the social and economic tensions that came into existence due to the lack of income (Szoboszlai, 1999; Bartal, 2001).

Revitalising the household economy

Unemployment and lack of income, especially in rural regions

Between 1989 and 1992, almost 30% of all jobs ceased to exist in Hungary and a million people became unemployed (Csoba, 2010). The majority were unskilled individuals or those who did not have a marketable profession. They were mainly commuters between the countryside and city, but due to the ever-narrowing labour market, they had to return to their home villages. With the transformation of socialist cooperatives, the previous cooperative members in the villages lost their livelihood and land property. The tradition of the household economy – the ability to be self-sufficient – slowly disappeared in these families. In addition to this, because of the de-urbanisation processes and gentrification of inner-city ghettoes, a selective migration started in the 1990s from urban to rural areas. Highly disadvantaged (mostly Roma) people bought properties in poor rural municipalities with low prices, where the labour opportunities were already decreasing. As a result, impoverishment processes started or were expedited, which led to the birth of new rural (mostly ethnic) ghettoes. More and more people had to rely on welfare transfers (mostly passive ones) from the local municipalities and the state. Since finding a job was hopeless, especially for unskilled workers living in smaller communities, individuals who had lost their job started to exit the labour market. They retired, became disabled or relied on the support of the social welfare system. The missing income gradually led to the impoverishment of these people and their communities. As a result, several leaders of small municipalities approached the ministry in charge to ask for support to start the organisation of agricultural activity among gradually pauperised, unemployed groups as early as the 1990s (Kovács, 1999; Serafin, 2015). They requested land, machinery, agricultural equipment and resources for promotional materials. The fact that due to the ageing population, increasingly larger areas had become uncultivated by the millennium also contributed to the establishment of the new programme. The SLP – having been started as a test programme in the early 1990s – was ratified as a benefit in kind in 1993 under the Act on Social Administration and Social Benefits (1993/III). Section 47(4) of the Act also declared that the provision of *benefits that help farming that caters for family needs* should be regulated by the communities in local government decrees.

Official objective and Theory of Change

The original goals of the SLP were to revive the household economy culture in order to reduce the disadvantage of the rural population, especially the long-term unemployed, individuals with reduced work capacity, large families and Roma people (EMET, 2016). In its original form, as a grass-roots movement, the SLP aimed at providing additional income and contributing to self-maintenance. Before 2010, the goal of leading to (greater) employment was not an inherent element of the SLP. However, the programme also had a significant impact on income replacement and activation (Bartal, 2001; Jász and Szarvák, 2005; Szoboszlai, 1999, 2003; Rácz, 2009). This was especially important in communities that were underpopulated, and where support for the unemployed population had been limited until then to passive benefits.

Over the years, the aims and tools of the SLP were under constant change by policymakers. Its focus moved from integration and improving living standards to increasing employability among people with multiple social disadvantages and supporting the creation of social cooperatives and local self-sustaining communities. The National Social Inclusion Strategy – having aimed to recover the country from the crisis of 2008 – promised to organise complex programmes regarding employment and to use active labour market policies to target specific groups and each individual. However, the period was instead characterised by the gradually increasing dominance of public employment programmes (Act CVI of 2011) and the substantial reduction of passive benefits. The reduction of passive benefits was not accompanied by the establishment of new inclusive services and the resources allocated to active labour market policies were decreased. Interventions other than public employment (training courses, consultation, training for job-seeking, etc) were radically diminished (Makay and Blaskó, 2012; Bakó et al, 2014; László, 2015). In these circumstances, local governments had a special role in including in the SLPs unemployed persons who were not yet prepared for engaging with their own business, starting or running social cooperatives, or participating in alternative self-sufficiency-oriented farming programmes such as household farms (Kelen, 2012; Fekete and Lipták, 2014; Tésits et al, 2015).

The main actors

Since 2011, the SLP has been under the Ministry of Human Resources (EMMI, 2014), which is currently responsible for social issues. Participation in the programme is voluntary and beneficiaries receive resources through calls for bids organised by the coordinators. In the 1990s, municipalities, Roma minority governments and civil organisations were entitled to apply to start SLP projects. However, over the years, the list of potential applicants has been expanded. Currently, public benefit organisations, social organisations participating in prominent public benefit activities, governmental partnerships and micro-regional partnerships can also apply for grants.

Although the SLP seems to include a wide variety of actors, it is the local governments who provide the programme's framework of operation. They are obliged to enact local decrees that regulate the operation tailored to local characteristics. The majority of the implemented projects are based on communities with a population below 2,000, where this programme – besides public employment – is the only means of local employment and activation (Jász and Szarvák, 2005; Váradi, 2015). The applicants are obliged to cooperate with Roma minority self-governments where they exist in the community. The reason behind the continuous governmental support of the programme since the 1990s is the increasing poverty among small communities where a large part of the population is of Roma origin. Families and participants can only join the programme through applying to municipalities and non-profit institutions. Of the participants, 62.7% are single parents or couples who are raising children, and an additional 16% are extended families where children are being raised as well. Only 8.3% of the participants are people who live alone and 11.5% of them consist of married couples not raising children in their household.

Financial framework of the programme

During its first 10 years (1993–2003), the SLP was financed by the domestic state budget. When Hungary joined the European Union (EU) in 2004, it was suggested that the SLP could be financed by EU Structural Funds, but this initiative was turned down on the grounds of a hidden subsidy to agriculture. Therefore, national resources have provided the financial basis for the programme since then. The annual budget is designed by the yearly central budget law. Between 26 March 2015 and 30 June 2016, this amount was equal to 130,000,000 HUF. This consisted of funds for equipment procurement and development (50,000,000 HUF) and garden culture and livestock-keeping projects (80,000,000 HUF). With this budget, 130 settlements were intended to be involved. Each project receives approximately 1 million HUF on average and includes 25–30 families. The support received by families is 30,000 HUF/year (approximately €100).

Activities and innovations

Selection of participants

The yearly calls for applications to the SLP do not specify criteria for potential participants of the programme. They only require applicants to be in a disadvantaged situation. As a result, the participating local governments can specify the conditions for selection themselves, which are then legislated in local regulations. This level of freedom is beneficial for many reasons as the communities can select the households to be supported based on their unique characteristics. This aspect is different from the 'universalism' of other programmes in Hungary.

Informing people through flyers about the SLP was undertaken in communities during the recruitment process, but it was usual practice to *recruit participants personally* by local government employees and mayors. In some municipalities, civil organisations or minority governments also played a significant role in the recruitment and selection process. The criteria of the selection had two basic aspects: first, what form of eligibility was preferred by local decision-makers at the time they began participating in the programme; and, second, what type of activity did they aim to engage in within the programme and what essential conditions did that have.

The most important feature is *the voluntary nature* of the selection process. In comparison to the majority of activation programmes in Hungary, in the SLP, both the municipalities and the families have to apply for the opportunity to take part. Indeed, there is an element of competition among the potential future target group members in order to be enrolled in the programme and to receive support. This is a significant factor in the motivation of participants. The SLP has also taken on the responsibility – as seen in the local selection criteria of five out of the eight local SLP projects in this study– to integrate another excluded group known as the 'outsiders'. After the millennium, as a result of population changes and migration processes, since young people had moved and older generations had passed away, many houses were left empty. These were occupied by 'strangers' arriving from other cities or communities. Involving them in the SLP significantly helped to integrate these families into the local community.

Activities of the SLP

The SLP – as its name implies – is a form of integration related to agricultural activity. It includes both crop production and livestock farming. Whether it is one or the other that is being focused on depends on the traditions that still exist in the community regarding household agriculture and the amount of land that is available for working on by the participants or the organising local governments. The supported activities of the SLP are listed in Table 10.1.

The support manifests in different forms in the different communities in the SLP. What is the same in all municipalities is that participants all receive a bag of seeds or breeding animals (mainly chickens). The significance of this is considered by many to be the fact that families with extremely low income do not have sufficient capital after the winter to finance the horticultural needs of the spring season (soil treatment, tools, seeds, pesticides, etc), so they do not even begin cultivating the gardens, even if there is land available around their house for cultivation. The seed packages or breeding animals are identical in most municipalities. There are cases, though, where the support is assembled according to the needs of the participants. In most cases, the budget of local SLP projects is not sufficient to

Table 10.1: The main activities of the SLP

The project publicises the opportunity to join
- disadvantaged people meet the eligibility criteria
- interested and motivated people apply voluntarily
- those applicants are selected that meet the eligibility criteria
- the participants and the municipality conclude a contract to participate in the programme
- the participants receive the seeds or breeding animals from the local government

Training is organised
- identifying training needs among the participants (personalisation)
- participation in vocational training organised by the local government
- mentoring during the training process

The project provides continuous support
- professional support from the coordinator
- personal attention from the mayor/notary
- participation of experts in the support process (eg veterinarian, gardener)
- providing chemicals and animal foods if needed
- providing special services (eg soil preparation, sales organisation)

The participants execute the activities
- producing food and products
- participating in project meetings
- development of household economy

cover the costs of support services. The municipalities supplement the support and organise a significant part of the services from their own resources. One of the most reputable services is the training for participants. It is organised in every community as a 20-hour training session. Besides general farming know-how, the training also included household management knowledge. The meetings with the mentors also provided an opportunity to share their experience regarding production/farming or to ask questions from the 'inspectors'. In the case of livestock-oriented programmes, having a vet available was very helpful.

Cooperation between the local actors

In the implementation of the programme – except for a few instances – the mayor plays a key role, in many cases, being the one and only decision-maker. The Roma minority government participates in the programme's delivery as an individual applicant in the case of two municipalities (Katmár, Magyargéc), while in the other municipalities, it acts as a compulsory consortium partner. There are also civil organisations, such as Katymár Rainbow Island Children's House and Rozsály Municipality Welfare Service Local Foundation. These are not strictly speaking non-governmental organisations (NGOs) as either their founder or their operator is the local government or one of its key members. The municipalities have seen considerable progress with regard to civil society but these organisations are not directly involved in the SLP.

The results and impact of the SLP

Evaluation of the impact of the SLP in the eight communities that we studied was based on interviews with experts (10) and with beneficiaries (50), as well as a survey of 153 households. There was evidence of both direct impacts (on beneficiaries and their families) and indirect impacts (on the communities). Direct impacts were increased confidence, improved ability to plan ahead, positive role models within families and the acquisition of skills relevant for securing employment. *The development of confidence and better self-image* was achieved through pride in new agricultural skills. Participants explained that their gardens produced the most beautiful vegetables. Some even bought incubators in order to breed poultry stock by themselves (see Box 10.1). They were able to share the yield (mainly eggs and vegetables) with their neighbours and also their adult children who had moved from home. Those families that had been dependent on others now became the ones giving away their goods. This revival of reciprocity has transformed the roles of the programme's participants in their community. There was also evidence of *a change of the dimension of time*. According to experts and participants, a new ability to plan ahead is typically gained within two years. The requirements for self-sufficiency after that time will be the availability of resources that make it possible to buy feed, as well as the substances needed for cultivation (seeds, sprays, soil treatment products, etc). In the case of a family that does not have any income or reserves, this is sometimes exactly what makes or breaks the achievement of their goals. For families suffering from multigenerational unemployment, a significant result of the SLP was the *passing on of positive role models* to children through a shift from the acceptance of passive benefits to value creation and self-sufficiency. A significant advantage of the SLP – one that is rarely present in other integration programmes – is that it makes starting the *improvement of labour market skills* and 'becoming an employee' possible on various levels suited to the circumstances of the participants.

Box 10.1: Growing produce

Participants in the SLP expressed pride in their new ability to provide food through their own effort, as illustrated in the words of two mothers:

> "Well, this is definitely a great amount of help for me. What we have received, I will now sow. I have planted potatoes in half of my garden, so if it turns out to be successful, I can definitely store those till next spring." (Panyola, single woman with two children)

> "The yield will last until next May for me, and I have produced it." (Katymár, who has four children)

Community reporter stories indicate that people are empowered to cultivate their own land in order for it to provide for their families and sometimes for other people who live in the villages. Pálma describes how in the village of Homrogd, there are about 1,000 inhabitants and around 60% of them live in a disadvantaged situation. She relates how the local government combined the cultivation of people's own gardens with parts of the village's land. The crops produced as part of this cultivation are utilised by the families involved in the SLP, and also shared with the community via the school and other local institutions.

A strong sense of local ownership of the programme comes out from most of the stories. Zita describes how in the village of Jászladány, over 30 families received chickens and feed as part of the programme. They rear the chickens in their own homes, using them to produce eggs and also to eat. Imre talks about how the expertise of local people is used to maintain the agricultural activities. In his village, the local government do not have enough money to buy a second tractor, so they are using more traditional methods, that is, horses. This relies on the horsemanship skills of a Roma man who lives in the village. He takes care of the horses so that they can transport the goods to and from the fields.

The indirect impacts were positive changes in the community image, improved community cohesion and an element of self-sufficiency in the communities and a new 'mindset' of less dependency (Jász et al, 2003; Rácz 2013). *Changes in the community image* occurred because the environment looked much tidier after neglect, which had not only posed aesthetic issues in the past, but also potential problems regarding health and public safety. It had seemed impossible for individuals to escape this situation as when they had tried to participate in crop cultivation or livestock farming, people stole from them or their work turned out to be useless because of the pests. One of the indirect effects of the SLP programme that is often praised besides the improved appearance of the communities is the creation *of proper ownership* and an *increase in public security*. The *improvement of community cohesion* came about through barter, which makes it possible for participants to turn up at the community's 'market' with the goods that they have acquired or produced. In the case of barter, the values of compensation are not controlled, but agreed by the constant and mutual communication of the parties. This permanent 'reciprocity' and constant communication strengthens involvement in the community and contributes to the improvement of the community's cohesion (Polányi, 1944). The community-building power of the programme was especially important in those municipalities where the cultivation activity also supported the involvement and *integration of newcomers*. *A change of mindset* was associated with the immense activity, independence and problem-solving ability required from the participants following initial support from the SLP. This is counter to the paternalist approach quite common among disadvantaged communities, which was partly determined by forms of behaviour inherited from the socialist era, but also by the subsequent welfare system that had accustomed people to receiving passive benefits. The SLP has contributed significantly to the *improvement of the community's self-sufficiency*, even through the smallest element of the programme, the revival of horticulture. According to experts, no self-sustaining community can be based on this programme element alone. However, the revival of the production culture has created an excellent foundation for the development of new programme elements that are significant with regard to self-sufficiency and employability.

Conclusions

In Hungary, the public employment programme – having been introduced widely as a means of dealing with the impact of the crisis on employment – is being implemented more and more widely as a temporary income replacement (Csoba, 2010; Koncz, 2012; Fazekas and Neumann, 2014). The rate of transition to the open labour market is only around 10% (Csoba and Nagy, 2012; Cseres-Gergely and Molnár, 2015). This state public employment model, which has a gradually increasing budget, cannot be financed in the long run. This is why it would be of great significance to have welfare models that could become independent from the support of the state, and that advocate self-sufficiency and self-maintenance. The SLP is potentially an exemplar that can ideally combine activation with a high degree of self-sufficiency and long-term sustainability within the framework of household farming. Indeed, the SLP provides cheap and innovative solutions to support the highly disadvantaged target group. A cost-effectiveness evaluation shows that a minimal contribution is needed, and through the efforts of the beneficiary, which is a key point in achieving the desired project outcomes, financially measurable results are generated (Csoba and Sipos, 2016). However, the widening of the successful SLP faces a number of obstacles. The most significant problem is the lack of means of production, especially the lack of land. Most of the disadvantaged families do not have their own land or garden. In recent years, the local government has given them land for cultivation. However, the land-use legislation has been changed unfavourably to the programme in the last few years. The privatisation of state-owned land was further advocated through the establishment of a loan programme (which is beneficial for farmers) in government decree 1765/2015 (X. 16.), which also increased the area of land being privatised while, at the same time, decreasing the area of land available for community use and the chances to expand the SLP. This legislative change significantly restricts the scope of the programme.

Another obstacle for the further development of the SLP is the *lack of resources* in the involved municipalities. The amount of funds available for the SLP – despite the high need for such a programme and its efficiency having been proved by many impact assessments – has not increased significantly over the past 25 years. Moreover, there are elements of the social benefit system that hamper motivations to become self-sufficient and the extension of the land programme. Free mass catering for children is ensured by the 1 September 2015 modification of Act XXXI of 1997 on child protection and family guardianship administration. In the view of one expert: "they got used to it, they got used to eating for free a long time ago … they have never paid for it … not even as early as nursery school".

Despite the difficulties of the SLP in its 25 years, it has become 'an essential part of disadvantaged communities' social policy (Serafin, 2015). Within this framework, the organisers of the programme operate a permanent support system for the participants, allowing them to receive support for several years and ensuring the personalised development and social integration of Roma, 'strangers' and socially excluded people. In this way, the form and schedule of the social and labour market integration of the individuals concerned is adjusted for each individual's situation. The original purpose of the programme – to improve the quality of life – has been achieved. Our research on the programme also proved that in the case of the most peripheral groups, the usual forms of punishment and sanction that have been the dominant motivational tools in Hungary over the last few years are unproductive; only positive motivation can work efficiently among the most disadvantaged target groups. Small steps, little risks, minor successes, these are key to the motivational system of the SLP, building on a high level of social interaction, activation and empowerment.

References

Bakó, T., Cseres-Gergely, Zs., Kálmán, J., Molnár, Gy. and Szabó, T. (2014) *A munkaerőpiac peremén lévők és a költségvetés* [*People on the verge of the employment market and the budget*], Budapest: MTA, KRTK Közgazdaságtudományi Intézet.

Bartal, A. (2001) *A szociális földprogramok – avagy az aktív foglalkoztatás- és szociálpolitika alternatívái a rurális térségekben* [*Social land programmes – the alternatives of the active employment and social policy in rural areas*], Acta Civitalis, Budapest: Civitalis Egyesület.

Cseres-Gergely, Zs. and Molnár, Gy. (2015) 'Public works programmes in the public employment system, 2011–2013 – basic facts', in K. Fazekas and J. Varga (eds) *The Hungarian labour market 2015*, Budapest: Institute of Economics, Centre for Economic and Regional Studies, Hungarian Academy of Sciences, pp 86–100. Available at: http://econ.core.hu/file/download/HLM2015/23.pdf

Csoba, J. (2010) '"Job instead of income support": forms and specifics of public employment', *Review of Sociology of the Hungarian Sociological Association*, 6(2): 46–69.

Csoba, J. (2015) *Decent work: Full employment: Utopia or chance of the 21th century*, Bremen: Wiener Verlag für Sozialforschung.

Csoba, J. (2017) 'A kertkultúra és a háztartás gazdaság szerepe a vidéki szegények társadalmi integrációjában – 25 éves a Szociális Földprogram' ['The role of garden culture and the household economy in the social integration of rural poor – 25 years of Social Land Program'], *Tér és társadalom*, 31(3): 85–102.

Csoba, J. and Nagy, Z.É. (2012) 'The evaluation of training, wage subsidy and public works programs in Hungary', in K. Fazekas and G. Kézdi (eds) *The Hungarian labour market, 2012: In focus: The evaluation of active labour market programs*, Budapest: Research Centre for Economic and Regional Studies, Hungarian Academy of Sciences and National Employment Non-profit Public Company, pp 55–79.

Csoba, J. and Sipos, F. (2016) 'The Social Land Programme. D4.2 evaluation report', CoSIE project report, Debrecen.

EMET (Emberi Erőforrás Támogatáskezelő) (2016) 'Szociális Földprogram' ['Social Land Programme']. Available at: http://www.emet.gov.hu/hatter_1/szocialis_foldprogram/

EMMI (Emberi Erőforrások Minisztériuma Szociális és Társadalmi Felzárkózásért Felelős Államtitkárság) (2014) *Magyar Nemzeti Társadalmi Felzárkózási Stratégia II. Tartósan rászorulók – Szegény családban élő gyermekek – Romák (2011–2020)* [*National strategy for social inclusion II: Persons in long-term need – Children in Poverty – Roma people (2011–2020)*], Budapest. Available at: http://www.kormany.hu/download/1/9c/20000/Magyar%20NTFS%20II%20_2%20mell%20_NTFS%20II.pdf

Fazekas, K. and Neumann, L. (2014) *The Hungarian labour market 2014*, Budapest: Centre for Economic and Regional Studies, Hungarian Academy of Sciences and National Employment Non-profit Public Company Ltd. Available at: http://www.krtk.mta.hu/publications/THE-HUNGARIAN-LABOUR-MARKET-2014/74/

Fekete, É.G. and Lipták, K. (2014) 'Közfoglalkoztatásból szociális szövetkezet' ['Social cooperative from public employment'], in M. Lukovics and B. Ziti (eds) *A területi fejlődés dilemmái*, Szeged: Szegedi Tudományegyetem, Gazdaságtudományi Kar, pp 123–42. Available at: http://www.eco.u-szeged.hu/download.php?docID=40071

Jász, K. (2003) 'Társadalmi kirekesztettség a szociális földprogramok tükrében' ['Social exclusion in the light of social land programs'], in Szoboszlai, Zs. (ed) *Cigányok a szociális földprogramban*, Budapest: Gondolat, pp 79–96.

Jász, K. and Szarvák, T. (2005) 'Az esélyegyenlőségi politika Janus-arca' ['The Janus-faced equal opportunity policy'], *Politikatudományi Szemle*, 14(2): 135–55.

Jász, K., Szarvák, T. and Szoboszlai, Zs. (2003) 'A szociális földprogram vidékfejlesztési hatásai' ['The effects of Social Land Programmes on rural development'], in T. Kovács (ed) *A vidéki Magyarország az EU csatlakozás előtt*, VI. Falukonferencia, Magyar Tudományos Akadémia Regionális Kutatások Központja, Pécs, pp 471–8.

Kelen, A. (2012) 'A szociális gazdaság új fejleményei a mai vidéki Magyarországon' ['Recent developments of social economy in today's rural Hungary'], *Magyar Tudomány*, 173(12): 1459–70.

Koncz, K. (2012) 'A válság hatása a foglalkoztatottság és a munkanélküliség alakulására az Európai Unióban és Magyarországon' ['The effect of the crisis on employment and unemployment in the European Union and Hungary'], *Munkaügyi Szemle*, 55(4): 12–24.

Kovács, I. (1999) 'A modellkísérlettől a hálózatig' ['From model experiment to network'], *Hírlevél*, 1: 3–4.

László, Gy. (2015) 'A foglalkoztatáspolitika új paradigmáinak működése' ['The mechanism of the new paradigms of employment policy'], *Munkaügyi Szemle*, 58(3): 19–21.

Makay, Zs. and Blaskó, Zs. (2012) 'Családtámogatás, gyermeknevelés, munkavállalás' ['Family support, child raising and getting a job'], in P. Őri and Zs. Spéder (eds) *Demográfiai Portré 2012: Jelentés a magyar népesség helyzetéről*, Budapest: KSH Népességtudományi Kutatóintézet, pp 45–57.

Nagyné Varga, I. (2007) 'A szociális földprogramok, mint a szociális szövetkezet alapítás lehetséges bázisai' ['Social Land Programmes as potential bases of creating social cooperatives'], *Szövetkezés*, 28(1/2): 56–65.

Polányi, K. (1944) *The great transformation. The political and economic origins of our time*, Boston, MA: Beacon Press.

Rácz, K. (2009) 'Útban a szociális gazdaság felé? Beszámoló egy produktív szociálpolitikai program eddigi eredményeiről' ['On the way to a social economy? State-of-the-art report on the results of a productive social political program'], *Kapocs*, 8(3): 18–29.

Rácz, K. (2013) 'Szegénységkezelés aktív eszközökkel. Egy produktív szociálpolitikai program két évtizedes működésének tapasztalatai' ['Poverty management with active means. A productive social policy programme is two decades experiences of its operation'], in K. Kovács and M.M. Váradi (eds) *Hátrányban, vidéken*, Budapest: Argumentum Kiadó, pp 135–56.

Serafin, J. (2015) *Szociális Földprogram* [*Social Land Programme*], Budapest: Manuscript.

Szoboszlai, Zs. (1999) 'A szociális földprogramok hatékonysága' ['The effectiveness of Social Land Programmes'], *Esély*, 11(3): 26–44.

Szoboszlai, Zs. (2003) 'A szociális földprogram roma kedvezményezetteinek társadalmi jellemzői' ['Social characteristics of Roma beneficiaries of social land program'], in Zs. Szoboszlai (ed) *Cigányok a szociális földprogramban* [*Gypsies in the social land program*], Budapest: Gondolat Kiadó.

Tésits, R., Alpek, B.L. and Kun, A. (2015) 'Az új típusú szociális szövetkezetek területileg eltérő foglalkoztatási szerepe' ['The varying roles of the new type of social cooperatives in employment based on geographical location'], *Területi Statisztika*, 55(3): 254–272.

Váradi, M.M. (2015) 'Szegénység, projektek, közpolitikák' ['Poverty, projects and policies'], *Tér és Társadalom*, 29(1): 69–96.

Vida, A. and Vidra, Zs. (2015) '"Ez is segély, csak máshogy hívják" Helyi szegénypolitikák: segélyezési gyakorlatok és a közmunka' ['"This is also benefit, just called another name" – local poverty policy: benefit practices and public work'], in T. Virág (ed) *Törésvonalak: Szegénység és etnicitás vidéki terekben*, Budapest: Argumentum Kiadó, pp 68–89.

Referenced legal sources

Act III of 1993 'A szociális igazgatásról és szociális ellátásokról' ['On social administration and social benefits'].

Act CVI of 2011 'A közfoglalkoztatásról és a közfoglalkoztatáshoz kapcsolódó, valamint egyéb törvények módosításáról' ['On public employment and the modification of Acts related to public employment or other issues']. Available at: https://net.jogtar.hu/jr/gen/hjegy_doc.cgi?docid=a1100106.tv

Government decree 1765 of 2015 (X1. 10) 'A "Földet a gazdáknak!" Program keretében az állami tulajdonú földek földművesek részére történő értékesítéséhez szükséges intézkedésekről szóló 1666/2015. (IX. 21.) Korm. határozat és az MFB Földvásárlási Hitelprogram bevezetéséről szóló 1765/2015. (X. 16.) Korm. határozat módosításáról' ['On the modification of 1666/2015 (IX. 21.) government decree on the necessary provisions for the sale of state-owned lands to farmers in the framework of "Lands to the farmers" programme and the 1666/2015 government decree on the introduction of the MFB Land Purchase Loan Programme']. Available at: http://www.kozlonyok.hu/nkonline/MKPDF/hiteles/MK15168.pdf

Social Investment and the causes of energy poverty: are cooperatives a solution?

*Michael Willoughby, José Millet-Roig,
José Pedro García-Sabater and Aida Saez-Mas*

Introduction

This case study looks at the example of a local energy cooperative and its relationships with local authorities to provide a Theory of Change and sustainable solutions that might be transferred to other agents in the energy chain. The price of all commodities for households in Spain has undergone a dramatic rise, yet the price of electricity in particular, as compared to other wealthier nations, such as France or Germany, has been even more remarkable (see Figure 11.1).

An unemployment rate of around 20% has meant profound changes in Spanish households. Around 35% of under 25s not in full-time

Figure 11.1: Comparative evolution of net price of electricity (euros/kWh) in European Union countries

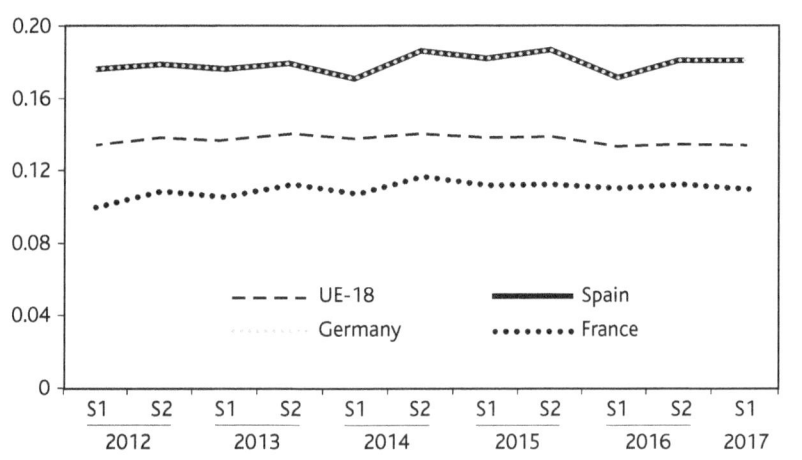

Source: Spanish Industry, Tourism and Digital Agenda Ministry (2017)

education were without work in mid-2017, which means that very few young Spanish people are able to live independently; they usually end up living with their parents and relying on them for all their basic needs, with the subsequent rise in costs for the household. The state, through a budget provided to local councils, provides benefits to people who run the risk of having their electricity supply cut off or who are liable for eviction from their property, both rented and owned. However, there is little evidence of state intervention in balancing the increasing polarisation of social well-being and crippling electricity prices (Bono, 2012). The so-called 'bono social' imposed on the large, controlling electric corporations, which took the form of subsidies for at-risk groups, has recently been rescinded. Not only that, but taxpayers will now be obliged to repay the estimated €188 million per year that the bono social provided to large families, pensioners and the unemployed, which consisted of a 25% reduction in their electricity bill.

The town halls in the bigger cities are beginning to launch new initiatives to attempt to tackle the root issues of energy poverty, such as poor housing conditions. Recent political swings in larger cities such as Madrid, Barcelona or Valencia have led to more of a focus on socio-economic issues despite austerity still being very much the order of the day, as well as widening gaps in the funding received by Spain's different regions. Unfortunately, the effects of the economic crisis are still fully visible and projects that look to install modern water heaters or better-insulated windows are isolated actions, due, in part, to budget restrictions as a result of austerity measures (Pavolini et al, 2015). Devolution of power to local councils may be high on the agenda in other European areas such as the UK (Richards and Smith, 2015), but in the case of Spain, there is already a high degree of devolved power through its 17 autonomous governments. The issue here is exactly how wealth is distributed and what the effect is for Social Investment initiatives under the strains of austerity measures that seem to affect some areas more than others. This, then, begs the question: to what extent is the government, at a regional or local level, investing in catering for the needs of those most at risk?

The Alginet Electric Cooperative

Within the atmosphere of general concern over rising levels of energy poverty shown by both the national and international experts that we interviewed for this case study, examples exist on a localised level that might point the way to potential solutions to energy poverty through

Image 11.1: The Alginet Electric Cooperative has been in existence since 1930

social innovation and investment, based, in part, on elements of public and private co-creation (Phimister et al, 2016). The region of Valencia in the east of Spain is home to some of the oldest and most established energy cooperatives in the country (Romero-Rubio and De Andres Díaz, 2016). The energy cooperative in the town of Alginet, which has a population of around 13,000, has become a reference point for social enterprise within the energy sector, both nationally and internationally. Due to the nature and mission of industry cooperatives and their inherent societal missions, they are close to the community and are able to engage in continuous dialogue with users.

As it says on its website, the Alginet Electric Cooperative, or CEA (Grup Cooperativa Elèctrica d'Alginet), has its origins back at the start of the 20th century, when electricity distribution had only one set criteria for installation, which was to be as profitable as possible. This meant that electricity only reached the major towns and industrial areas. However, in 1930, a group of businessmen from Alginet, with a registered capital of 150,000 pesetas (just over €900), paid for the line to bring electricity to the people and constituted the Alginet Electric Cooperative on 24 November 1930. The cooperative is a member of the Federation of Electric Cooperatives of Valencia. The registered name of the company is Suministros Especiales Alginetenses Coop V., and its offices are located in the centre of the town, a fact that does not seem noteworthy at first sight, but, in fact, lies at the heart of the Theory of Change proposed in this study.

The statutes of the cooperative declare that it is inspired by the cooperative values of self-help, self-responsibility, democracy, equality, equity and solidarity declared by the International Cooperative Alliance (see: http://ica.coop/es). Cooperative principles are the guidelines by which they implement those values, and they are as follows:

- voluntary and open membership;
- democratic management by the members;

- economic participation of the partners;
- autonomy and independence;
- education, training and information;
- cooperation among cooperatives; and
- interest in the community.

This list of intentions as to the role of cooperatives within the community, which may seem like any number of declarations found in statements of corporate social responsibility, is key to understanding how the cooperative model might help to form the Theory of Change for the energy sector.

Commitment to sustainable energy

European Union (EU) directives for countries to reach 20% of total production through renewable energies (European Commission, 2009) and a greater social awareness of the environmental benefits of renewable energies led to major changes in the source of energy sold by the cooperative. Even before this directive, the CEA had installed a small photovoltaic plant high up in the mountainous area of the town in 2006 as part of its commitment to a sustainable energy model. Currently, other solar power plants inject clean energy into the Alginet network for a total of 1200 kW/h. Such was the interest among its members in sourcing green energy that, since October 2015, 100% of the energy it supplies to the town comes from renewable sources (wind, sun and hydraulic power).

Social Investment by the Alginet cooperative in conjunction with the local administration

In a small town such as Alginet, without a lot of industry or investment in an autonomous community that has been particularly hit hard by the economic crisis (González et al, 2016), there are a sizeable number of families who are living at the limit of their economic possibilities. Such families are subsisting well below the stipulated €7,000 yearly income established by the regional government as the yardstick for those living in poverty. Part of the conversations undertaken with the senior management of the cooperative dealt with questions pertaining to the actions of the cooperative as regards social protection and how these are related to the actions of local government. Important lessons can be learnt that are applicable to all sections of society in creating models that are both economically viable and, more importantly in the context of an ongoing economic crisis, pay close attention to human needs.

The energy cooperative as food bank

The National Institute for Statistics (INE) carries out periodic surveys known as the Active Population Survey. According to recent data (SEPE, 2017), an estimated 1.5 million unemployed people in Spain receive no type of financial benefit whatsoever from the state. The consequences of these figures are potentially catastrophic and thus the role of the social economy is of utmost importance. The organisation of food supplies for the needy in Alginet is a perfect example of how the public administration, private entities from the social economy and third sectors can work together.

Within the town, there are three agents that act as providers of food supplies to people who are unable to pay the cost of their basic needs: the first is the town hall (Ajuntament d'Alginet); the second is the registered charity Cáritas, which is a confederation of Catholic relief, development and social service organisations operating in over 200 countries and territories worldwide; and the third is the CEA. Benefits provided by the town hall tend to be cyclical in order to share around the budget for providing food assistance, which means that people who rely on the town hall for basic nutritional needs will periodically have to turn to other sources for aid. Charities such as Cáritas do what they can but they are reliant upon resources that do not enjoy a constant flow. The cooperative of Alginet currently provides essential food supplies to around 90 families.

In a collaborative agreement reached with local shops, they provide those in need with food tokens that they can then cash in for a variety of foodstuffs. As with the price of electricity, they are able to negotiate the products in their shopping baskets to suit their needs at a given time if they have not used some of a particular product and want to substitute it for another. The advantage that the cooperative has over the other entities is that its income and resources are sustainable, and even growing. With 98% of households in the town as its members, and being a not-for-profit cooperative, it is able to plough resources back into the town and its citizens.

The impact of these measures is hard to gauge in monetary terms but the investment in social capital is sizeable for a cooperative the size of the CEA. The return on that investment is that they help to feed 90 families each month who would otherwise have little other choice but to relocate, and then with no guarantee of

Table 11.1: Distribution of the budget of the CEA for social initiatives

Recipient of financing from the CEA	Amount in euros
Donations to local charities and associations	83,000
Internet access (the cooperative provides subsidies for connection to the internet with an associated firm, Ago Telecommunications, to reduce the cost of internet access)	94,000
Tokens for food and school materials	189,000
Electricity rebates for the over 65s (every three months, the cooperative discounts €25 from the electricity bills of pensioners)	150,000

finding sustainable work. They also pay for the electricity of around 10 families who live in conditions of extreme poverty, a question that we go on to address.

Key findings and impact

In the first conversation we held with the president of the cooperative, he stated that: "As I told the Commission on Energy Poverty of the Parliament of Valencia, in Alginet, there is no energy poverty and while the cooperative still exists, there won't be any". Despite appearing to be a somewhat bold statement, there are data that back up this opinion. The success of the cooperative is based on its closeness to the community, and the fact that there is a real, human connection between the cooperative and the community. As in other sectors, such as retail, small businesses have to carve out a niche in comparison with large corporations who can sell goods at a lower cost or provide greater convenience by offering a wider range of products under one roof. A face-to-face relationship with customers is an essential element in tackling social problems, as this case exemplifies. The cooperative president went on to say: "Firstly, we need to attend to people as people. What is unacceptable is that someone in a desperate economic situation has to talk to someone they don't know, cannot see or, even worse, talk to a machine". A number of previous studies have looked at the effect of front-line service quality on consumers in other contexts (eg Andersson et al, 2016), but in the context of continued hardship, the challenges of maintaining front-line service quality are even greater. In cases where cooperative members are having difficulty in paying bills or are unaware of the options open to them, there is a person employed full-time whose responsibilities focus almost entirely on dealing with low-income families.

Financial investment by the CEA in the local community

As mentioned in the previous section, one major difference between the small cooperatives and the large corporations is the active role that they play at the heart of the community. They are not looking to make a profit in the same way as their giant counterparts. They need enough turnover to be self-sufficient and the rest is ploughed back in to reducing electricity bills and supporting local causes. The CEA helps to finance tokens for meals, school materials, cultural associations, sporting associations, charities, local events and pensioner electricity rebates, among other activities.

Most of the data gathered for the evaluation of the processes involved in the cooperative originate from in-depth guided interviews with managers and staff at the cooperative, triangulated with documents provided by members of the organisation. These guided interviews lasted over two hours and gave researchers an in-depth view of how the cooperative operates within the local community. We also designed a second questionnaire to guide conversations with consumers and members of the community in order to triangulate the information received from organisational members, based on some of the concepts contained in the Servqual model (Parasuraman et al, 1994).

Often, customer care on the part of large corporations involves a system of automatic options via recorded messages, and users may become overly frustrated with the process. The result is that after the two-month stipulated time allowed for the non-payment of bills, many homes are eventually without electricity, with the subsequent hardship that that entails for those living close to or under the poverty line. In order to reconnect to the grid, large electricity companies charge a minimum of €165, along with the demand to repay the accumulated debt. This may mean bills of over €500 for families with little or no resources. At the CEA, they attempt to avoid cutting the electricity supply at all costs.

According to managers of the CEA, before consumers are threatened with having their electricity supply cut off, there needs to be a process, a dialogue by which the needs of community members are expressed and each individual story is heard. They are aware that energy poverty and poverty in general cannot be solved by one action. Households now have three or four adults living in the home as children do not have the means to leave home when they are over 18. Some of them have no working members at all, while, as mentioned earlier, social benefit coverage is extremely low. First, the policy of the cooperative is to ensure fluid communication with its members. They attempt to ensure that cooperative members (consumers) know the names of all the employees, which creates an atmosphere of trust. Bearing this premise in mind, the process to avoid energy poverty for those using the CEA as their distributor and commercial agent is as follows: in many cases, there is some kind of income in the household, but the date of payment is not favourable to the dates on which they receive their income or benefit. The administrative staff ask customers to come into the cooperative's offices to work together to produce a timetable via which payment can be made. This means not only that the date of payment is flexible, but also how much the consumer pays at a given moment. For example, if they have a monthly bill of €60 that has been returned by the bank due to lack of funds, they can personally go to the offices of the cooperative and negotiate how much they will pay that month and establish a timetable for paying the rest. It is often the case that those who are unable to find employment have a low level of education, and also social skills. They therefore find it difficult to explain their situation to someone attending their call from the types of call centres used by large corporations.

Managers report that a large proportion of the problems related to payment are avoided using this simple method. One manager commented:

> "We are not reducing poverty in one go, we are stopping the downward spiral of someone whose electricity has been cut off and whose debts start to mount up for reconnection, etc. You are managing to keep them in the circuit; this could solve perhaps 50% of the payment problems we deal with."

Consumption is already reasonably low, which leaves little room to negotiate different behaviours on the part of the consumer, though this remains an integral part of the cooperative's policy. In cases where families have no available income and little or no benefit, the president of the cooperative deals personally with cases of more extreme poverty and negotiates with the consumer over how they can deal with the problem. He sits down with the customer to examine the energy consumption of the household with an extract of their typical consumption. Using the example of a family that consumes an average of 359 kw per month, he informs the house owner that consumption must be reduced to 250 kw per month and reduces the contracted power capacity to what might be an average of 4.75 to as low as 1.75 (for his account of negotiating with a customer, see Box 11.1).

Box 11.1: The president of the cooperative negotiates with a customer

"We ask if they have a water heater, an electric stove, washing machine or other household appliances. Certain appliances, such as fridges, we tend not to discuss as they cannot be economised, despite accounting for a large proportion of household energy consumption. We inform them their habits around the house need to change to save energy. If they put the water heater on, they can't use the oven or the washing machine, and are basically limited to using one of these types of appliance at a time. The consumption of electric light is extremely important, and people need to learn to be frugal with their use of electric light, only having lights on when they are really needed. Habits are hard to break, but when the choice is between having no electricity at all or reducing consumption, in our experience, everyone is capable of adapting. When we get consumption down to roughly half what they were previously consuming, we tell them that we will continue to closely monitor their electricity usage through dialogue and via our smart meters, but the cooperative will pay for their electricity. In other words, if they show that they are capable of reducing their consumption to a minimum, they will not be billed for the electricity they use."

The threshold set for each of these cases is dependent upon the individual situation of each user, taking into account factors such as the number of people in the household, household income and whether there are individual needs to cover, such as a disability:

> "We ask them to come in at the end of the month and again review the extract. We take a human approach to this process. We are an energy distributor and commercial agent but we are also an integral part of the community. We ask them how they have got along in the past month. We commonly hear people complain that they had used up their quota by the 24th or 25th of the month. We encourage them to keep trying to change their habits and often in the conversation we have at the end of the second month, they have kilowatts left to spare. It is a matter of education, dialogue and community."

The policy is drastic but effective. The person charged with dealing with customer payments told us:

> "Given the complexity of the Spanish electrical sector [see Costa-Campi, 2016], and its system of production,

distribution and commercialisation, the avenues left available for change are limited. Managers at the CEA indicate that the margin for lowering energy costs via reducing the actual costs of energy production are narrow. In the case of smaller producers, they need to make the necessary profit to keep their businesses afloat, and the cost of production depends greatly on how they produce the energy they put on the market."

If we go back to the original statement of the general manager of the CEA, "in Alginet, there is no energy poverty", we can use this statement as our starting goal and work towards a model whose concepts might be taken on board by the ruling bodies of the Ministry of Energy, or the large corporations. In the model illustrated in Figure 11.2, the last line of policies shows those currently carried out by the CEA.

The bottom line of the Theory of Change shows the policies and actions carried out by the energy cooperative, while the middle line shows the positive outcomes of these actions. The direction of the relationships between the concepts is shown by the arrows and how, potentially, they can lead not only to the eradication of energy poverty, but also to improvement in social awareness and of the needs of society in general. By humanising the types of service that people receive for basic commodities and providing policies and triggers for different courses of interaction, the cooperative model provides solutions that the state does not or cannot fulfil.

The way forward

The case of the CEA can be regarded as a standalone case of Social Investment on the part of a private enterprise, despite the fact that there is an element of collaborative effort towards social protection between a variety of institutions (local government, non-governmental organisations [NGOs] and the cooperative). Vandenbroucke et al (2011) argued that the Social Investment impetus was more essential than ever given current demographic trends, and examples such as the CEA make it patently obvious that this change cannot only come from the public sector.

As in other sectors in Spain, the Social Investment paradigm for the energy industry remains unclear. The major stakeholders appear to be functioning according to their own agendas, and there is no common goal that galvanises all the agents into any sort of joint

Figure 11.2: Theory of Change for the Spanish electric sector based on a cooperative model

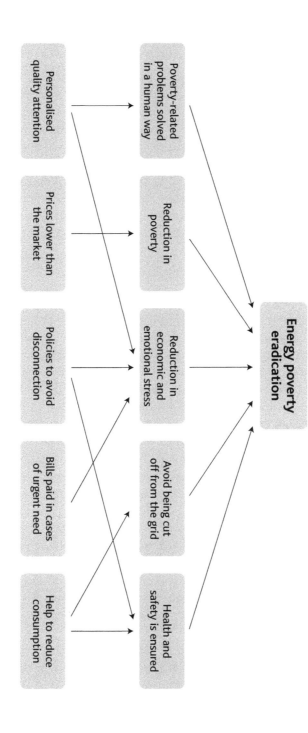

action. The result of this lack of coordinated effort is that in a society where the need for social protection is currently at its highest since the civil war, little or no investment is coming from the state. The majority of Social Investment energy-related actions are compensatory and do not generally provide a long-term solution, for example, if people are unable to pay their monthly energy bills due to long-term unemployment. Social protection initiatives tend to be led by local town halls and funded by regional government due to the three-tier system of government. Some experts reflect on the fact that the policymakers in central government are far removed from the needs of local communities (Navarro, 2006), and thus the policies needed to strengthen and embody the Social Investment paradigm are missing.

In the search for examples of Social Investment in the energy sector in Spain, it gradually became clear that the region of Valencia was home to some of the oldest and most established energy cooperatives in the country, and that if collaborative Social Investment was to be found anywhere, it would be with these institutions. The cooperative in Alginet has become a reference point for social enterprise within the energy sector, both nationally and internationally. Due to the nature and mission of industry cooperatives, they are close to the community and are able to engage in continuous dialogue with users. Some residents of the town of Alginet commented that going to the offices of the energy cooperative was like going to buy their bread at the local bakery: a natural act that forms a part of their daily lives precisely because the cooperative ensures that it actively participates in events that affect the lives of citizens.

Cooperative members all point to the personalised treatment that they receive from the customer care service in Alginet. In our interviews with consumers, 'I always have access to personalised help and advice on issues concerning electricity' received the largest number of maximum scores, indicating the added value of the human capital of the cooperative dedicated to customer care and, in this case, to advising consumers on how to reduce their energy consumption and determining ways of meeting costs that are workable for the customer. In the same vein is 'Employees at the cooperative show willingness in solving my problems'. Members of the cooperative feel assured that, whatever their circumstances, they will have the opportunity to explain their situation and that their voices will be heard. They feel safe in the knowledge that employees will take the necessary action to find a rapid solution to any economic or organisational difficulties that they encounter. Lessons can be learnt here by large corporations who provide the great majority of electricity directly to the consumer. With great business in terms of public services comes great responsibility, and the human factor seems to be largely forgotten in a public service area that, under the right conditions and management, can respond adequately to the needs of consumers.

In cases of long-term unemployment or poverty, where all possibilities of benefit coverage have been exhausted, one clear message comes from the users: the feeling that they are just another number among the millions who need the help of social services leads to increased frustration, and even to depression in some cases (for stories from Innovative Social Investment: Strengthening Communities in Europe (InnoSI) project interviewees on employment and poverty, see: www.communityreporter.net). It could be argued that for the larger corporations, such a personalised relationship with their customers is simply unattainable. If we look again at Alginet, a town with a population of 13,600 people is served by one office, and at least one member of 98% of all households in the town is a member of the cooperative and has regular contact with the organisation. As suggested by the president of the CEA, for the large electric companies with a yearly turnover of more than €16,000,000,000, face-to-face attention for a number of clients, for example, with one front-line service employee per 10,000 inhabitants in the areas where they have a distribution monopoly, would be a start in improving human relationships. Building human relationships takes time, but there needs to be a starting point. Dealing with issues of poverty and the related stress of having electricity cut off, with the subsequent high costs of reconnection, are symptoms of the desperate situation of many left in the wake of the economic crisis, and a change in the humanistic values of the large corporations would be welcome if the example of this energy cooperative and others like it can be used as a yardstick.

Even in this case, there are clear examples where improvement in collaboration between the social economy and the public administration is necessary. The case of Cáritas and the CEA providing food to those who can no longer be covered by the scheme in place at the town hall is more a case of social innovation to plug a gap not filled by state-run organisations. Under limited budgets, politicians say that their hands are tied and that they wish they were able to provide security to all those at risk. Managers at the CEA admitted that more could be done to improve relations with the local government despite the joint intervention in social protection. Co-creation and a cooperative model, under the correct circumstances and the right method, might provide some answers that have been lacking on the provision of energy services in Spain and around Europe.

References

Andersson, P.K., Gustaffson, A., Kristensson, P. and Wastlund, E. (2016) 'The effect of frontline employees' personal self-disclosure on consumers' encounter experience', *Journal of Retailing and Consumer Services*, 30: 40–9.

Bono, E. (2012) 'El decrecimiento sostenible, crisis ecológico-económica, desigualdad y economía social, CIRIEC-España', *Revista de Economía Pública, Social y Cooperativa*, 76: 181–96.

Costa-Campi, M.T. (2016) 'Evolución del sector eléctrico español', ICE La economía española en el reinado de Juan Carlos I March–June, No. 889–890.

European Commission (2009) 'Directive 2009/28/EC of the European Parliament and the Council of 23 April 2009 on the promotion of the use of energy from renewable sources and amending and subsequently repealing Directives 2001/77/EC and 2003/30/EC'.

González, E., Cárcaba, A. and Ventura, J. (2016) 'Weight constrained DEA measurement of the quality of life in Spanish municipalities in 2011', *Journal of Social Indicators Research*. Available at: https://doi.org/10.1007/s11205-016-1426-y (accessed 27 November 2016).

Navarro, V. (2006) *El subdesarrollo social de España. Causas y consecuencias*, Barcelona: Anagrama.

Parasuraman, A., Zeithaml, V. and Berry, L. (1994) 'Reassessment of expectations as a comparison standard in measuring service quality: implications for future research', *Journal of Marketing*, 58(2): 6–17.

Pavolini, E., León, M. and Guillén, A. (2015) 'Welfare rescaling in Italy and Spain: political strategies to deal with harsh austerity', *Comparative European Politics*, 13: 56.

Phimister, E., Vera-Toscano, E. and Roberts, D. (2016) 'The dynamics of energy poverty. Evidence from Spain', *Economics of Energy and Environmental Policy*, 4(1): 153–66.

Richards, D. and Smith, M.J. (2015) 'Devolution in England, the British political tradition and the absence of consultation: consensus and consideration', *Representation*, 51(4): 385–401.

Romero-Rubio, C. and De Andres Díaz, J.R. (2016) 'Sustainable energy communities: a study contrasting Spain and Germany', *Energy Policy*, 85(10): 397–409.

SEPE (Servicio Público de Empleo Estatal) (2017) 'State employment service statistics on benefit coverage'. Available at: http://www.sepe.es/contenidos/que_es_el_sepe/estadisticas/datos_estadisticos/prestaciones/tasa-cobertura-prestaciones.html (accessed 30 December 2017).

Spanish Ministry for Energy, Tourism and the Digital Agenda (2017) 'Net price of electricity for domestic use across the EU'. Available at: http://www.minetad.gob.es/es-ES/IndicadoresyEstadisticas/DatosEstadisticos/IV.%20Energ%C3%ADa%20y%20emisiones/IV_12.pdf (accessed 29 December 2017).

Vandenbroucke, F., Hemerijck, A. and Palier, B. (2011) *The EU needs a social investment pact*, OSE Opinion Paper No. 5, Bruxelles: European Social Observatory.

TWELVE

Social Investment in theory and praxis: a 'quiet revolution' in innovative local services?

Andrea Bassi, Susan Baines, Judit Csoba and Flórián Sipos

Introduction

This book has presented empirical evidence from in-depth, evaluative case studies in 10 European countries. In this concluding chapter, we highlight outstanding themes from the case studies and then go on to put forward a few implications of this research, intended to inform experts, stakeholders and interested readers. Nearly two decades ago, Esping-Anderson and colleagues (2002) made a case for a new welfare state that in the face of heightening uncertainties, would adopt a generational life-course logic. An emerging Social Investment paradigm became widely acknowledged, informed European Union (EU) policy (European Commission, 2013) and became influential worldwide (Deeming and Smyth, 2017). There is now a shared understanding in scholarship and policy of a Social Investment paradigm, albeit sometimes more in the form of 'engaged discord' (Hemerijck, 2017: 5) than thoroughgoing consensus.

We begin this chapter by reminding the reader (traveller) of the main stopovers that we took them to visit in this book. It has been a daring journey across 10 European countries (from south to north and from west to east) in order to see social innovation initiatives in the Social Investment policy framework. Thematically, we followed, in turn, the policy domains of early interventions in the life course, active labour markets and social solidarity. Cases were selected because, based on initial understandings of the vision of the projects and programmes, they fitted the Social Investment paradigm and literature, and because there was some evidence of innovation. Most importantly, there was the opportunity for learning.

We started in the north-east part of Italy, in a geographic area that goes from the Apennines mountain chain to the Adriatic seaside, visiting the city of Bologna and the small towns of Serramazzoni and Comacchio. In each of those places, we saw examples of innovation and good practice in Early Childhood Education and Care (ECEC). Then, we moved north-west to Greater Manchester in England, where we learned about the local implementation of a national programme intended to turn around the lives of families with multiple problems. After this, we went north-east to the city of Gothenburg in Sweden and gained insight from an innovative form of collaborative partnership to address the urgent challenges of integrating immigrant children who arrive in Sweden without parents. Turning to active labour markets, we moved eastwards to Turku in Finland, where we learned about how multi-agency One-Stop Guidance Centres contribute to the reduction of youth unemployment and the empowerment of young adults. Then, we took a long trip to the very south of Europe in order to analyse an integrated intervention in Greece for addressing the issue of youth unemployment. In the central part of Europe, we saw the successful labour market integration of refugees and asylum seekers in the city of Münster in Germany, and innovative support for homeless people seeking work in Wroclaw, Poland. Finally, we visited examples of Social Investment with an emphasis of social solidarity. In the Netherlands, we saw the Green Sticht, a socially mixed neighbourhood in the Utrecht new town extension of Leidsche Rijn. We went eastwards to Hungary to analyse the Social Land Programme, supporting poor households in rural areas to acquire competences in household agriculture. We concluded our journey in the south-east part of Spain to look at an energy cooperative in the small town of Alginet.

Following this introduction, we examine the 'quiet revolution' (Hemerijck, 2015) of Social Investment visible in the case studies along each of the following dimensions (adapted from Evers and Brandsen, 2016): governance; ways of addressing service users; ways of working and of financing; social justice; and, finally, nurturing, sustaining and expanding social innovations. *New forms of governance* is about the changing roles and responsibilities of different actors, highlighting new forms of cooperation and networks, and also considering the interaction of national and sub-national levels. *Ways of addressing service users* mainly relates to social capital, personalisation and co-creation. *Ways of working* involves some revision of professional roles but – much more prominently – the 'substantive economy' as a significant resource. *New ways of financial resourcing* were uncommon in the case studies but some examples are discussed. *Social justice* is shown to be a main driver for some participants. The final section brings these themes together to revisit models of *social innovation* in order to reflect on what can be learned from the case studies about nurturing, sustaining and expanding social innovations in the context of Social Investment.

New forms of governance

Claims to innovation in the Innovative Social Investment: Strengthening Communities in Europe (InnoSI) case studies almost always invoked new participants, and new combinations of participants, entering into unfamiliar interactions and relationships. Theories of Change identified social challenges as too big and complex for one agency, and that users' needs do not conform to professional and organisational boundaries. Troubled Families in Greater Manchester, UK (Chapter Three), and the Youth Guarantee in Finland (Chapter Five) established new ways of inter-working mainly across different professional fields in public services that had tended to work in separate silos, helping to achieve a more effective and efficient operation on a local level. More complex, cross-sectoral partnerships, collaborations and networks demonstrated some success at achieving 'collaborative advantage' (Huxham, 2003; Huxham and Vangen, 2013) to meet common Social Investment aims.

In case after case, there were examples of the redistribution of implementation roles, often expanding the importance of social economy actors. MAMBA in Germany, for example, brought new opportunities through the coming together of five organisations with divergent goals and priorities, which ranged from the championing of refugee rights to resolving skill shortages in the craft sector (Chapter Seven). In MAMBA, new services were devised and delivered with input from the public, social economy and private sectors, as was also the case with early years services in Emilia-Romagna in Italy (Chapter Two). In Gothenburg, Sweden, on the other hand, only the public and social economy sectors were involved (Chapter Four). In that city, an entirely new way of partnering between a local authority and non-profits was created, superseding established models of grant giving and contracting. In Wroclaw, Poland, the leading role taken by a social-economy organisation was, in itself, innovative (Chapter Eight).

Multi-organisational and cross-sectoral activity in InnoSI comprises various configurations, ranging from entirely informal cooperation (eg between a social-economy organisation, businesses and public services in Wroclaw, Poland) to formally constituted partnerships (partnerships between idea-based and public organisations, as in Sweden) and integrated services (Troubled Families in Greater Manchester, UK). These 'innovations in governance' have in common that they are conceived and implemented above the level of a single agency, and are able to tap into new resources (Moore and Hartley, 2008; Hartley, 2015). Examples of how such innovations in governance successfully accessed new resources include:

- securing opportunities for building human capital through real work experience in 'Assistance from A to Z' in Poland;
- the pooling of funds in partnerships between idea-based and public organisations in Sweden;
- operating shared services in the Youth Guarantee in Finland; and
- the exchange of information and databases in Troubled Families in the UK.

Social-economy groups are mainly engaged in delivery in InnoSI case studies but some try to step up to influence policy. This was so in MAMBA in Germany, where in addition to case-based work, the network members undertake awareness-raising to sensitise the public, officials and employers to the precarious situation of refugees. In the partnership for supporting young migrants in Sweden, non-profit leaders told evaluators that they have gained greater abilities to influence local policy though the partnership with the local government.

In some countries in which research for this book was undertaken, notably, Italy, Spain and Germany, the role of regions is very pronounced. In other countries with more unitary national welfare traditions (the Netherlands, Finland and the UK), there has been a recent transfer of national responsibilities to sub-national levels. An increasing role for local-level institutions is illustrated in the Youth Guarantee in Finland, where there was new freedom for municipalities to organise services for younger people not in employment, education or training. The programme framework, however, was created on the national level and operated within national regulations. Troubled Families is a national programme funded by central government across England but local authorities are expected to deliver it in accordance with local conditions. The recent devolution deal with Greater Manchester has made it part of a broader programme of public service reform within that subregion, and the national policy agenda seemed largely irrelevant in the boroughs of Greater Manchester (Chapter Three). The Green Sticht in the Netherlands (Chapter Ten) and 'Assistance from A to Z' in Poland (Chapter Eight) involved the local, context-specific reorganisation of services and supporting networks for vulnerable people. A rather different dynamic was present in the

Social Land Programme in Hungary (Chapter Nine), where it was low financial investment by central government that forced innovative elements on the local level. National policy and regulation were prominent in the case study for combating youth unemployment in Greece (Chapter Six). A national aim of reducing structural obstacles in migrant policy was significant in MAMBA in Germany. Although innovative features of MAMBA include services designed and carried out locally, the form and many features of the programme were determined nationally and its future is vulnerable to political change at the national level.

New ways of working: professional change and the 'substantive economy'

Innovations in governance and ways of combining services result in changing demands on front-line service staff. Professionals in more integrated services may be required to relocate to new workplaces, where they are situated alongside others from different occupations and agencies while still employed by their original organisations, as was the case for workers in the Finnish One-Stop Guidance Centres for young people. Some entirely new professional roles have been created. In the Troubled Families programme in Greater Manchester, as a result of service integration, case workers now operate across long-established professional and service boundaries. Such service integration can make employees worried about their professional identities and the continuation of their jobs, as we heard in Greater Manchester. A different kind of new work role is that of the 'accompanist' supporting unemployed homeless people in Poland. 'Accompanist' is a part-time paid role and most of the post-holders take it on in addition to their existing jobs, which are often in services for homeless people. Research for this case study revealed that many accompanists put in much more work than they are paid for, making this a partially volunteer role.

The most dramatic changes in ways of working encountered in the case studies in this book were not new roles for professional workers; rather, they were in the wide variety of unpaid work that supported the programmes and sometimes made them possible. In the previous section under governance, we discussed how social-economy organisations made an important and distinctive contribution to new forms of collaboration and partnership with public agencies, sometimes also alongside private sector involvement. InnoSI cases involved many different kinds of social-economy organisations, including international non-governmental organisations (NGOs), social enterprises, local activists and faith groups. None of this was surprising as InnoSI set out with an interest in the social economy and expectations that it would be active in the implementation of Social Investment. Rather less anticipated was the extent to which this was only one aspect of the ways in which the wider 'substantive economy' was deeply embedded in local Social Investment initiatives.

Polányi (1976) is a reference point for the substantive economy (see Table 1.2 in Chapter One). Gibson-Graham (2006: 59–60) has more recently taken on the challenge of 'widening the identity of the economy to include all those practices excluded by a strong theory of capitalism'. To do this, the image of an iceberg is used. At the tip of the iceberg are the activities usually regarded as 'the economy', waged labour, market exchange and for-profit enterprise. Below the surface lie all the other practices by which people produce, exchange and distribute value – those characterised in the 'substantive economy'. These practices include volunteering, mutual aid, self-provisioning, care-giving and community activism, all of which have a strong presence in the chapters of this book. Indeed, in some cases, non-financial inputs (mainly unpaid work on the part of citizens) are essential to make Social Investment initiatives viable.

Volunteering is present particularly when social-economy partners are able to access local traditions of giving time to others. This is the case, for example, in Münster, Germany, where many long-established Catholic and Protestant institutions are active in helping refugees. Although involving volunteers is characteristic of many social-economy organisations, not all do so and social economy and volunteering should not be conflated. One of the non-profit partners in the partnerships between idea-based and public organisations in Sweden did not normally use volunteers, but called upon retired members of staff to meet the partnership's needs for skilled counsellors. There are many reasons for volunteering. Religious faith can be a strong factor for volunteering to help people perceived as unfortunate, for example, supporting refugees in Münster and homeless people in Wroclow. Other groups of unpaid workers, in contrast, are united around a shared interest, as was the case with the mothers who worked together to create new facilities for their children in a small town in Emilia-Romagna, Italy. This is in the tradition of self-help and mutual aid, which is distinct from volunteering as a form of philanthropy directed towards people seen as 'other' (Hardill and Baines, 2011). It reflects the distinction between horizontal solidarity and charity previously discussed in the introduction to Part C.

Ways of financing

There is an overall lack of innovation in the financing of the Social Investment programmes reported in this book. Most are financed wholly or mainly through public sources from national government and/or the EU. The continuation of the initiatives dependent on fixed-term funding streams from these sources is always insecure. There are also a few elements of financial input from the private and charitable sectors. Mixed sources of funding were preferred by some innovators. The founders of the Green Sticht, for example, were determined to avoid over-dependence on public funds because of the uncertainty it entails. They secured finance from a social housing corporation and a loan from an international foundation, in addition to a contribution from local government and a European Structural Fund grant.

Although Social Investment is intended to generate future benefits and outcomes, there is very limited focus in the case studies on understanding or demonstrating the return on investment generated through the financing of these programmes. In this respect, the use of Payment by Results (PbR) in the UK stood out as exceptional because payments to a provider (in the case of Troubled Families, a local authority) are partly dependent on documenting the achievement of specified outcomes. The outcomes-based funding model of Troubled Families is just one of many versions of PbR mechanisms that have been trialled in the UK and elsewhere (Albertson et al, 2018). Unlike some other PbR schemes, it does not involve incentivising private providers and it is certainly not a fully fledged implementation of risk transfer from the public to the private sector (Warner, 2013).

Throughout the cases reported in this book, financial constraints on local government were stressed by decision-makers and front-line workers. InnoSI case studies offer some small-scale instances of ways to activate new resources. The Green Sticht has become financially self-reliant. The Foundation owns the real estate and generates income by renting out rooms in the residential/working community. In addition, it operates social enterprises on site: a restaurant, a furniture workshop, a thrift store and catering for neighbourhood festivities. In Hungary, some 'entrepreneurial municipalities' involved in the Social Land Programme are using socially produced goods (pasta, jam, garlic, paprika powder) to generate income and/or to provide resources for the community. The case of Alginet Electric Cooperative in Spain (Chapter Eleven) stands out as a successful initiative that has achieved the Social Investment goals of long-term welfare improvement (combating fuel poverty) and citizen activation without any form of state funding.

Ways of addressing service users: personalisation, co-creation and social capital

Personalisation

Overall, the interventions covered in this book were person-centred in ways that reflect an active welfare paradigm and the principle of 'preparing' rather than 'repairing'. This is consistent with the demands of user-led organisations, academics, policymakers and advocacy groups for a way of thinking about social interventions that rejects standardised services (Jenson, 2012; Künzel, 2012; Prandini, 2018). At its simplest, personalisation means that public services respond to the needs of individuals rather than offering standardised solutions said to be typical of welfare bureaucracies (Needham, 2011). In the labour market activation programmes reported in Part B, in particular, local decision-makers and service providers invariably articulate a stark distinction with 'one-size-fits-all' interventions that have failed in the past. In their Theories of Change, they identify the dysfunction of overly specialised systems that consist of many branches and 'silos', and the need to make up for missing services and institutions, for example, 'tailored, participant-focused measures' are a central element of MAMBA in Germany.

Deeper personalisation implies the active involvement of service users in reciprocal relationships with providers, for example, the ethos of the Youth Guarantee (Finland) is to not only work with young people as individuals and respond to their needs, but also involve them in shaping their own services. In Emilia-Romagna, new early childhood services were developed to respond to specific local contexts but with more emphasis on community participation and empowerment than individual service users as 'customers'. In Valencia, Spain, the energy cooperative delivers services in a personalised way that larger energy providers do not. It does this through its visible presence within the community and through intensive work with those unable to pay bills to reduce their energy usage, raising their awareness of consumption and empowering them to control that aspect of their lives in the longer term. More radical, however, is the relationship between provider and consumer inherent in the cooperative membership model built on principles of solidarity (Ridley-Duff and Bull, 2016).

Co-creation

The turn to personalisation in welfare has been criticised for a lack of focus upon relationships, community life and responsibilities (Fox, 2012; Prandini, 2018). Co-creation has much in common with deep personalisation in emphasising the capacities and knowledge of people who receive services. It goes further in locating them as creators of value in conjunction with service providers (Alves, 2013). In co-creation, people who use services work with professionals to design, create and deliver them (Social Care Institute for Excellence, 2015). It overlaps with the notion of co-production, which has the more limited meaning of service users taking on some of the work done by practitioners (Social Care Institute for Excellence, 2015). Both are present, for example, in the Green Sticht community in the Netherlands. The accommodation is managed directly by residents with some support from professional staff (co-production). Formerly homeless people were involved from the beginning in the development of the Green Sticht and currently participate in decision-making about the direction of the Foundation (co-creation). 'Co-creation' in public services implies profound changes in relationships between the state and the individual. Producer and consumer roles, in particular, blur and overlap. These are changes that invariably heighten the importance of the substantive economy previously discussed.

Co-creation was not part of some of the personalised interventions covered in this book where there were very widely different power positions, as was the case in 'Assistance from A to Z' in Poland, and where paternalistic elements are dominant in the country's welfare models, as in Hungary. Perceived lack of skills and motivation of intended beneficiaries can make co-creation challenging but not impossible. Following the logics of empowerment and democracy close to their hearts, social-economy partners in the programme for welcoming young unaccompanied minors in Sweden were clear from the outset that they wanted to include the young people themselves in planning joint activities. For this purpose, they formed a reference group to represent their views but there was some self-criticism within the partnership that they did not manage to involve the young people enough. The partnership learned lessons from low uptake of the first set of work experience services they offered and devoted more time to involving the reference group in further developing those services.

Social capital

Social capital materialises in the structure of relationships between actors, and stimulates individual action (Coleman, 1988). The target groups of the interventions in this book were typically said by professionals and decision-makers to be characterised by a narrow scope of relationships and mainly passive behaviour. Extending and enriching their connections was seen as an effective means to improve their social status and to activate them. By involving local employers in providing work experience, 'Assistance from A to Z', for example, helped homeless people to establish new contacts, acquaintances and even friendships. An additional value not originally anticipated was changing the attitudes of people employed in those workplaces by breaking down their stereotypes of homeless people.

Some interventions, especially but not only regarding solidarity (Part C of this book), explicitly aim to improve communities through advancing social capital (Putnam, 2000). There is evidence of some success in this, with notable examples of initiatives where enhanced social capital helps to strengthen aspects of the public sphere. In Hungary, the exchange of goods and services by barter encouraged by the Social Land Programme strengthens involvement in the community and contributes to reducing tension between locals and 'outsiders', who are mainly poor Roma people relocated from cities. The Green Sticht in Utrecht (the Netherlands) has built trust not only within the community itself, but also between the formerly homeless, vulnerable residents and other workers and residents in the neighbourhood. The early childhood centre in the small Italian town of Comacchio offers a space where people of different generations, ethnicity, religions and cultures can meet in a safe and controlled environment.

Social justice

Social justice is one the sharpest points of contention in debates about Social Investment, especially in relation to activation. The primary goal of activation that has been increasingly used since the 1990s is to encourage and support the re-entry of the unemployed and other non-working, inactive groups into the labour market. The instruments used include a variety of solutions providing stronger incentives for work, as well as the widespread application of services supporting job search and employment (Bonoli, 2010). As the most influential theorist of activation policy, Giddens (1998) adopted the philosophy of activation from the Danish labour market policy model from the early 1990s and made it one of the central elements of the socially investive state. The idea of 'no rights without obligations' became one of the defining slogans of welfare policy at the turn of the millennium. The fiscal crisis of 2008 gave fresh impetus to activation policies with the main aims of ensuring budgetary balance, to increase the responsibility of citizens in securing their own livelihood and to reduce dependence on welfare. The emphasis in Social Investment on the productive function of social policy and an overly narrow interpretation of activation can be seen as subordinating social justice goals to economic ones (Smyth and Deeming, 2016). For advocates of Social Investment, the life-course perspective is inherently supportive of social justice because most people will be vulnerable at some point in their lives (Hemerijck, 2017).

At national and international levels, economic justifications of Social Investment reform agendas appear to weigh more heavily than societal ones. This was confirmed in expert national interviews undertaken for InnoSI (Barnett et al, 2016). The case studies paint a very different picture at the local level. This is partly explained by the involvement of value-driven social-economy organisations. Social justice rather than economic efficiency is typically their motivation, as we saw, for example, in MAMBA in Germany, ECEC services in Italy, the Green Sticht in the Netherlands and partnerships between idea-based and public organisations in Sweden. In Hungary, where the social economy is weaker, it was local elected representatives responsible for implementing the Social Land Programme who questioned national policies prioritising labour market outcomes over more social ones. This street-level view of Social Investment in practice is consistent with recent scholarly perspectives on it as a tool to enhance human capabilities and social justice, and not only to increase productivity (Bonvin and Laruffa, 2017; Morel and Palme, 2017).

Nurturing, sustaining and expanding innovations for Social Investment

Empirical evidence about the characteristics of social innovations in welfare across Europe highlights non-standard answers to non-standard risks, as well as vulnerabilities associated with transitions through the life course, and people's strengths and assets (Ewert and Evers, 2014). All these resonate strongly with the claims of Social Investment. Emphasis on the active welfare user in the Social Investment paradigm is consistent with the importance now given in innovation studies to ways to bridge the gap between designers and users (see Voorberg et al, 2015). Concepts of co-production and co-creation in public services are inspired by business practices mainly in technological innovation, such as 'design in use' (McLoughlin et al, 2012) and 'user-led innovation' (Von Hippel, 2005). Bonvin and Laruffa (2017) draw upon a very different set of ideas from the anthropological foundation of the capability approach (Sen, 2001) to articulate three central anthropological dimensions: human beings as 'receivers', 'doers' and 'judges'. Receiver and doer dimensions broadly relate, respectively, to being a beneficiary of material and social support, and to active participation in work (understood as including but not limited to joining the labour market). Very importantly, these are complemented by the 'judge' dimension, which 'refers to the fact that human beings are able to say what has value in their eyes and that this should be taken into account when designing policies aimed at enhancing their capabilities' (Bonvin and Laruffa, 2017: 8). They do not actually use the terms 'co-production' and 'co-creation', but nevertheless offer a rich language for expressing recognition of the legitimate knowledge of service beneficiaries and the need to create spaces for their participation, and that of collective entities representing them, in service innovations.

In the analysis of Westley and Antadze (2010), social innovation occurs in the domains of 'resources, routines, authority flows, and beliefs'. The Social Innovation Compass (Bassi, 2011) starts from this categorisation, cross-referencing it with the reflections of Hochgerner (2011) who, drawing on Parsons (1971), proposes four key labels to classify social innovations in terms of new combinations of social practices. These are 'roles', 'relations', 'norms' and 'values' (Hochgerner, 2011). The Compass is structured around four main dimensions of social innovation: 'resources' (material, human and financial), 'authority flows', 'routines' and 'beliefs, values and conceptual frameworks'. These four domains are presented graphically as the Social Innovation Compass in Chapter Two (see Figure 2.1) and discussed in relation to the ECEC services in Emilia-Romagna, Italy.

The 'Compass' framework allows us to analyse the influences of and interactions between new elements of social practices. There is evidence that social innovations are more effective (and sustainable) when they activate processes of change in all the four dimension of the Compass (Bassi, 2011; see also Chapter Two). Social innovations supporting Social Investment reforms may be initiated at the local level, often in the social economy and driven forward by 'social entrepreneurs' who identify unmet needs and assemble resources. Social entrepreneurs who do this are typically not 'heroic' individuals, as Amin (2009) has noted from earlier studies of the social economy. The charismatic figure of Ab Harrewijn, who inspired the Green Sticht and died 2002, is exceptional in this book. The social entrepreneurs we encountered were groups such as the mothers who initiated new childcare in Emilia-Romagna and front-line professionals in non-profits working with unaccompanied migrant children in Gothenburg, Sweden. The idea of routines is often used to explain resistance to change. To explore how change in routines comes about, Westley and Antadze (2010) refer to 'institutional entrepreneurs', who pursue and achieve change in the established institutional logics of services or professions (Battilana et al, 2009). Again, these change agents may not be individuals. An example from this book is the new ways of configuring mixed housing projects that are emerging in the Netherlands with the influence of the various partner organisations in the Green Sticht.

Case-study evidence suggests that systematic change usually needs sponsors from the political level and continuity in the form of public funding (authority flows). Significant actors may be local 'policy entrepreneurs', who devote time and effort to promoting a particular solution to an apparently intractable problem. The mission-driven non-profit leaders and municipal administrators who together promoted the partnership for working with immigrant minors took on this role in Sweden, where their innovative model has inspired new partnerships. There are opportunities for social innovations to be mainstreamed when a crucial role is played by agencies of the public administration, as in the Italian case of ECEC services. This does not always happen, as we saw in MAMBA in Germany, for example, where the achievements of the local network are vulnerable to changes at the political level. As a counter-example, the Spanish energy cooperatives demonstrate one way in which the social economy can help to shape the future of welfare in the absence of state funding and in the face of national policies that are not well aligned.

Influence on 'beliefs, values and conceptual frameworks' is something that social organisations often aspire to. For this reason, it is important to them not to be mere deliverers of local welfare programmes, but to try to bring about change through wider education and lobbying activities. This is much more daunting than other levels of innovation. An outstanding example is the case of Comacchio in Emilia-Romagna, where a long-standing lack of attention to early childhood education was turned around by the successful interaction of international, national, regional and local actors. There were also some achievements in challenging attitudes to homeless people in Utrecht and Wroclaw, and to Roma in rural villages of Hungary.

Policy implications

The body of new evidence from the InnoSI case studies reported in this book has begun to incorporate social innovations into debate surrounding a 'Social Investment state', and to push them towards reflection on sub-national contexts (Ewart and Evers, 2014). In particular, it has foregrounded the importance of the social economy and, rather less predictably, the much wider 'substantive' economy. It is perhaps something of a paradox that Social Investment (with its emphasis on labour markets) relies, in practice, on so much non-marketised time and activity. In most analyses of Social Investment, all this typically lies out of sight, below the iceberg (see Gibson-Graham, 2006). It leaves unanswered questions about the sustainability of voluntary action in the long term, and how to compensate the work of citizens who may not be a part of mainstream work, but still perform valuable and impact-laden services for the community (Klemelä, 2016).

In addition to the case studies reported in this book, InnoSI teams interviewed national policy experts and analysed policy documents in 10 countries (Barnett et al, 2016). Overall, there was awareness of Social Investment as a perspective on welfare, albeit with variations from country to country. In the UK, and to a lesser extent in Germany, it competes with 'social impact investing' but is rather better recognised in Southern and Eastern Europe in response to EU economic incentives (Barnett et al, 2016). At the sub-national levels at which the research reported in this book was undertaken, the concept of Social Investment was almost unknown. Nevertheless, the evidence documented from the case studies in Chapters Two to Eleven is consistent with the presence of a 'quiet revolution' in innovative welfare (Hemerijck, 2015) in the form of capacitating services devised and delivered at sub-national levels. This is true in the sense that local projects, pilots and experiments were dedicated to the principles of Social Investment. In other words, they can be seen as 'investments' in human capital and/or promoting the long-term resilience of individuals, families or communities. Some were guided by national and European-level priorities, and a few influenced change beyond their immediate local context.

The evidence from Chapters Two to Eleven presents a mixed picture of how social innovation practices are beginning to contribute to welfare state reforms that fit the Social Investment paradigm. Generally, it is at the margins in particular initiatives. There have been some examples of replication but the uptake of innovations at a system level is not well advanced. Many researchers and stakeholders see potential for greater use of social innovation to drive welfare state reform and are looking for ways to achieve this (Brandsen et al, 2016; Reynolds et al, 2017; Sabato et al, 2017). For Reynolds et al (2017), this implies opening up innovation processes to a broader range of people and organisations. Evers and Brandsen (2016) emphasise the strong links of social innovations to specific and local contexts. They argue for more focus on the cumulative effect of small initiatives, and less on success in the sense of wider take-up and mainstreaming. All these commentators emphasise the overwhelming importance of experimentation, adaptation and ways of nurturing learning (Sabel et al, 2017). The evidence from this book offers examples of how innovations can be kept alive by energetic knowledge exchange and shared capacity building (as in the partnership for the reception of unaccompanied minors), and by collective reflection and self-evaluations, as occurs within the Green Sticht community.

Overall, there was little monitoring of outcomes and returns on financial and other investments. The UK case study was an exception in that it deployed an outcome-based funding model (PbR). This is not a panacea that can be wholeheartedly recommended for other contexts. There are many criticisms of the principles of PbR and indications that it has not so far delivered on its promises (Albertson et al, 2018). PbR is consistent with the usage of the term 'social investment' in the English-speaking world to refer to new financial instruments for funding social programmes rather than to the Social Investment paradigm. There has been little dialogue to date between these meanings of 'social investment'. While the Social Investment Package (European Commission, 2013) advocates such financial innovations, Barbier (2017), as discussed in Chapter One, argues that they should be strenuously resisted by supporters of Social Investment. The conversation, however, has barely started as yet.

Critics have warned that the Social Investment paradigm is not pro-poor and may drive economic rationales to replace human rationales (Deeming and Smyth, 2015). Case studies reported in this book set out to benefit some of the most vulnerable and stigmatised social groups, often with elements of compensation. Nevertheless, they demonstrate success for initiatives with a socially investive and innovative character in tapping into new capacities and resources. They do this in ways that support personalised interventions to assist the poorest and most disadvantaged (non-EU migrants, Roma, people with physical or mental health problems) and achieve some positive outcomes for individuals and communities. There are also some (albeit often incomplete) instances of co-creation. These legitimate the knowledge of people who receive public services, and nurture their participation in service innovation and decision-making. All this does not, of course, overthrow concerns regarding the productivist stance of Social Investment, but it adds to a much richer picture of what implementation of its principles can look like. This book has enhanced what we know by taking the unusual step of viewing Social Investment from a sub-national perspective and listening to the voices of front-line providers and intended beneficiaries.

References

Albertson, K., Fox, C., O'Leary, C. and Painter, G. (2018) *Payment by Results and Social Impact Bonds: Outcome-based payment systems in the UK and US*, Bristol: The Policy Press.

Alves, H. (2013) 'Co-creation and innovation in public services', *The Service Industries Journal*, 33 (7/8): 671–82.

Amin, A. (2009) 'Extraordinarily ordinary: working in the social economy', *Social Enterprise Journal*, 5(1): 30–49.

Barbier, J. (2017) '"Social investment": with or against social protection', in A. Hemerijck (ed) *The uses of social investment*, Oxford: Oxford University Press.

Barnett, S., Bailey, D. and Fox, C. (2016) 'A provisional overview of public policy according to "social investment" from institutional perspectives'. Available at: http://innosi.eu/the-state-of-the-art-of-social-investment/

Bassi A. (2011) 'Social innovation: some definitions', *Boletin CIES* [Centro de Investigación de Economía y Sociedad], n. 88 (March).

Battilana, J., Leca, B. and Boxenbaum, E. (2009) 'How actors change institutions: towards a theory of institutional entrepreneurship', *Academy of Management Annals*, 3(1): 65–107.

Bonoli, G. (2010) 'The political economy of active labor-market policy', *Politics & Society*, 38(4): 435–57.

Bonvin, J.-M. and Laruffa, F. (2017) *Towards a normative framework for welfare reform based on the capability and human rights approaches*, Re-InVEST Working Paper Series D4.1, Leuven: RE-InVEST.

Brandsen, T., Cattacin, S., Evers, A. and Zimmer, A. (eds) (2016) *Social innovations in the urban context*, Berlin: Springer International Publishing.

Coleman, S.J. (1988) 'Social capital in the creation of human capital', *The American Journal of Sociology*, 94(Supplement: Organizations and Institutions: Sociological and Economic Approaches to the Analysis of Social Structure): 95–120.

Deeming, C. and Smyth, P. (2015) 'Social investment after neoliberalism: policy paradigms and political platforms', *Journal of Social Policy*, 44(2): 297–318.

Deeming, C. and Smyth, P. (eds) (2017) *Reframing global social policy: Social investment for sustainable and inclusive growth*, Bristol: The Policy Press.

Esping-Andersen, G., Gallie, D., Hemerijck, A. and Myles, J. (eds) (2002) *Why we need a new welfare state*, Oxford: Oxford University Press.

European Commission (2013) 'Towards social investment for growth and cohesion – including implementing the European Social Fund 2014–2020', COM (2013) 83 final, Brussels.

Evers, A. and Brandsen, T. (2016) 'Social innovations as messages: democratic experimentation in local welfare systems', in T. Brandsen, S. Cattacin, A. Evers and A. Zimmer (eds) *Social innovations in the urban context*, Berlin: Springer International Publishing, pp 161–80.

Ewert, B. and Evers, A. (2014) 'Blueprints for the future of welfare provision? Shared features of service innovations across Europe', *Social Policy & Society*, 13(3): 423–32.

Fox, A. (2012) *Personalisation: Lessons from social care*, London: RSA.

Gibson-Graham, J.K. (2006) *A post capitalist politics*, Minneapolis, MN: University of Minnesota Press.

Giddens, A. (1998) *The third way: The renewal of local democracy*, Cambridge: Polity Press.

Hardill, I. and Baines, S. (2011) *Enterprising care? Unpaid voluntary action in the 21st century*, Bristol: The Policy Press.

Hartley, J. (2015) 'Eight and a half propositions to stimulate frugal innovation', *Public Money & Management*, 34(3): 227–32.

Hemerijck, A. (2015) 'The quiet paradigm revolution of social investment', *Social Politics*, 22(2): 242–56.

Hemerijck, A. (2017) 'Social investment and its critics' in A. Hemerijck (ed) *The uses of social investment*, Oxford: Oxford University Press.

Hochgerner, J. (2011) 'The analysis of social innovations as social practice'. Available at: https://www.zsi.at/object/publication/1566/attach/The%20Analysis%20of%20Social%20Innovations%20as%20Social%20Practice.pdf

Huxham, C. (2003) 'Theorizing collaboration practice', *Public Management Review*, 5(3): 401–23.

Huxham, C. and Vangen, S. (2013) *Managing to collaborate: The theory and practice of collaborative advantage*, London: Routledge.

Jenson, J. (2012) 'Redesigning citizenship regimes after neoliberalism: moving towards social investment', in N. Morel, B. Palier and J. Palme (eds) *Towards a social investment welfare state*, Bristol: Policy Press, pp 61–88.

Klemelä, J. (2016) 'User-driven development of local public services in Kainuu, Finland', InnoSI Policy Briefing. Available at: http://innosi.eu/wp-content/uploads/2017/04/FINLAND-Kainuu.pdf

Künzel, S. (2012) 'The local dimension of active inclusion policy', *Journal of European Social Policy*, 22(1): 3–16.

McLoughlin, I.P., Maniotopoulos, G., Wilson, R. and Martin, M. (2012) 'Inside a "digital experiment" co-producing virtual services for older people', *Scandinavian Journal of Information Systems*, 24(2): 3–26.

Moore, M. and Hartley, J. (2008) 'Innovations in governance', *Public Management Review*, 10(1): 3–20.

Morel, N. and Palme, J. (2017) 'A normative foundation for the social investment approach?', in A. Hemerijck (ed) *The uses of social investment*, Oxford: Oxford University Press.

Needham, C. (2011) 'Personalization: from story-line to practice', *Social Policy & Administration*, 45(1): 54–68.

Parsons, T. (1971) *The system of modern societies*, Englewood Cliffs, NJ: Prentice-Hall.

Polányi, K. (1976) *Az archaikus társadalom és a gazdasági szemlélet* [*Archaic society and the economic approach*], Budapest: Gondolat Kiadó.

Prandini, R. (2018) 'The person-centred turn in welfare policies: bad wine in new bottles or a true social innovation?', *International Review of Sociology*, 28(1): 1–19.

Putnam, R.D. (2000) *Bowling alone. The collapse and revival of American community*, New York, NY: Simon and Schuster.

Reynolds, S., Gabriel, M. and Heales, C. (2017) *Social innovation policy in Europe: Where next?*, London: NESTA.

Ridley-Duff, R.J. and Bull, M. (2016) *Understanding social enterprise*, London: Sage.

Sabato, S., Vanhercke, B. and Verschraegen, G. (2017) 'Connecting entrepreneurship with policy experimentation? The EU framework for social innovation', *Innovation: The European Journal of Social Science Research*, 30(2): 147–67.

Sabel, C., Zeitlin, J. and Quack, S. (2017) 'Capacitating services and the bottom-up approach to social investment', in A. Hemerijck (ed) *The uses of social investment*, Oxford: Oxford University Press.

Sen, A. (2001) *Development as freedom*, Oxford: Oxford Paperbacks.

Smyth, P. and Deeming, C. (2016) 'The "social investment perspective" in social policy: a longue durée perspective', *Social Policy & Administration*, 50(6): 673–90.

Social Care Institute for Excellence (2015) *Co-production in social care: What it is and how to do it*, SCIE Guide 51, London: SCIE.

Von Hippel, E. (2005) *Democratising innovation*, Cambridge, MA: MIT Press.

Voorberg, W.H., Bekkers, V.J. and Tummers, L.G. (2015) 'A systematic review of co-creation and co-production: embarking on the social innovation journey', *Public Management Review*, 17(9): 1333–57.

Warner, M. (2013) 'Private finance for public goods: social impact bonds', *Journal of Economic Policy Reform*, 16(4): 303–19.

Westley, F. and Antadze, N. (2010) 'Making a difference: strategies for scaling social innovation for greater impact', *The Public Sector Innovation Journal*, 15(2): article 2.

Index

Note: page numbers in *italic* type refer to Figures; those in **bold** type refer to Tables.